LUNA LAPIN

Stitched with Kindness

New Friends to Make and Stories to Share

Sarah Peel
With short stories by Grace Machon

DAVID & CHARLES
— PUBLISHING —

www.davidandcharles.com

Contents

Introduction

We are delighted to welcome you back into Luna Lapin's little world for a fifth time! I want to start this book by extending my heartfelt gratitude to you. Over the years, your unwavering trust and support have made this journey not just an adventure but a true pleasure. Luna would be proud of the kindness, creativity, and effort you all pour into your stitching and each other.

This book was born in 2024, a year that turned out to be one of the hardest of my life. It was filled with unexpected challenges, including the profound loss of my mum (Grace's nanny) – the very root of my creativity and of Grace's love of stories. We had hoped for a quiet year to refocus and rediscover our creativity, but life had other plans. We've often said that Luna is exactly where she needs to be, especially when we need her most, and this has proven true even for us.

Over the years, so many of you have told us stories of the restorative qualities of hand-stitching, of how, in dark moments, Luna and her menagerie of felt friends have helped ease broken hearts, soothe sadness and distract from illness. These stories keep me stitching and make me extremely proud to head this incredible studio of dressmaking in miniature. My favourite stories, though, are of those of kindness and personal wins – from being brave enough to enter your village fair to making your first human-sized dressmaking project, as well as the gifts you give your friends.

In the following pages, you will find not just hours of stitching, but stories of kindness that mirror the wonderful community we have built together.

Thank you for sharing this journey with us and for your willingness to embrace surprises and each other's unique paths. Together, we continue to weave a tapestry of kindness and creativity that we know Luna will celebrate. Who knows what's next?

Sarah

x

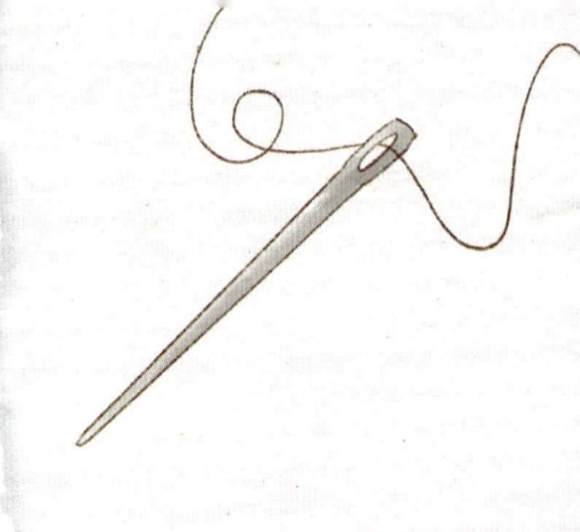

Materials

This section describes the materials and equipment you will need to make the projects in this book.

BASIC SEWING KIT

- Sewing needle, tapestry needle, darner needle (for sewing heads to bodies), and doll needle (for sewing on legs and arms)
- Sewing threads to suit projects, including embroidery threads
- Pins, safety pins, and fabric clips
- Sharp scissors for fabric and scissors for paper
- Fabric marker (e.g. water-soluble pen or chalk)
- Adhesive tape (for joining pattern pieces)
- Turning tool for pushing out small shapes (a knitting needle or chopstick will do)
- Iron and pressing cloth
- Sewing machine with selection of feet, including a walking foot
- Overlocker (not essential but a great timesaver)

BEFORE YOU START

Look at the You Will Need list for the project and gather supplies. To help eliminate mistakes, read through all of a project's instructions first and highlight any areas that need more focus. Press your fabric to ensure it is flat and easy to work with (see Techniques: Pressing Techniques).

FABRICS

Various fabric types have been used for the projects in the book and here is some advice on using them.

Felt

Felt fabric is not a woven fabric; it is formed by the agitation of fibres and therefore will not fray when cut. However, not all felts are made equal; choose a felt that has wool in it, and look for a thickness of about 1.5mm (1⁄16in) – definitely no thicker. I adore the softly marled tones used for Luna and her friends, which are either 100% wool or a wool and rayon blend (see Suppliers). Felt doesn't have a grain, so you can move your pattern pieces around as you choose.

Knitted and Jersey Fabrics

This category encompasses a huge number of fabric types that share a common characteristic – they stretch. If this is your first time using stretch fabrics, try cutting up an old T-shirt to have a go. It may sound scary but actually sewing with jersey is quick, easy, and fun, although a cotton jersey will be more stable and easier to start with than a viscose jersey.

When cutting out, the stretch needs to go across the pattern pieces. To maintain the stretch in the seams, use a small zigzag or stretch stitch on your machine. A ballpoint or jersey needle prevents fibre damage and laddering but is not essential for such small garments. Take great care not to stretch the fabric as you put it through the machine to avoid ugly wavy seams (a walking foot can help here). Seams do not need to be finished or pressed flat.

Velvet

Velvet has a 'pile' but the even cut of this woven tufted fabric creates a flat, smooth surface with a soft feel and beautiful rich colours. It has a tendency to shift and creep under your machine foot, so always prepare your seams well with tacking (basting). Changing the pressure on your machine foot will also help cope with this bulkier fabric. Velvet can be quite springy, so don't worry too much about pressing; if you do need to press, use a scrap piece of velvet pile-side down as a pressing cloth.

Linen
The oldest recorded fabric in human civilisation, linen is made from flax plant fibre and has a low impact on the environment. It has a relaxed, softly rumpled finish and is stable to cut and sew in these tiny garments; however, it comes in many weights, so choose a lighter, pre-washed type to achieve the detail in Maurice's Baker's Smock. Use a pressing cloth when ironing to avoid the seams glazing.

Boiled Wool
I like to think of boiled wool as the grown up version of felt. The fabric is knitted but then finished in the same way as felt, with heat and agitation of the fibres, so it can be left with raw edges and unfinished seams to give a relaxed, lightweight but warm garment. It can be expensive but usually you don't have to allow extra, for hemming, facings, etc. The key to a good finish is to cut the shapes smoothly.

Bouclé
This describes a fabric with a nubby texture and you'll find that there are different types available. The word 'bouclé' comes from the French verb 'boucler' meaning 'to curl'. Bouclé does have stretch qualities so you will need to control the stretch when you are sewing it to non-stretch felt when making the donkeys, Sidney and Sol. By nature, it is a thick fabric, so you might have to adjust your machine foot pressure, or use a walking foot if you have one.

Faux Fur
Imitation fur comes in many different pile lengths (i.e. the length of the fur) and you will need to choose a fabric that is appropriate for the project.

When cutting out, snip the backing fabric only and then pull the shapes apart to minimise floating fibres. When sewing, changing the pressure on your machine foot will help cope with this bulkier fabric. When you have sewn your seams, use a comb or a strong pin to tease the fibres out of the seam.

Techniques

This section describes the basic techniques used for the projects. Each project is given a difficulty rating with the You Will Need lists – one leaf for easy projects, working up to three leaves for more difficult ones.

LAYOUTS

Layout diagrams are given for the projects as a guide for the amount of fabric needed, but if you have a different shape of fabric you will need to be flexible. Take note of which pattern pieces need to be cut out more than once and pin these onto double thickness fabric. The pattern pieces and layouts give this information so follow them carefully.

PATTERNS

All patterns are supplied full size in a section at the back of the book called The Patterns. Please follow the guidelines there for using the patterns.

CUTTING OUT

Time spent on accurate cutting will really improve your end result. Use a good quality pair of scissors that are suitable for (and reserved for) fabric. I tend to use the part of the blades that are closer to my hand to start cutting – this gives me better control and allows me to make a longer cut, as I have the rest of the blades to travel through the fabric. I only use the tips of the scissors when I am marking notches or for really fiddly bits.

TRANSFERRING MARKINGS

Mark the notches shown on the patterns with either a tiny snip in the fabric or by using a water-soluble pen or chalk marker. Mark any triangles with a tiny snip at the centre. Mark any dots on the patterns with either a water-soluble pen or tailor's tacks. The triangles and dots are position markers. The notches can be there to mark a position or to help you ease around curves so please be accurate when you are snipping them. Once you have marked the positions, unpin the pattern pieces from the cut fabric and store them together when you are sure you have cut them all out.

RIGHT SIDE AND WRONG SIDE

Printed fabrics and some plain fabrics have a right side and a wrong side, and this is shown in the illustrations and referred to in the instructions. Felt normally has no definite right or wrong side, but I have referred to right and wrong to help you sew.

FINISHING RAW EDGES

You could use an overlocker or a machine zigzag stitch to finish the raw edges of the seams on woven fabrics. The items in this book are small ones that are not going to be washed, so this is optional. Because of the nature of felt and boiled wool, the edges do not need to be finished. You will find that some fabrics fray more easily than others – for example, velvet and hessian. Using a product such as Fraystop will help.

HAND SEWING STITCHES

Hand sewing is relaxing, portable and allows you to focus on something creative. Luna and her friends are sewn by hand (mostly!) and you could aim to complete a limb each night or perhaps take one on your commute to work. I have used various stitches, as described here. Always start and finish with either a knot in the fabric or a couple of small stitches made in the same place.

Overstitch / Whipstitch

I use an overstitch (also called whipstitch) to sew felt pieces together. Use a single thread thickness and make sure you sew consistently, that is, the same distance between stitches and the same depth in from the edge, about 0.2cm (1⁄16in) into the felt.

Bring the needle through to the front and then sew from back to front, repeating and working from right to left if right-handed (see **Fig.1**) or left to right if left-handed. As you pull the thread through you will feel the tension as the thread is drawn and you can then continue to the next stitch. The thread will sink into the felt.

Fig.1

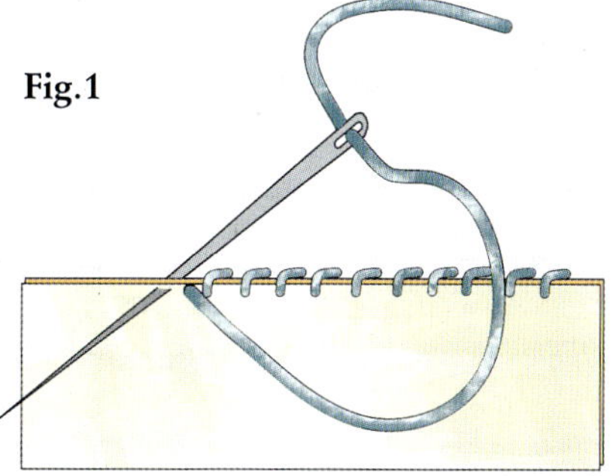

Satin Stitch

Satin stitch is an embroidery stitch that is good for creating blocked-out shapes in contrast colours. Use between three and six strands of the embroidery thread, depending on how bold you want the contrast stitch to look.

Following **Fig.3**, draw out the outline of the shape you are going to fill. Use the needle to pass backwards and forwards from outline to opposite outline. Try to keep your stitches parallel to one another and don't pull the stitches too tight.

Fig.3

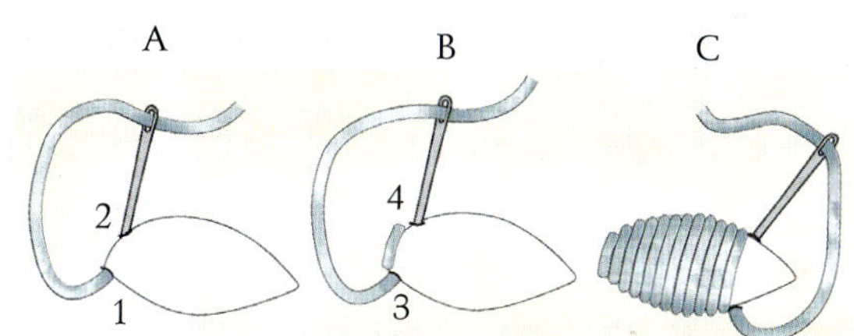

Backstitch

Backstitch is used to sew two pieces of fabric or felt together with a seam allowance. Backstitch is a good replacement for machine sewing if you wish to sew the garments by hand. Use a single stand of toning sewing thread in your needle.

Following **Fig.2**, bring the needle up at point 1 and then back to point 2. Bring it out at the top again beyond point 1 at point 3, and then back through at point 4, which should be very close to or in the same place as point 1. Repeat along the seam.

Fig.2

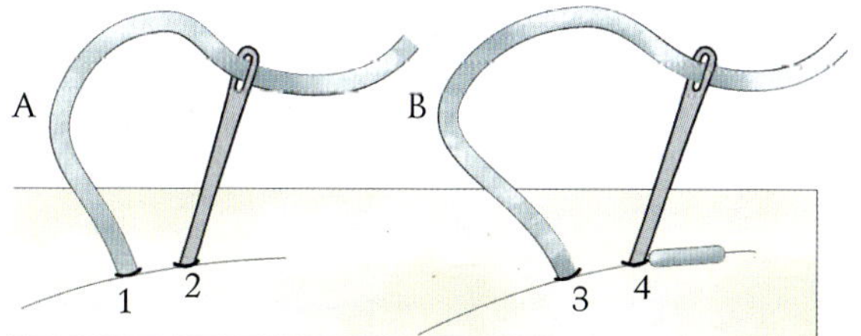

Slip Stitch / Ladder Stitch

A slip stitch (also called ladder stitch) is used to join two fabrics when you don't want the stitches to show. Following **Fig.4**, secure the thread onto a bulkier part of the project – a seam allowance or the fold of a hem. Now pass your needle through a tiny amount of the main fabric and then travel diagonally into the back of the other fabric piece. Come down directly into the main fabric again, pick up a small amount again and travel diagonally across to the second fabric again. Repeat along the edge.

Fig.4

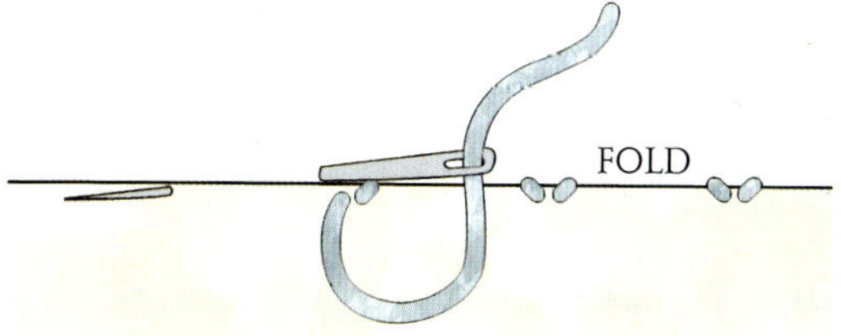

MACHINE SEWING TECHNIQUES

I recommend sewing the clothes for Luna and her friends on a sewing machine as this will give a more professional and even finish. For these projects it is assumed that you have the basic skills of machine sewing. However, here are a few tips on how to sew small items.

The Right Stitch

Test your fabrics first – for example, a cotton lawn will react differently to a faux fur under the machine and you may need to adjust the stitch length or tension.

'Donkey' or Stitch Starter

If you find that with small projects and fine fabrics your fabric tends to disappear down into the needle plate at the start of a seam, you could use what's called a 'donkey'. Fold over a piece of scrap fabric so it's about 5cm (2in) square and a few layers thick and start your line of sewing on this. Butt the project up to the donkey and continue sewing onto the project – reversing as in Securing Your Stitching, below, but without involving the donkey. You can snip the threads to detach the donkey at the end of the seam and use it again and again.

Securing Your Stitching

Always use your machine reverse function to start and finish seams as this will stop your seams from coming undone. The reversing should only be for two to three stitches – if you stitch any more than this then you probably will have lost the line of stitching anyway.

Seam Allowance

It is amazing how many people come to my Make Friends with Your Sewing Machine classes who don't know what the little parallel grooves are on the footplate of the sewing machine. These are your sewing guidelines and before you start sewing you should identify which line is right for the recommended seam allowance. So, if sewing with a 1cm (⅜in) seam allowance, you should be feeding the sewing through the machine so the raw edges are on the right-hand side of the presser foot and are running along the 10mm groove. If you are working to a narrow 0.5cm (¼in) seam allowance, use the edge of your presser foot as the guide for the edge of the fabric.

Using the Hand Wheel

Instead of using the foot pedal, using your hand wheel to make the last few stitches before a point you are aiming for can really improve your accuracy and confidence. Always turn the wheel towards you.

Pivoting at a Corner

To make a crisp, accurate 90-degree corner when you are sewing, at the point of the corner leave the needle down in the fabric, lift the presser foot and move the fabric around at a 90-degree angle, and then continue sewing.

Coping with Curves

Sewing a curve is easier if you are using your seam guidelines. Slow down to control your sewing more easily and if you need to realign what you are doing, leave the needle down in the fabric, lift the presser foot and move the fabric slightly to bring the curve back in line. You may find that you have a speed setting on your machine or foot pedal, so if it helps you should slow the speed down whilst you practise new techniques. A needle down function on your machine is invaluable for working on curves, such as when inserting sleeves into a garment.

Easing

There are times when it feels like you are squeezing more fabric on one side to match less fabric on another side. This can occur, for example, if you are setting in a sleeve or sewing a curve onto a straight piece of fabric. To help with easing there are two different techniques, as follows:

METHOD 1

This is the normal dressmaking technique. Change your stitch length to be the longest possible. Do not reverse at the beginning or end, and then on the longer looking side (normally the curved side), sew two rows of stitching. Row 1 should be 0.3cm (⅛in) from the raw edge. Row 2 should be 0.5cm (¼in). Now grab the sewing threads from one end of the upper side of the fabric and gently pull to slightly gather up the fabric. Do the same with the other ends, but make sure you don't have actual gathers, just more tightness. Now you can pin and sew to the other piece of fabric and eventually remove the initial stitching. Remember to change your stitch length back to normal first though.

METHOD 2

This is the factory method. Take the tighter (usually the straighter piece of fabric) and put snips 1cm (⅜in) apart along the edge of the fabric, which are a little bit shorter than the seam allowance allowed. This will lengthen the edge of the fabric and allow it to stretch to the longer curved piece.

Staystitching

Staystitching is a foundation step to keep your fabric from stretching. Sew using a normal length straight stitch just inside the given seam allowance so that your stitches will be hidden. Sew without reversing at the beginning or end so that you can easily remove the stitches if necessary.

Edgestitch

An edgestitch is a line of stitching that is very close, about 0.1cm–0.2cm (approx. 1/32in–1/16in) away from a seam or folded edge. It is used to decorate or strengthen a seam. An easy way of establishing a guideline for edgestitching is to move your needle across to the left-hand position; then use the groove in the centre of the presser foot as the seam guideline. Stitch slowly to keep the stitching even.

Topstitch

A topstitch is a line of stitching that is close, about 0.4cm–0.5cm (approx. 3/16in) away from a seam or folded edge. It is used to decorate or strengthen a seam. Use the edge of the presser foot as your seam guideline. Edgestitching and topstitching can be used together to create a twin needling effect.

Making Buttonholes

Buttonholes are a finishing touch to garments and an important fastening function, but in this tiny world it might be difficult to create them. So have a think about your capabilities and practise on your machine with some scrap fabric first to check it is up to the job. You could just as easily use buttons and press stud fasteners.

If you are having a go, a sewing machine with a computerised function (where you can put in the length of buttonhole required) will work, as will machines where you turn a knob for each stage of the buttonhole, but a machine which has a foot where the button drops into the back to determine the buttonhole length will not work as the button is too small to be detected. Once the buttonhole is completed, cut through the small area between the zigzag stitches carefully using an unpicker. To do this safely, place pins at each far end of the buttonhole, but just before the wide end bar of stitching. This will stop the unpicker from accidentally cutting further.

MAKING A TOGGLE BUTTON AND LOOP

Erik's Duffle Coat has traditional toggle loop fastenings that are easy to make. Following **Fig.5**, make a knotted loop using a length of waxed cord – the loop should be roughly 1cm (⅜in) deep with tails of about 1.5cm (⅝in). This is the fastening loop. For the toggle button, thread a piece of waxed cord through the holes in the toggles, allowing for a loose loop on one side of the toggle and 2cm–3cm (¾in–1⅛in) tails on the other side. Pass the tails through the loop and pull the cord tight so the loop sits snug to the toggle. Trim the tails to 1.5cm (⅝in) long.

Fig.5

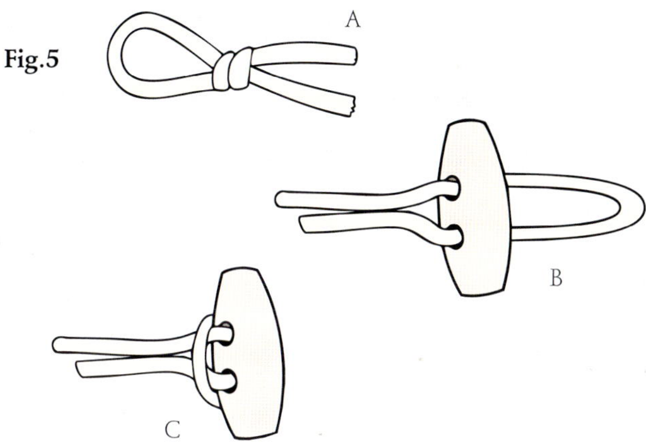

PRESSING TECHNIQUES

An iron is as valuable to the sewing process as the sewing machine itself. Make sure you have a pressing cloth available to cover your project as you feel necessary. Keep scrap fabric to test the temperature and the use of steam before you work on your project. Some seams will be too small to press, but it's worth making the effort, depending on the shape, to set the seam first by pressing the seam flat. Then open up the fabric and use the nose of the iron to either open up the seam allowances and press flat, or to flatten the seam allowances together in one direction.

If you are working on turning out a shape – the collar on Luna's Shirtwaister Dress, for example – after trimming your seam allowances as per the instructions, turn through and use your thumb and fingers to roll the seam right out onto the edge of the shape before pressing with the iron.

Throughout the pressing process, your fingers will be working near the hot iron, so do take care.

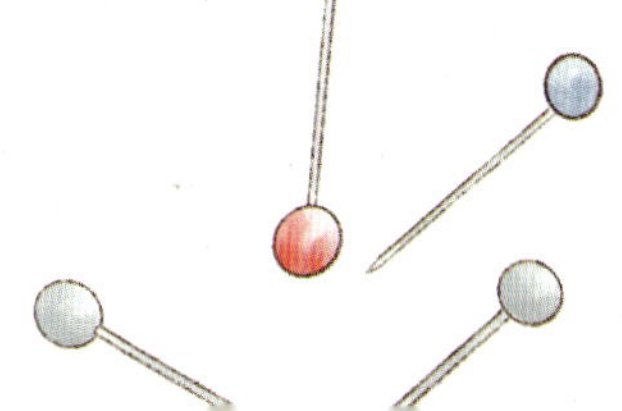

LUNA LAPIN AND THE *Perfect Picnic*

Though she wouldn't ever admit it, Luna Lapin had not been looking forward to her tenth birthday. The whole Lapin family had planned to celebrate with Granny's second cousins in the Netherlands, but Alfie had broken his arm climbing a tree, and they had had to cancel their trip. Alfie and Luna had made so many birthday plans. Riding their bikes, going on merry-go-rounds, and eating birthday pancakes at a world-famous pancake house. Oh, and the windmills! Luna was going to miss the windmills and canal boats, too! Now, there was nothing to do and no one to play with. Alfie's arm wasn't going to be better for weeks, and their mum was so worried. To make matters worse, they had to take Alfie to the hospital so that Luna would spend the whole day just with Granny.

As a rule, Luna didn't sulk, but on the morning of her birthday, she didn't wake up her best self. "Wake up, birthday girl!" said Granny, her voice breaking through Luna's sleep. Luna groaned. "Look, I know today isn't all you wanted it to be, but I thought we could maybe go for a picnic?"

Luna's ears poked up from under the covers. All days were better with a picnic! "Will there be dandelion sandwiches?" she asked.

"Luna Lapin, do you think I, Celeste Lapin, would put together a picnic without dandelion sandwiches? Now, get dressed. Today calls for an excellent outfit. I have made you something – it is with your presents."

On the end of her bed was a pile of gifts. First, Luna opened her mum's card containing the promise of weekend birthday pancakes. Luna knew her mum was sad about missing her birthday, but it didn't make her feel better. The 30 brightly coloured pencils and a new sketchbook cheered her a little. Luna made a mental note to be less materialistic now that she was ten, but they were the nicest pencils she had ever seen, and they even came with a beautiful engraved silver tin! Alfie's card simply read, "Sorry I ruined your birthday", and Luna giggled as she unwrapped the beaten-up kite that was not only Alfie's pride and joy but the reason he was climbing a tree in the first place!

Granny gave Luna a beautifully wrapped parcel. Inside was a gorgeous lilac dress – just like Granny's. Luna loved it. She couldn't wait to fill her pockets with daisy chains, perfectly round pebbles, and pine cones that she could draw later.

Luna dressed and joined Granny in the kitchen. The smell of freshly baked carrot cake filled the room. "You look lovely, Luna. Could you grab me the pickled onions from the pantry?" she said, kissing her between the ears.

Luna's mood had lifted considerably, and she hurried to help. Together, they packed the picnic basket full of treats: crisp lettuce, sweet strawberries, and, of course, carrot cake. Granny had even made a special camomile cordial, Luna's favourite.

With the basket packed and a colourful blanket tucked under Granny's arm, they set off towards the meadow by the river, through the tall grass, oxeye daisies, poppies, and cornflowers. The smell of dog roses and birdsong filled the air with a sense of early summer. As they walked, Luna almost forgot about the windmills and canals she should have been exploring.

"Granny, we aren't dressed for a picnic," Luna proclaimed. Granny was wearing her favourite lilac dress with a pretty white collar. The white collar was part of Granny's signature style, but this dress was nothing ordinary. Luna thought it might be the most lovely Granny had ever looked. In their matching lace dresses, they looked a rather dashing pair! "Oh, how I wish Mum and Alfie were here."

"I know, Poppet," Granny replied. I am so sorry about your trip. I promise to make your birthday as special as possible. There are some folks you should meet."

Luna could hear the music rising from over the hill. Slow and joyful. The sort of music fairies might play to trick you into dancing with them... At ten, Luna knew it probably wasn't fairies, but the rhythm was so otherworldly, she couldn't be sure. "What is that music, Granny?"

"Why don't you run ahead and find out?" Granny replied.

Luna ran over the brow of the hill cautiously. After all, she didn't want to get caught in a fairy ring on her birthday! Alfie would never forgive her for going on that sort of adventure whilst he was in the hospital. There was something unusual on the river below: a small collection of canal boats. Each painted in vibrant colours, tulips growing in boxes along the windowsills. The barges were carefully moored, and rabbits had set up a camp in the meadow. Fairy lights dripped between boats and trees, and music danced in the wind. The rabbits seemed to dance as they walked. Kits darted and hopped between the boats as if water wasn't to be afraid of.

"Who are they, Granny!?" Luna gasped. Before she could answer, a plump white-and-black rabbit appeared in front of them and, like Granny, the echoes of age tipped her fur. She wore a gingham dress with a gathered skirt and a romantic sleeve. Luna could tell it was handmade with love and expert stitches.

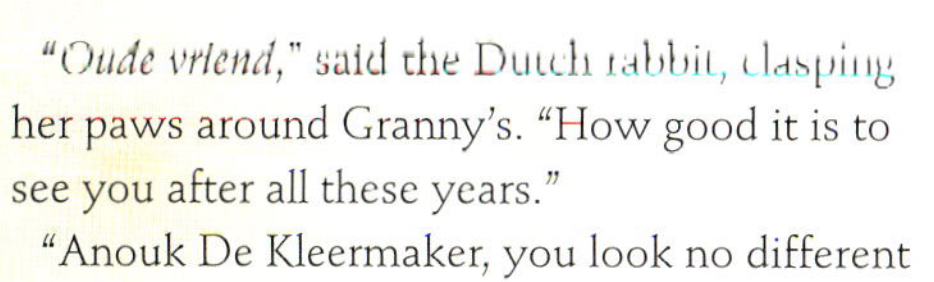

"*Oude vriend,*" said the Dutch rabbit, clasping her paws around Granny's. "How good it is to see you after all these years."

"Anouk De Kleermaker, you look no different than you did when we were ten! Taller, maybe?" said Granny.

"It is the freedom of the water, Celeste. It keeps us small and strong. How are you? You must tell me everything! And Luna, I hear it is your birthday today. *Gefeliciteerd*!"

Anouk kissed Luna on her cheeks three times, and Luna immediately felt the warmth of her heart.

"You know, it is my birthday today, too! Since you couldn't make it to us, I thought we could bring you a little touch of the Netherlands. My granddaughter is about the same age as you. *Schatje*, come meet Luna."

"*Hoi*," said a small rabbit with cute little ears and a striking black-and-white face. Tulip looked just like her Oma Anouk.

"Hello, Tulip," said Granny. "This is Luna. She is a little bit quiet but very, very kind. I think you will be good friends one day, just like your Oma and I. You know, we were girls together once."

"I like your dress," said Luna nervously. Tulip's dress – white with little embroidered flowers all over it and two bows tied down the front – was so pretty! Luna would have to ask Granny to make her one just like it.

"Girls, please could you fetch the, how do you say it… *aardbeientaart?*"

"*Ja Oma*!" said Tulip as she took Luna's paw. Luna had never been on a boat before. She wasn't sure that rabbits and rivers were a natural fit. The thought of all her fur getting wet made her shiver. The planks leading onto the boat looked very thin. Tulip chatted to her as she skipped over the plank with ease.

"Okay, just be brave," thought the little rabbity hare as the plank wobbled beneath her. "I DID IT!" Luna declared as her paws made contact with the deck.

The boat was beautiful, all jewel tones and richly coloured fabrics. "That's my room," said Tulip, pointing to a beautiful dark pink space with little bears and flowers painted on the walls. Luna couldn't help but stare. When she got home, she would practise drawing until she got as good as whoever had painted these murals.

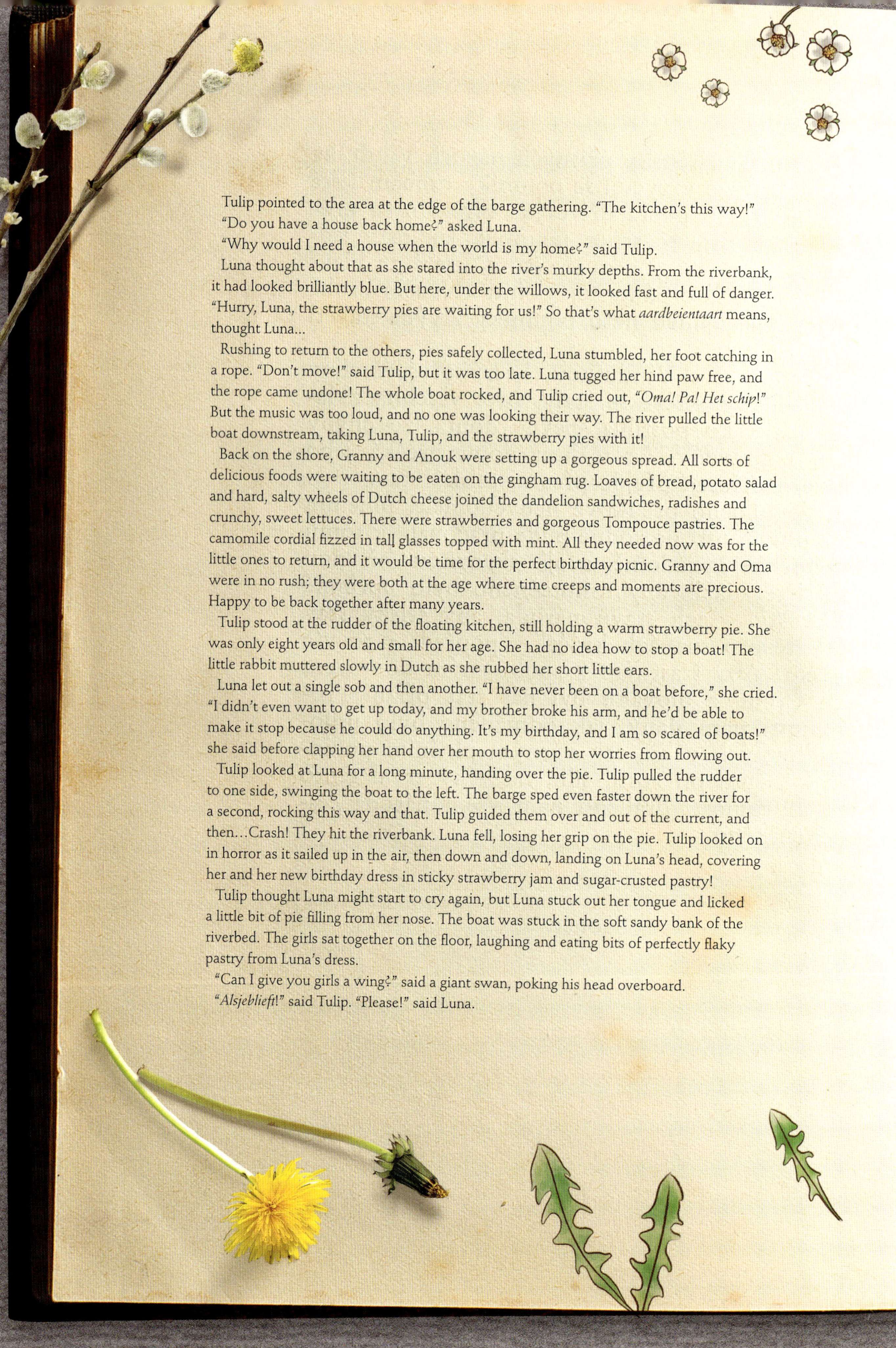

Tulip pointed to the area at the edge of the barge gathering. "The kitchen's this way!"

"Do you have a house back home?" asked Luna.

"Why would I need a house when the world is my home?" said Tulip.

Luna thought about that as she stared into the river's murky depths. From the riverbank, it had looked brilliantly blue. But here, under the willows, it looked fast and full of danger. "Hurry, Luna, the strawberry pies are waiting for us!" So that's what *aardbeientaart* means, thought Luna...

Rushing to return to the others, pies safely collected, Luna stumbled, her foot catching in a rope. "Don't move!" said Tulip, but it was too late. Luna tugged her hind paw free, and the rope came undone! The whole boat rocked, and Tulip cried out, *"Oma! Pa! Het schip!"* But the music was too loud, and no one was looking their way. The river pulled the little boat downstream, taking Luna, Tulip, and the strawberry pies with it!

Back on the shore, Granny and Anouk were setting up a gorgeous spread. All sorts of delicious foods were waiting to be eaten on the gingham rug. Loaves of bread, potato salad and hard, salty wheels of Dutch cheese joined the dandelion sandwiches, radishes and crunchy, sweet lettuces. There were strawberries and gorgeous Tompouce pastries. The camomile cordial fizzed in tall glasses topped with mint. All they needed now was for the little ones to return, and it would be time for the perfect birthday picnic. Granny and Oma were in no rush; they were both at the age where time creeps and moments are precious. Happy to be back together after many years.

Tulip stood at the rudder of the floating kitchen, still holding a warm strawberry pie. She was only eight years old and small for her age. She had no idea how to stop a boat! The little rabbit muttered slowly in Dutch as she rubbed her short little ears.

Luna let out a single sob and then another. "I have never been on a boat before," she cried. "I didn't even want to get up today, and my brother broke his arm, and he'd be able to make it stop because he could do anything. It's my birthday, and I am so scared of boats!" she said before clapping her hand over her mouth to stop her worries from flowing out.

Tulip looked at Luna for a long minute, handing over the pie. Tulip pulled the rudder to one side, swinging the boat to the left. The barge sped even faster down the river for a second, rocking this way and that. Tulip guided them over and out of the current, and then...Crash! They hit the riverbank. Luna fell, losing her grip on the pie. Tulip looked on in horror as it sailed up in the air, then down and down, landing on Luna's head, covering her and her new birthday dress in sticky strawberry jam and sugar-crusted pastry!

Tulip thought Luna might start to cry again, but Luna stuck out her tongue and licked a little bit of pie filling from her nose. The boat was stuck in the soft sandy bank of the riverbed. The girls sat together on the floor, laughing and eating bits of perfectly flaky pastry from Luna's dress.

"Can I give you girls a wing?" said a giant swan, poking his head overboard.

"Alsjeblieft!" said Tulip. "Please!" said Luna.

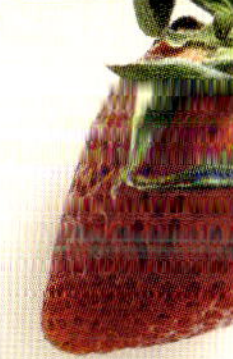

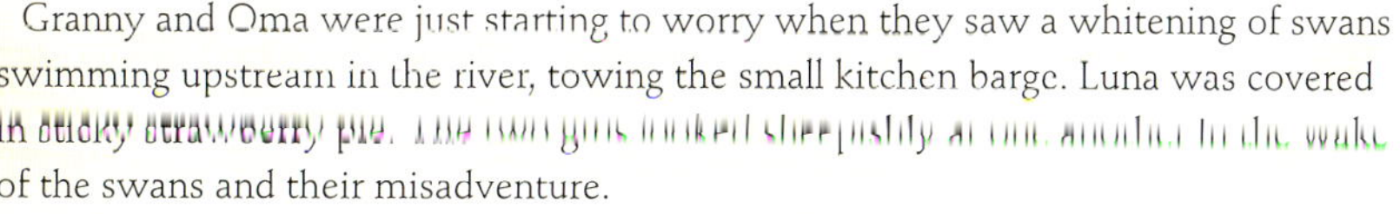

Granny and Oma were just starting to worry when they saw a whitening of swans swimming upstream in the river, towing the small kitchen barge. Luna was covered in sticky strawberry pie. The two girls looked sheepishly at one another in the wake of the swans and their misadventure.

"Goodness me!" said Granny. "You have had quite a day."

"Oma, do you think you have something Luna could wear?" asked Granny.

Anouk chuckled. "*Ja,* let me find it – Tulip, help Luna rinse off."

The river's water was cool against Luna's fur. It felt so good to be clean.

"Tulip, could you teach me to swim this summer?" Luna asked shyly. Though quiet and kind, she was still a sister, and she couldn't wait to show Alfie that she could swim, but he couldn't!

The group finally sat down to enjoy their picnic. Luna borrowed a stripey linen two-piece from Tulip and was very glad to be out of her sticky clothes. A strawberry tart took pride of place in the middle of the rug. "I thought I had ruined it!" Luna exclaimed.

"There is a Dutch proverb that says, never make only one *aardbeientaart,*" Oma said with a wink.

The rest of the afternoon slipped into the evening in a delightful haze of laughter, stories, and shared treats. The Dutch rabbits were fantastic company. Luna and Tulip played together, jumping from boat to boat. It was much easier in trousers! Tulip's Pa even taught them how to steer a runaway barge. The swans stayed to enjoy the music. Granny danced with all her cousins. As the sun began to dip towards the horizon, casting a golden glow over the meadow, Luna felt a deep sense of contentment.

"Let's not leave it so long next time, *oude vriend,*" Anouk said as she said goodbye.

"Today was wonderful, Granny," Luna said, reaching for her paw as they climbed the hill home.

"Happy tenth birthday, Luna," Granny replied, her voice filled with warmth. "It's days like these that remind us how lovely life can be."

Luna's Shirtwaister Dress

YOU WILL NEED

- **34cm (13³/₈in) x 145cm (57in) wide embroidered 100% cotton fabric with scalloped selvedges**
- **30cm (12in) x 15cm (6in) of white cotton poplin**
- **15cm (6in) of 18mm (¾in) wide bias binding**
- **Three 8mm (³/₈in) pearly buttons**
- **Two press stud fasteners**
- **Basic sewing kit (see Materials)**

Use a 0.5cm (¼in) seam allowance, unless a different amount is stated.

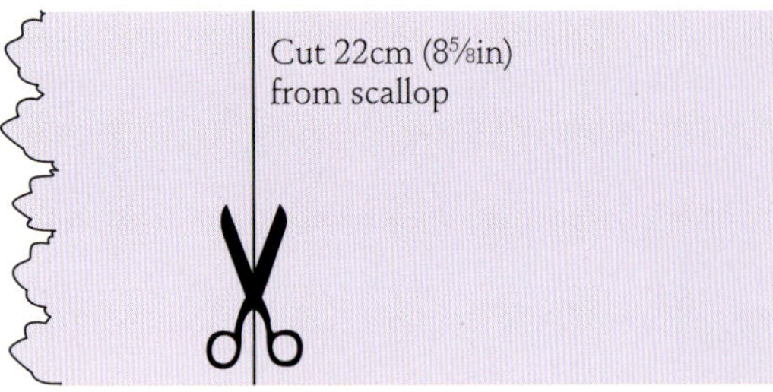

Fig.1

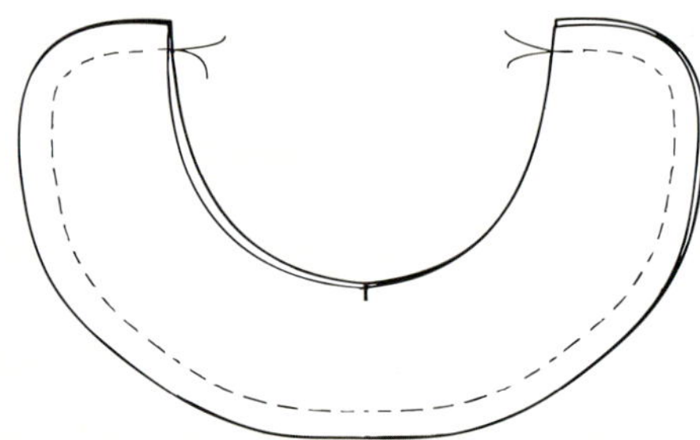

Fig.2

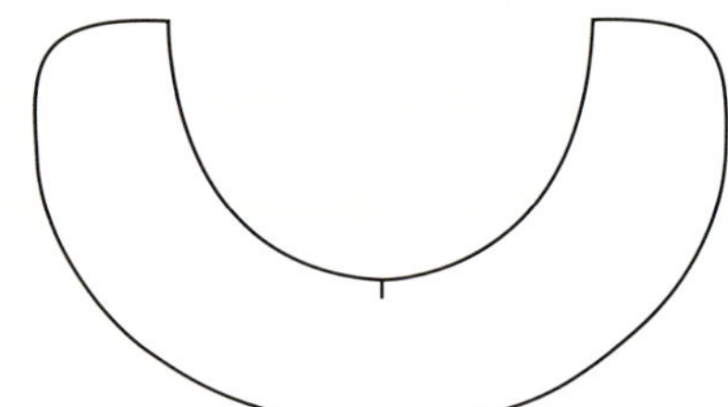

Fig.3

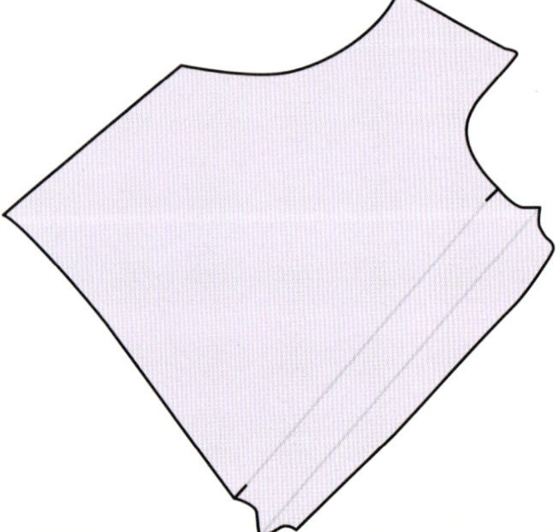

Fig.4

CUTTING OUT

1 Lightly mark a line 22cm (8⅝in) from each scalloped edge of the embroidered fabric and cut out (**Fig.1**). These are the front and back skirt pieces, each measuring 34cm x 22cm (13⅜in x 8⅝in).

2 Cut out the pattern pieces (see The Patterns) from the remaining fabric, placing them depending on the challenges of your chosen fabric, cutting the fronts and sleeves separately to mirror them. (We chose a voile heavily embroidered with flowers; pattern pieces were placed so these wouldn't cut onto a neckline or make a hem bulky.) Mark notches with a tiny snip and transfer any other pattern markings.

3 Fold the cotton poplin in half to cut out the collar pieces. Mark the notch with a tiny snip.

MAKING UP

Making the Collar

1 Match up the collar pieces, right sides together, and sew around the outside curve (**Fig.2**). Trim seam allowance and turn through. Press flat, so the seam is to the edge and the shape nicely rounded (**Fig.3**).

Sewing the Shoulder Seams

1 First, prepare the front pieces. Working on each in turn, fold over the inside edge to the wrong side by 1cm (⅜in), to the first dashed line, and press. Then fold over again by another 1cm (⅜in) to the notches, and press (**Fig.4**). With right sides together, match one front shoulder seam to one back shoulder seam and sew together, then repeat on the other side (**Fig.5**). Finish seams and press towards the back.

Attaching the Collar

1 Pin collar to right side of neckline; match edges using the centre back snip to guide you. The front edges will finish 0.5cm (¼in) from the inside pressed line on the fronts. Tack (baste) in place (**Fig.6**).

2 Using the memory of the folds already pressed and working on each side in turn, fold the front edge back along the inner fold (wrong side of folds facing up) (**Fig.7**), then turn one fold back on the other (right side of fold facing up), covering the end of the collar, and pin in place (**Fig.8**).

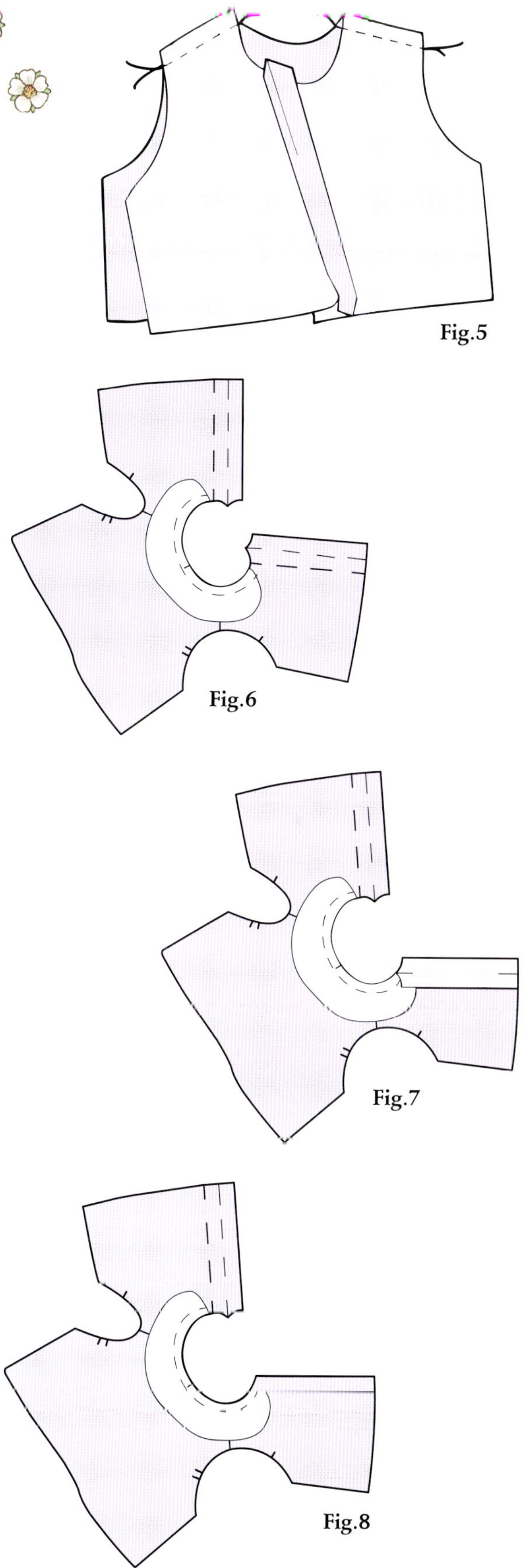

Fig.5

Fig.6

Fig.7

Fig.8

Fig.9

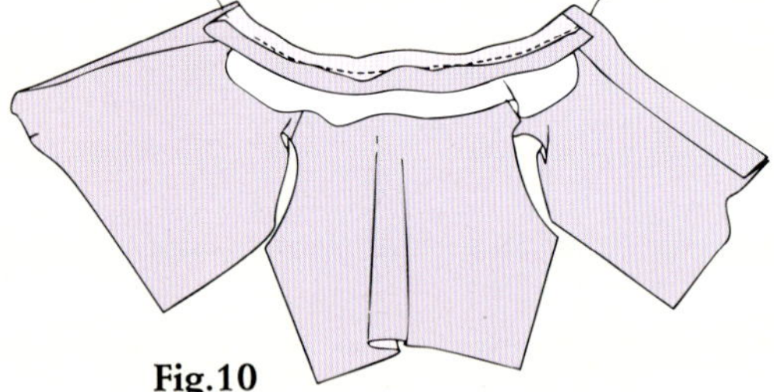

Fig.10

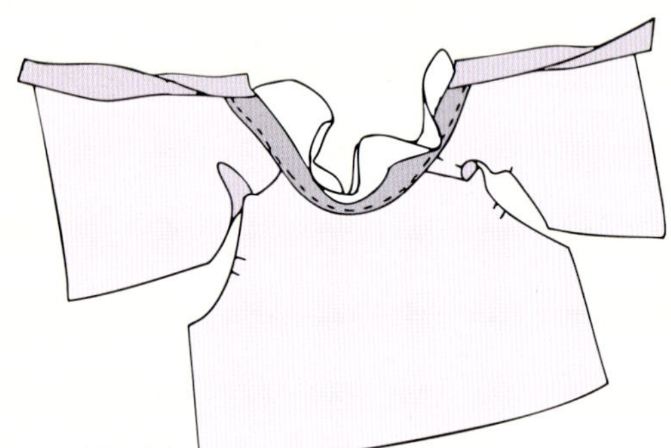

Fig.11

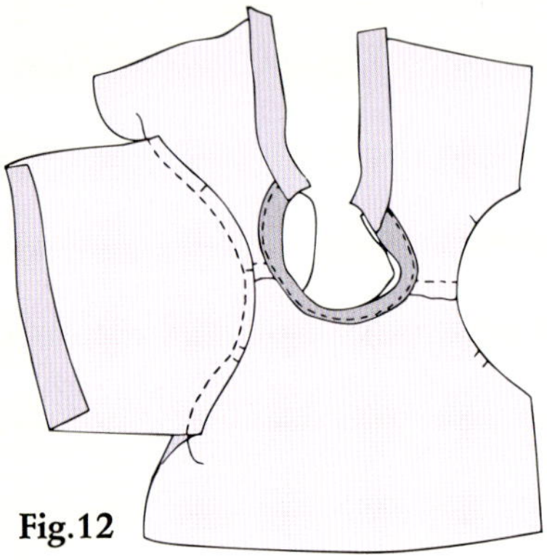

Fig.12

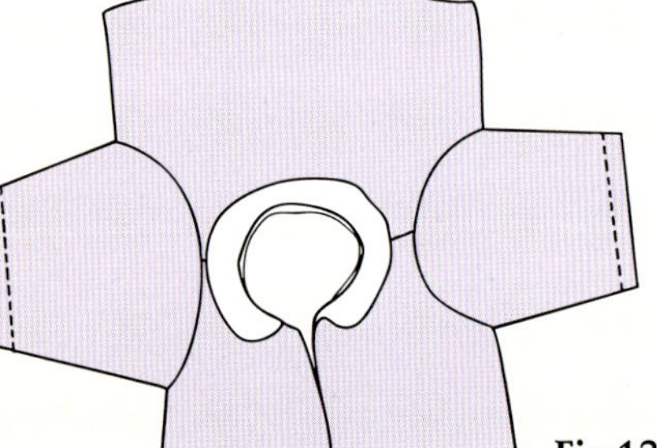

Fig.13

3 Now take your strip of bias binding and cut off one folded edge along the valley of the fold (**Fig.9**). With the wrong side of the bias facing up, match and pin the cut edge to the edge of the neckline, sandwiching the collar – make sure the bias overlaps the folded-back edge on the fronts by at least 0.5cm (¼in). Sew through all layers along the neck edge (**Fig.10**).

4 Trim the corners of the bias binding to reduce the bulk and snip into the seam allowance in curved parts to allow for turning through; trim the neck seam allowance back to 0.2cm (1/16in).

5 To turn through, push the front corners out to the right side and bring the folded edge of the bias binding down to the wrong side to cover all the raw edges. Pin and then hand or machine sew the bias binding in place, tight to the fold, starting and finishing at the inside edge of the front plackets (**Fig.11**).

Sewing the Sleeves

1 First, finish the raw edge of the sleeve hem using an overlock or zigzag stitch. Then hem the sleeves by turning 1cm (⅜in) to the wrong side. Press and edgestitch through all the layers close to the finished edge.

2 With right sides together, match one sleeve to the armhole using the notches to position, with the double notch indicating the back. Pin in place and sew together (**Fig.12**). Repeat with the other sleeve. Finish the seam (overlock or zigzag stitch), then press seam towards the sleeve.

3 There is just one more thing to do before moving on to make the skirt. With the top right side facing you as seen in **Fig.13**, overlap the right-hand side front as worn over the left-hand side front at the hem by 1cm (⅜in) and staystitch in place.

Making the Pleated Skirt

1 Working along the top (un-scalloped edge) of one skirt piece, measure 4cm (1½in) out from the centre to each side and fold the fabric in to meet the point from which you measured; pin the inverted box pleat in place. Measuring out from the centre each time, make two inward-facing pleats to each side. For the first pleat, measure 4.5cm (1¾in) away, and bring fabric over so that the fold is 1.75cm (¾in) away from the centre; pin in place. For the second pleat, measure 6cm (2⅜in) away, and bring fabric over so that the fold is 3cm (1⅛in) away from the centre; pin in place. (Note, the distance between pleats may need to be adapted slightly for the fabric you have chosen, to ensure that any interesting embroidered details are not lost in the pleats.) The width of the skirt top should measure 15cm (6in). Staystitch or tack (baste) in place (**Fig.14**). This completes the front skirt.

2 Repeat step 1 with the second strip of scalloped-edge fabric to create the back skirt, replicating the spacing of the pleats and ensuring that the skirt top measures 15cm (6in).

Attaching the Skirt to the Bodice and Sewing the Side Seams

1 With right sides together, match the pleated top of the front skirt to the front bodice, making sure the sides run smoothly into one another and that the centre fronts match. Sew together with a 1cm (⅜in) seam allowance **(Fig.15)**.

2 Repeat step 1 to sew the back skirt to the back bodice **(Fig.16)**. Finish the seam with overlock or zigzag stitch, then press towards the bodice.

3 With right sides together, match up the sleeve hems, underarms, waist, and skirt side seams, pinning as you go, then sew together (**Fig.17**). Finish the seam with overlock or zigzag stitch, then press towards the back as far as you can.

FINISHING OFF

1 Sew the three buttons on the right-hand side (as worn) of the bodice, using the pattern as a guide to positioning. Position one half of a press stud beneath each button and sew in place. Then sew the other half of each press stud in place onto the left-hand side of the bodice as worn.

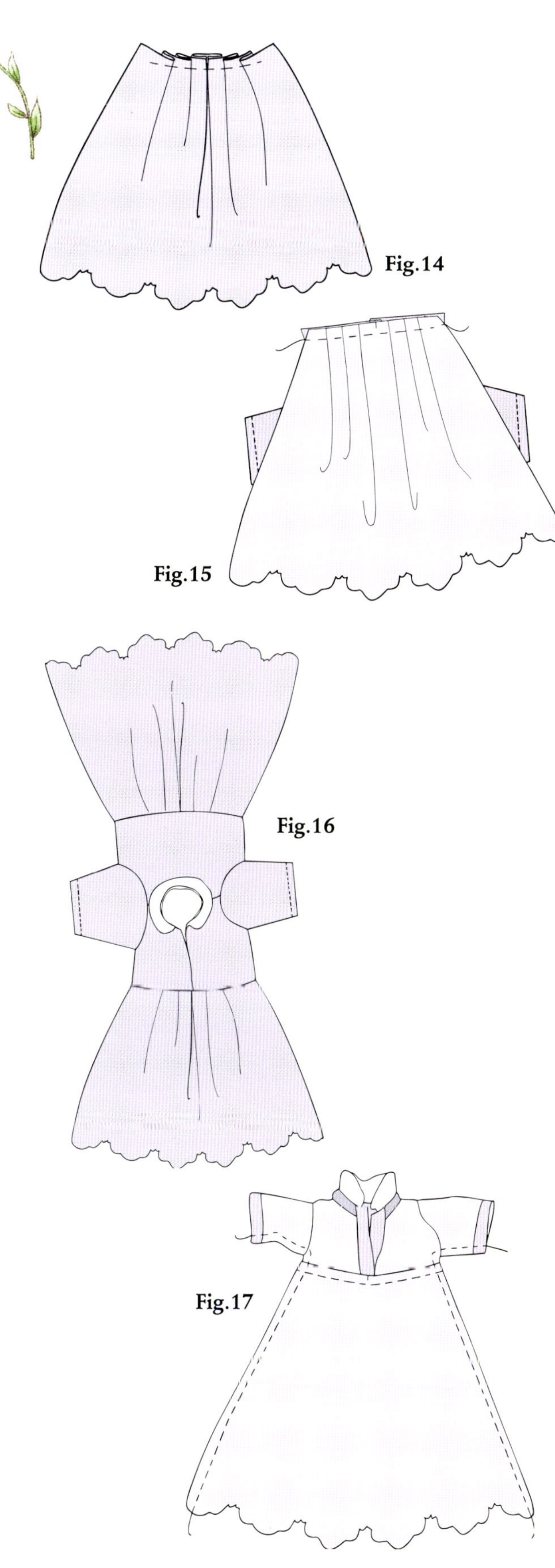
Fig.14

Fig.15

Fig.16

Fig.17

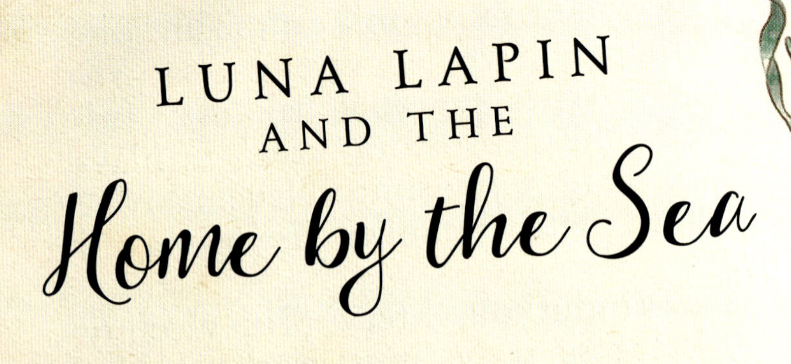

LUNA LAPIN AND THE *Home by the Sea*

The rain wouldn't let up, and something was definitely wrong with the car. It was Christmas Eve, long past sunset, and Alfie was struggling to feel any trace of the holiday spirit. The car sputtered and lurched before giving up entirely, leaving them stranded in the middle of nowhere.

"Stay in the car, Pepper," Alfie said, jumping out of the driver's seat to search for a torch. The back of the car was packed with presents, each one carefully chosen for their family. Alfie and Pepper had been on their way home from their honeymoon, hoping to arrive at Granny's cottage hours ago. But now, in the relentless downpour, it was clear they wouldn't make it. The landscape around them was unrecognisable – just darkened fields and endless rain.

Pepper had felt for a while that they'd taken a wrong turn, though it was hard to tell through the storm. The car let out one final groan and fell silent. Up ahead, a faint glow flickered from a distant second-floor window perched high on a hill.

Pulling coats tight around them, Alfie and Pepper braved the wind and rain, running towards the light. Pepper could taste salt on the air. "Alfie! Are we near the sea?" she asked. As they reached the summit, the sound of crashing waves answered her question. Saltwater stung their fur as the wind lashed against them, making it painfully clear just how far from home they were.

A faded sign – Shale Cottage Guest House – hung from a gatepost near the house. Pepper's spirits lifted briefly, only to drop again when she saw the smaller notice beneath it: No Vacancies. But Pepper believed in the kindness of strangers, especially at Christmas. Surely, in weather like this, room would be found for two wet, weary travellers. Alfie approached the front door, knocking harder than he intended, shaking the Christmas wreath. Rain dripped from his fur as he turned to Pepper, "I'm so sorry, darling. This isn't how I imagined our honeymoon would end."

No one answered the door. Alfie knocked again, louder this time, desperation creeping into his voice. When there was still no response, he leaned his head against the door and pleaded, "Please, we just need to use a phone. Help us!"

The wreath fell into his hands, but there was still no answer.

"We can use the blanket we got for Granny and pile on all our clothes," Pepper suggested, ever the optimist. "We'll make an adventure of it." But Alfie couldn't bear the thought of his gentle wife, who slept under two duvets, even in summer, curled up freezing in the back of their broken-down car on Christmas Eve.

As he tried to reattach the wreath, the door creaked open. A chocolate-brown donkey, wearing long johns and looking half-asleep, peered out. "What are you doing with our wreath? And why are you so wet?"

Before Alfie could respond, another donkey, sandy-coloured, in matching pyjamas, appeared behind him. "Sid! Don't be rude! Let them in, for goodness sake! What are you two doing out in this weather? Come inside, come in, you sweet soggy things!"

Inside, the warmth enveloped them like a hug. The home smelled of honey, saltwater, and warm oats. Alfie and Pepper were quickly wrapped in soft towels, the fire crackling beside a large Christmas tree decorated with handmade ornaments. Three stockings hung from the mantle, but Alfie couldn't help noticing Sidney's gaze drifted to the third one, which remained empty.

The sandy-coloured donkey, who introduced himself as Sol, carried a tray of steaming mugs. Sidney took his with a tired smile, while Sol perched on the arm of his chair, close enough that their shoulders touched.

Alfie and Pepper recounted their journey – the storm, the car breaking down, their desperate search for shelter. Sol listened with kind eyes, his hand resting on Sidney's knee. "Well," Sol said warmly, "you can stay as long as you need. Can't they, Sid?"

Sidney, though clearly lost in thought, nodded. "Yes, of course."

Sol continued, "We've had quiet Christmases for years now. It'll be nice to have some company. Besides, we can't let you spend your first Christmas together in the rain."

Sol showed Pepper to a cosy room with a tall iron bed topped with a patchwork quilt. Pepper sighed, taking in the old-world charm. "This could've been the perfect Christmas if we weren't so stranded," she mused.

Sol smiled at her. "You know, Christmas isn't always about everything going right – it's about the people you spend it with." He hesitated for a moment, then added, "We've had too many quiet Christmases. Sidney… well, Christmas is hard for him. He invites his brother every year, but he never comes."

Pepper frowned sympathetically. "That's so sad," she said.

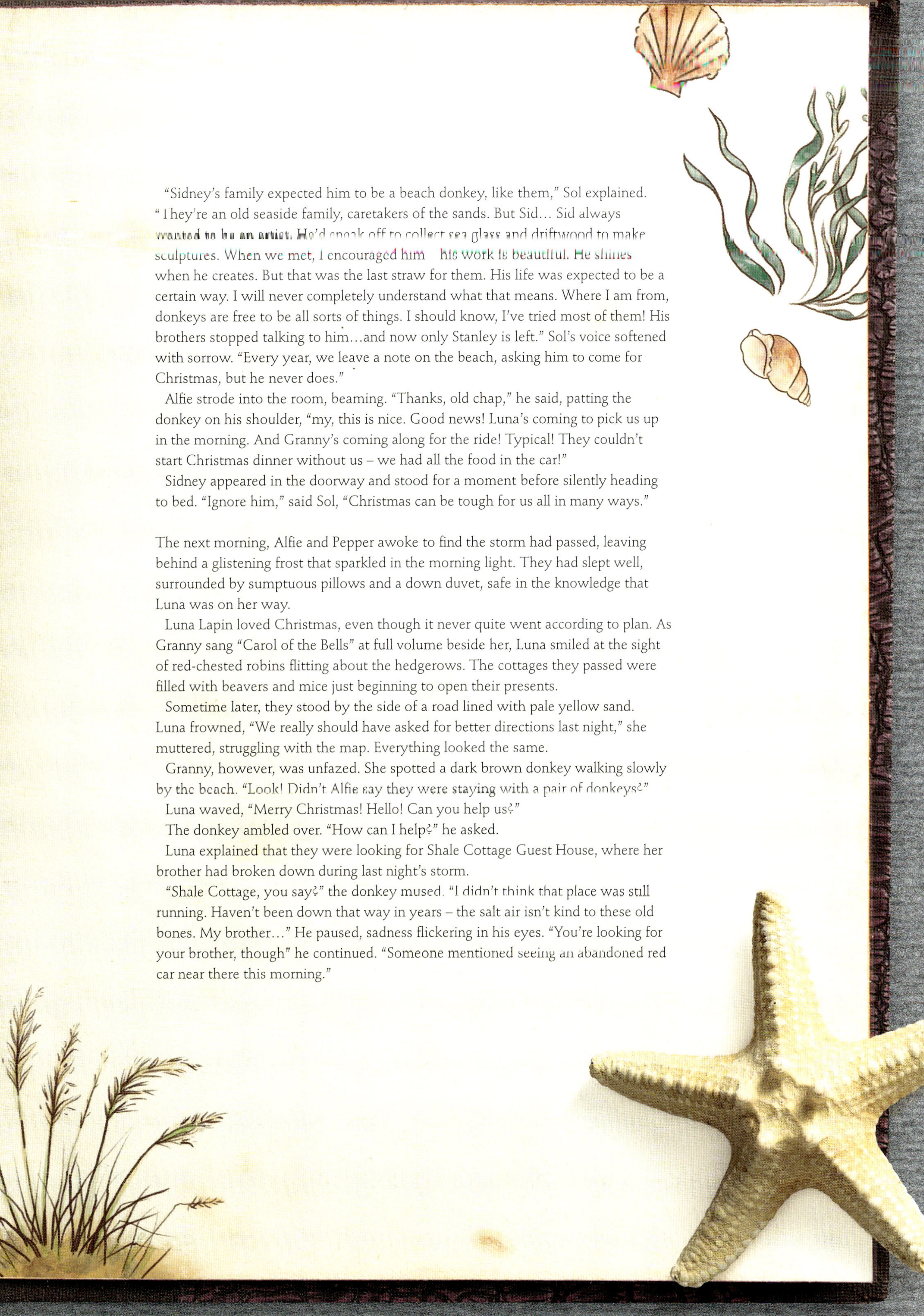

"Sidney's family expected him to be a beach donkey, like them," Sol explained. "They're an old seaside family, caretakers of the sands. But Sid… Sid always wanted to be an artist. He'd sneak off to collect sea glass and driftwood to make sculptures. When we met, I encouraged him his work is beautiful. He shines when he creates. But that was the last straw for them. His life was expected to be a certain way. I will never completely understand what that means. Where I am from, donkeys are free to be all sorts of things. I should know, I've tried most of them! His brothers stopped talking to him…and now only Stanley is left." Sol's voice softened with sorrow. "Every year, we leave a note on the beach, asking him to come for Christmas, but he never does."

Alfie strode into the room, beaming. "Thanks, old chap," he said, patting the donkey on his shoulder, "my, this is nice. Good news! Luna's coming to pick us up in the morning. And Granny's coming along for the ride! Typical! They couldn't start Christmas dinner without us – we had all the food in the car!"

Sidney appeared in the doorway and stood for a moment before silently heading to bed. "Ignore him," said Sol, "Christmas can be tough for us all in many ways."

The next morning, Alfie and Pepper awoke to find the storm had passed, leaving behind a glistening frost that sparkled in the morning light. They had slept well, surrounded by sumptuous pillows and a down duvet, safe in the knowledge that Luna was on her way.

Luna Lapin loved Christmas, even though it never quite went according to plan. As Granny sang "Carol of the Bells" at full volume beside her, Luna smiled at the sight of red-chested robins flitting about the hedgerows. The cottages they passed were filled with beavers and mice just beginning to open their presents.

Sometime later, they stood by the side of a road lined with pale yellow sand. Luna frowned, "We really should have asked for better directions last night," she muttered, struggling with the map. Everything looked the same.

Granny, however, was unfazed. She spotted a dark brown donkey walking slowly by the beach. "Look! Didn't Alfie say they were staying with a pair of donkeys?"

Luna waved, "Merry Christmas! Hello! Can you help us?"

The donkey ambled over. "How can I help?" he asked.

Luna explained that they were looking for Shale Cottage Guest House, where her brother had broken down during last night's storm.

"Shale Cottage, you say?" the donkey mused. "I didn't think that place was still running. Haven't been down that way in years – the salt air isn't kind to these old bones. My brother…" He paused, sadness flickering in his eyes. "You're looking for your brother, though" he continued. "Someone mentioned seeing an abandoned red car near there this morning."

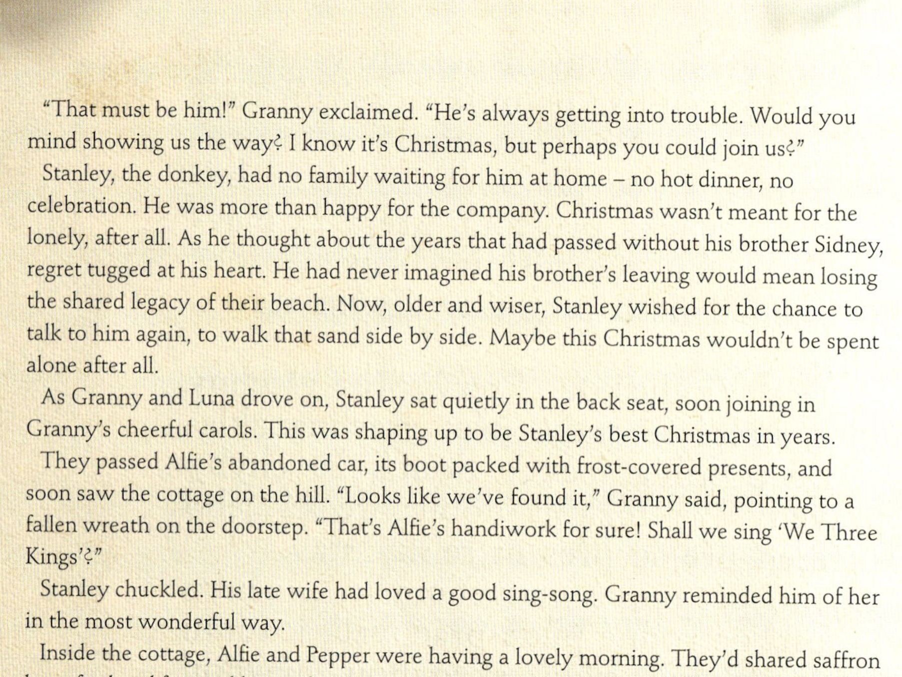

"That must be him!" Granny exclaimed. "He's always getting into trouble. Would you mind showing us the way? I know it's Christmas, but perhaps you could join us?"

Stanley, the donkey, had no family waiting for him at home – no hot dinner, no celebration. He was more than happy for the company. Christmas wasn't meant for the lonely, after all. As he thought about the years that had passed without his brother Sidney, regret tugged at his heart. He had never imagined his brother's leaving would mean losing the shared legacy of their beach. Now, older and wiser, Stanley wished for the chance to talk to him again, to walk that sand side by side. Maybe this Christmas wouldn't be spent alone after all.

As Granny and Luna drove on, Stanley sat quietly in the back seat, soon joining in Granny's cheerful carols. This was shaping up to be Stanley's best Christmas in years.

They passed Alfie's abandoned car, its boot packed with frost-covered presents, and soon saw the cottage on the hill. "Looks like we've found it," Granny said, pointing to a fallen wreath on the doorstep. "That's Alfie's handiwork for sure! Shall we sing 'We Three Kings'?"

Stanley chuckled. His late wife had loved a good sing-song. Granny reminded him of her in the most wonderful way.

Inside the cottage, Alfie and Pepper were having a lovely morning. They'd shared saffron buns for breakfast and listened to Sol's tales of Christmases from around the world. Sidney was greatly cheered from the night before. Alfie laughed heartily as Pepper smiled back at him with adoration. This Christmas hadn't turned out so bad after all. The sound of familiar voices singing outside caught Pepper's attention.

"O star of wonder, star of light, star with royal beauty bright, westward leading, still proceeding, guide us to thy perfect light."

Luna, Granny, and Stanley made their way slowly up the last of the steep steps, belting out carols filled with festive joy. The door swung open, and the cottage's occupants joined in the song. Sidney froze when he saw Stanley standing behind Luna, eyes closed, lost in the moment.

"Stanley?" Sidney's voice trembled as he rushed towards his older brother.

Stanley's eyes snapped open, his expression stern. "What are you doing here?"

"I live here, you old mule! Didn't you know?" asked Sidney.

Stanley looked confused. "You live here? I had no idea. You never invited me."

"We left you an invitation on the beach every year," Sidney explained. "It was always still there on Boxing Day."

Stanley sighed. "I can't walk that far anymore. The cold gets into my bones. I didn't even know you had come home," his voice cracking under the weight of missing years.

Sidney's face softened. "How could I not come home? The sea here is as much mine as yours. I'm sorry, Stanley. I should have made sure you knew."

Stanley shook his head. "Don't be sorry. I have more to apologise for. All that time..."

Sidney stepped aside, showing Stanley the inside of the home he had built alongside Sol. "You are here now," he said, and though there was much still to say, their long years of separation were washed away like the tide.

"Perhaps you'd all like to stay for Christmas dinner," said Sol, Sidney's partner, breaking the silence. "Those two look like they have a lot to discuss, and I could use the company."

Luckily, Alfie's car was full of carrots and Brussels sprouts, and soon everyone was peeling and chopping their way to a festive feast.

After dinner, the group strolled down the beach, full of mulled wine and figgy pudding. Stanley, Sidney, and Sol, clad in matching striped swimsuits, braved the icy sea, laughing like the children they once were as they plunged into the water. Luna, less courageous, giggled from the shore as the frigid waves tickled her paws.

Granny, wrapped in a blanket, watched them from her camping chair, pride swelling in her heart. How proud she was of her family, their kindness and generosity, not just on Christmas Day but every day.

Pepper stood beside Alfie, her heart full. As she placed a hand on her belly and splashed Alfie playfully, she smiled to herself, knowing that next Christmas would be even more special.

Sidney's Long Johns

YOU WILL NEED

- 37cm (14½in) x 70cm (27½in) pointelle jersey
- 26cm (10¼in) of 25mm (1in) wide bias
- Small amount of iron-on interfacing
- Three 1cm (⅜in) shell buttons
- Three press stud fasteners (optional)
- Basic sewing kit (see Materials)

Use a 0.5cm (¼in) seam allowance, unless a different amount is stated.

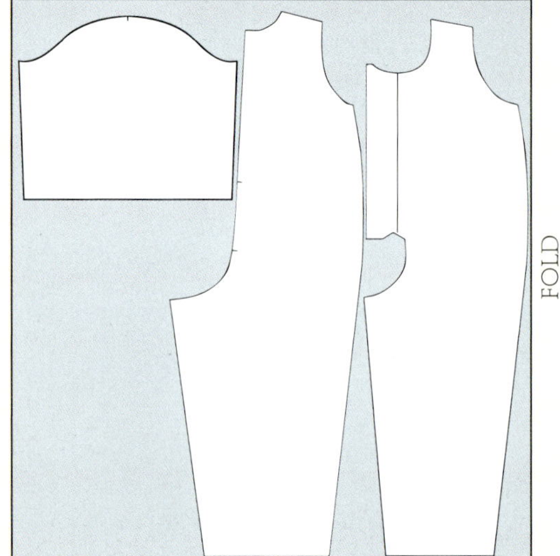

Fig.1

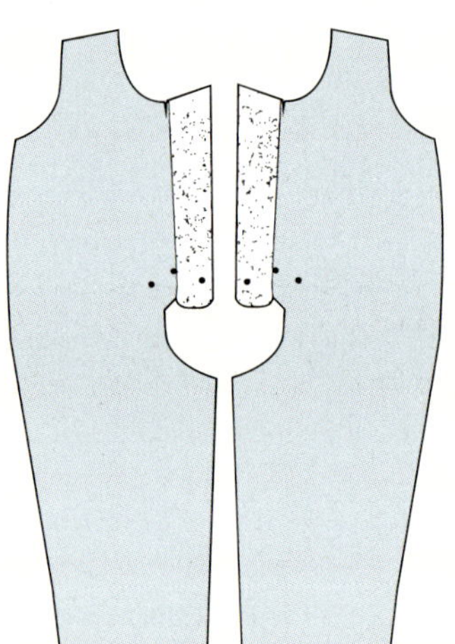

Fig.2

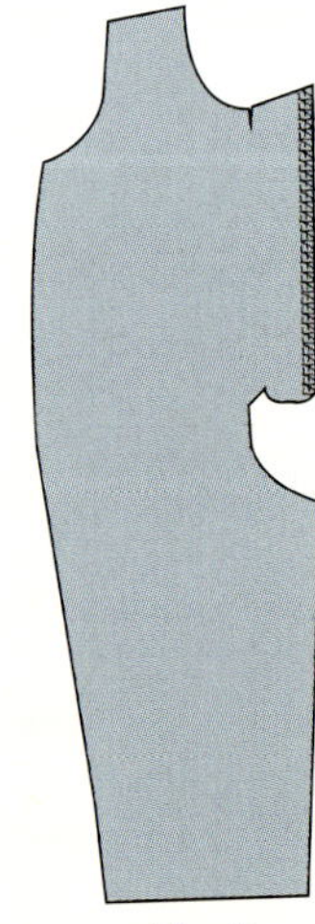

Fig.3

CUTTING OUT

1 Fold the jersey fabric in half with right sides together. Pin your cut-out pattern pieces (see The Patterns) onto the fabric using **Fig.1** as a guide. Cut all pieces as stated on the pattern. Mark notches on the back and sleeves, preferably with a water-soluble marker pen, or by making a small snip into the fabric.

2 Use the placket pattern (see The Patterns) to cut two pieces (one and one reversed) from the interfacing.

MAKING UP

Preparing and Sewing the Front Placket

1 Take the front pieces and establish the wrong side of the fabric. Apply the iron-on interfacing along the placket area of each piece (see **Fig.2**), laying the interfacing glue-side down and using a stamping (up-down) movement to fuse it in place with a medium-hot iron.

2 Mark the dots and notches from the front pattern piece using a water-soluble marking pen or with tailor's tacks. Overlock or zigzag stitch the placket extension edge on each front piece in turn (**Fig.3**).

3 Working on one of the front pieces, fold the placket back on itself so the right sides are together and the 'A' dots are aligned. Sew from dot B on the folded edge to dot A, which will mark the end of the front rise stitching (**Fig.4**). Don't overshoot dot A as this will affect how smoothly the placket sits.

4 Turning the front piece over, carefully snip into the seam allowance close to dot A (**Fig.5**). Then trim away the seam allowance at the bottom of the placket stitching. Push the placket through to the right side, to give a crisply turned corner.

5 Repeat steps 3 and 4 on the other front piece to give a mirror image (**Fig.6**).

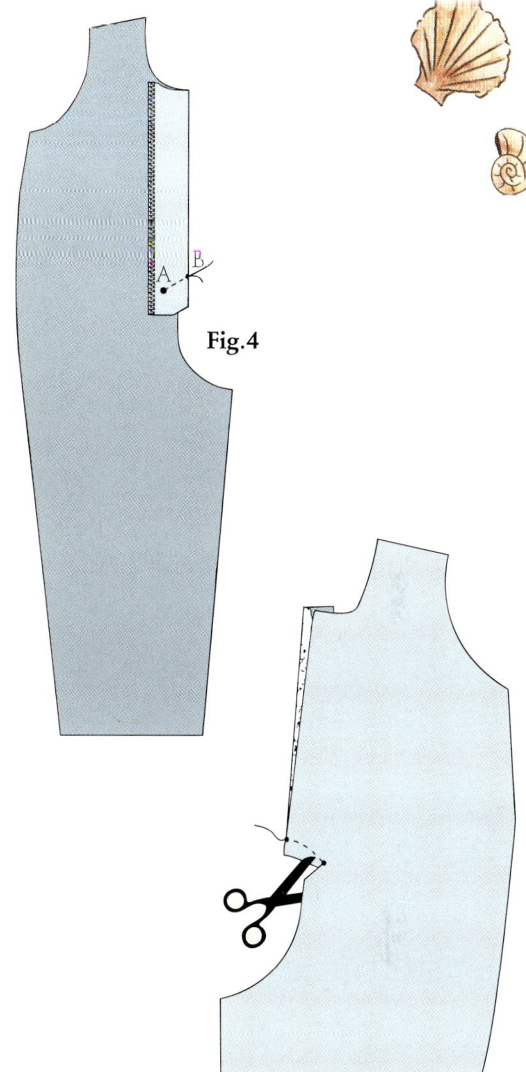

Fig.4

Fig.5

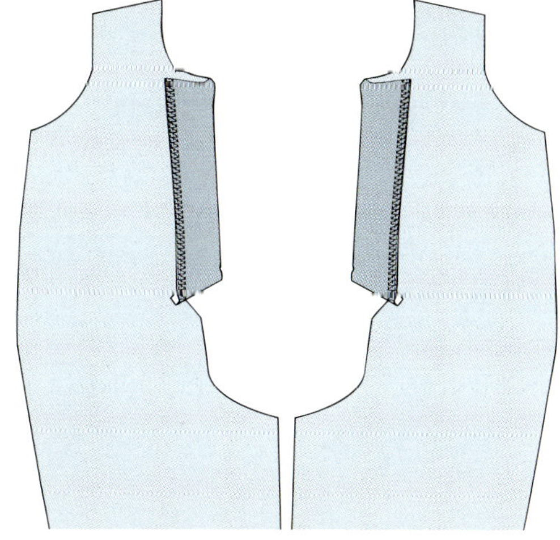

Fig.6

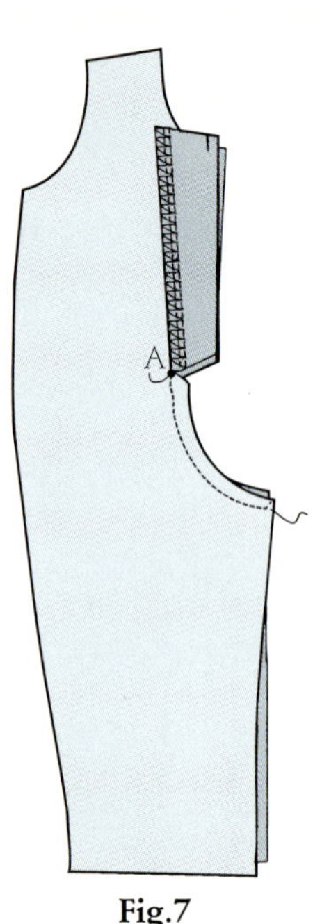

Fig.7

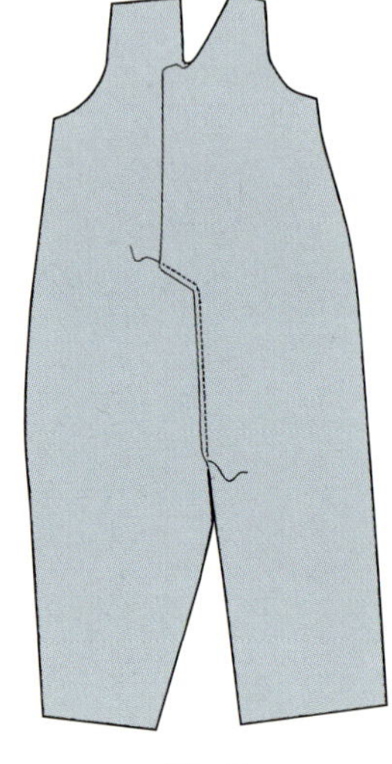

Fig.8

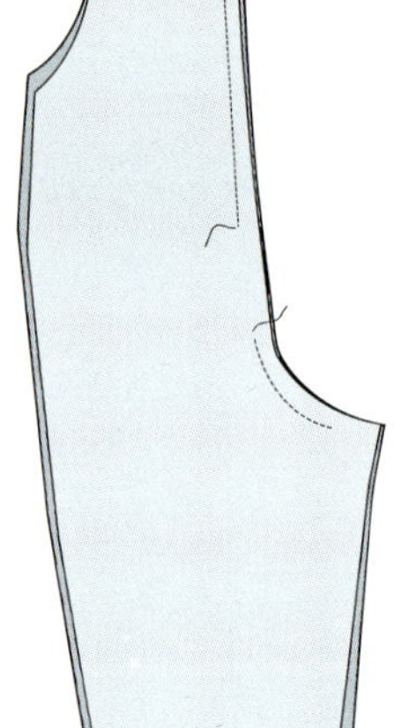

Fig.9

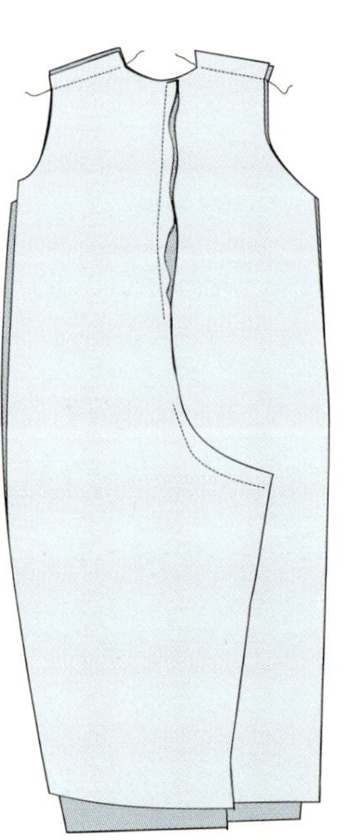

Fig.10

Sewing the Front Rise and Securing the Placket

1 With right sides together, match and pin the front rise and sew together, starting at dot A (**Fig.7**).

2 Turning the joined fronts to the right side up, bring the left extension (as worn) over the right-hand side (as worn). Pin, then sew in place, using an edgestitch, starting at the turned corner. If you wish, you can pivot at the front rise seam and edgestitch the front rise also, catching the seam allowance underneath (**Fig.8**). In a human garment, this would add strength to the seam.

Sewing the Centre Back Seam

1 Take the back pieces and, with right sides together, match and pin the centre back seams; then sew together, stopping and starting at the notches to leave a tail gap (**Fig.9**).

Sewing the Shoulder Seams

1 With right sides together, match and pin the front shoulders to the back shoulder seams, then sew together (**Fig.10**).

Sewing the Sleeves

1 To hem the sleeves, turn 1cm (⅜in) to the wrong side of each sleeve and zigzag stitch in place, taking care not to stretch the fabric as you sew. (Make a note of your hemming zigzag settings to that you can be consistent throughout the project.)

2 With right sides together, match and pin one sleeve onto each armhole (the sleeve notch should match the shoulder seam) and sew in place (**Fig.11**).

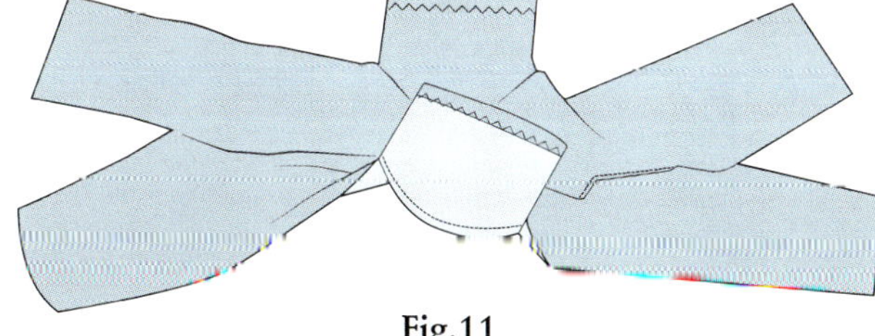

Fig.11

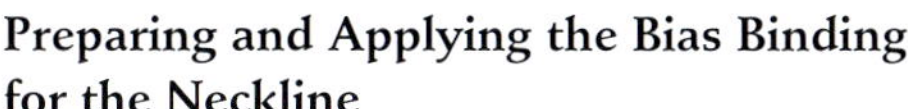

Preparing and Applying the Bias Binding for the Neckline

Note: The garment as shown is finished with bias binding on the neckline as described in the steps that follow. However, if you prefer a faster finish without the bias, see Alternative Method for Sewing the Neckline.

1 Trim one side off the bias binding using the inner raw edge as a guideline. This will leave you with a narrower bias to work with that has one flat edge and one folded edge. Use an iron to set the bias into a curve, focusing on stretching the folded edge and compressing the flat edge (**Fig.12**).

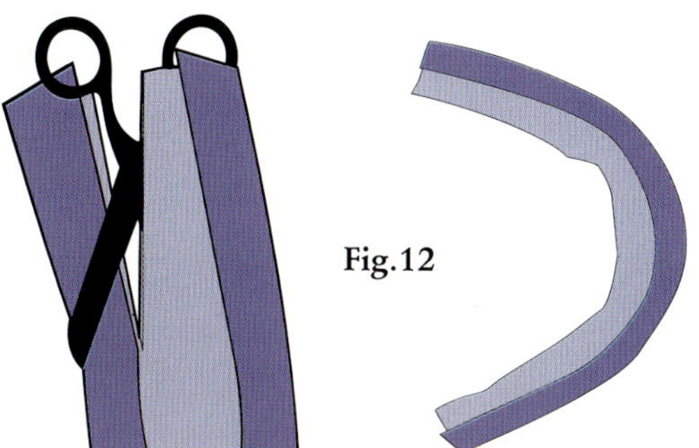

Fig.12

2 Fold the front placket extensions back on themselves to the wrong side and pin in place. Then, with right sides together, pin the flat edge of the bias binding to the neck edge, trimming to be a little short of the folded ends (**Fig.13**). Sew in place, then trim the excess seam allowance away at the fronts and snip into the seam allowance as necessary.

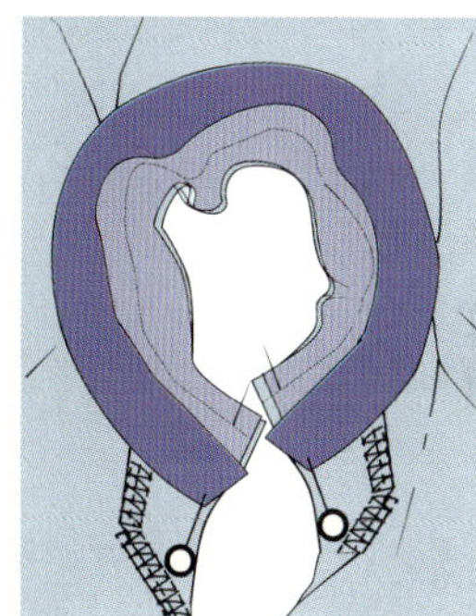

Fig.13

3 Push the front plackets out to the right side and press the bias back to the wrong side of the neckline. Sew with a stretch (or zigzag) stitch or a straight edgestitch to hold the bias down (**Fig.14**).

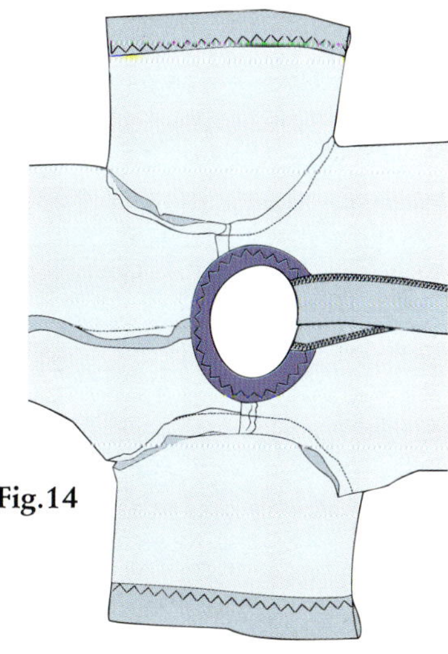

Fig.14

Alternative method for sewing the neckline

1 To sew the neckline without bias binding, simply fold the front placket extensions back on themselves to the wrong side and sew with a 0.5cm (¼in) seam allowance, trim and push out to the right side. Then turn back 0.5cm (¼in) around the rest of the neckline, press and zigzag or stretch stitch in place.

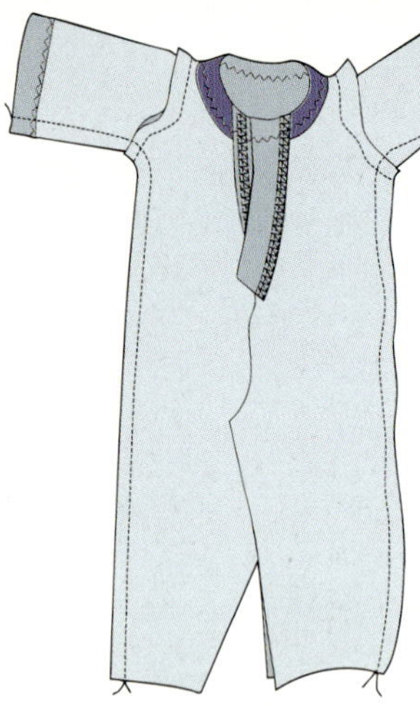

Fig.15

Fig.16

Fig.17

Fig.18

Sewing the Side Seams

1 With right sides together, match the underarms and body side seams, then sew together (**Fig.15**).

Sewing the Inside Legs

1 First hem the legs. Turn 1cm (⅜in) to the wrong side of each leg hem and zigzag stitch in place, taking care not to stretch the fabric as you sew (**Fig.16**).

2 With right sides together, pin the front to the back along the inside leg taking care to match the rise seam and hems, then sew together (**Fig.17**).

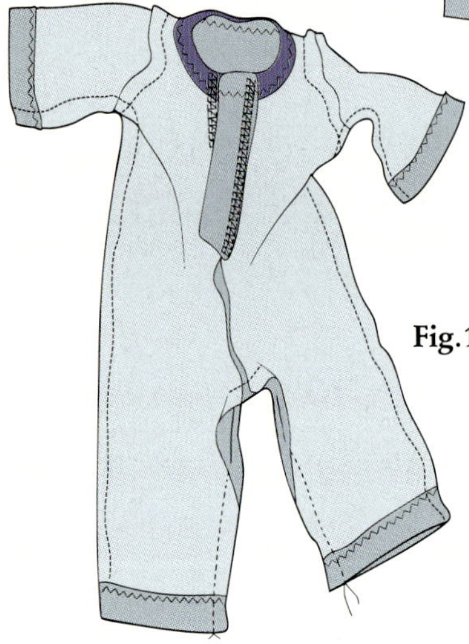

FINISHING OFF

Note: There are two alternative methods for finishing the garment with fastenings, but if you want to avoid buttonholes, then Method 2 is the one for you.

Method 1

1 Using the pattern as a guide to positioning, sew three buttons on the right-hand side as worn. Sew on with double thread, through the placket facing to hold it in position. Make three small buttonholes about 1.2cm (approx. ⅜in) long on the left-hand side as worn. Cut through the buttonholes carefully (**Fig.18**).

Method 2

1 Using the pattern as a guide to positioning, sew three buttons on the left-hand side as worn. Position one half of a press stud beneath each button and sew in place. Then sew the other half of each press stud in place onto the right-hand side as worn.

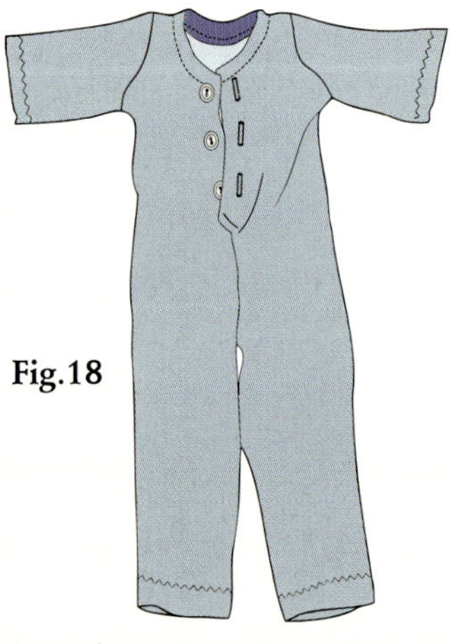

Sol's Bathing Suit

YOU WILL NEED

- **28cm (11in) x 70cm (27½in) striped sweatshirt fabric**
- **26cm (10¼in) of 25mm (1in) wide bias binding**
- **Small amount of iron-on interfacing**
- **Three 1cm (3/8in) buttons**
- **Three press stud fasteners (optional)**
- **Basic sewing kit (see Materials)**

Use a 0.5cm (¼in) seam allowance, unless a different amount is stated.

CUTTING OUT

1 Fold the sweatshirt fabric in half with right sides together. Pin your cut-out pattern pieces (see The Patterns) onto the fabric using **Fig.1** as a guide. Take care laying out the pattern pieces to ensure your stripes line up on the fronts and backs. Cut all pieces as stated on the pattern Mark notches on the back and sleeves, preferably with a water-soluble marker pen, or by making a small snip into the fabric.

2 Use the placket pattern (see The Patterns) to cut two pieces (one and one reversed) from the interfacing.

MAKING UP

Please refer to Sidney's Long Johns.

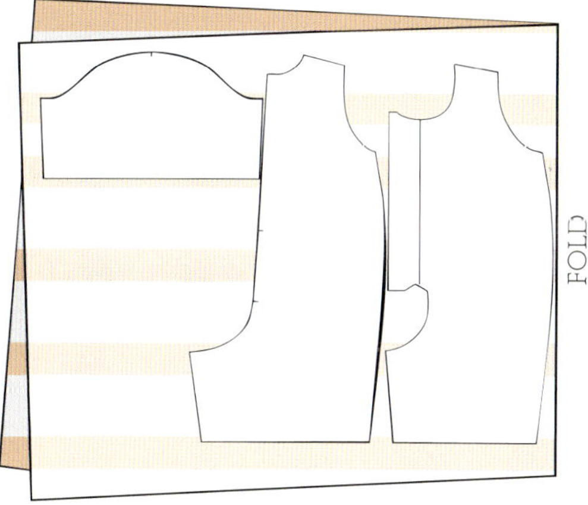

Fig.1

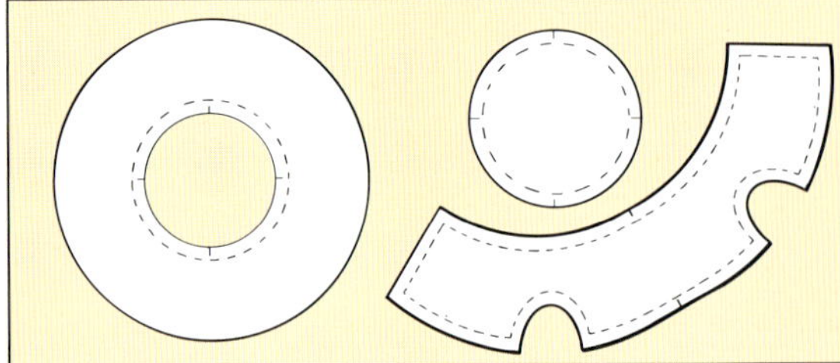

Fig.1

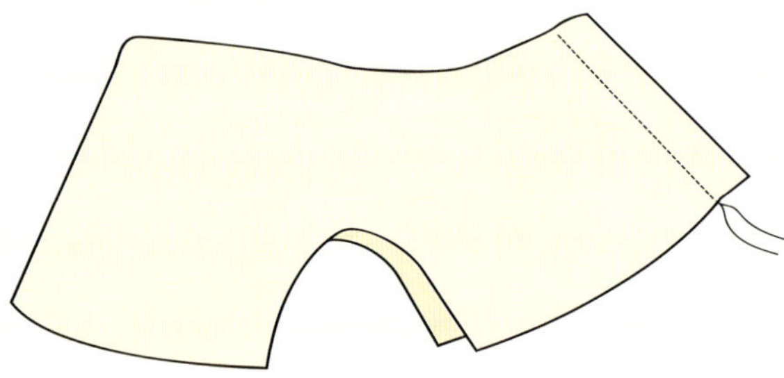

Fig.2

Sol's Straw Hat

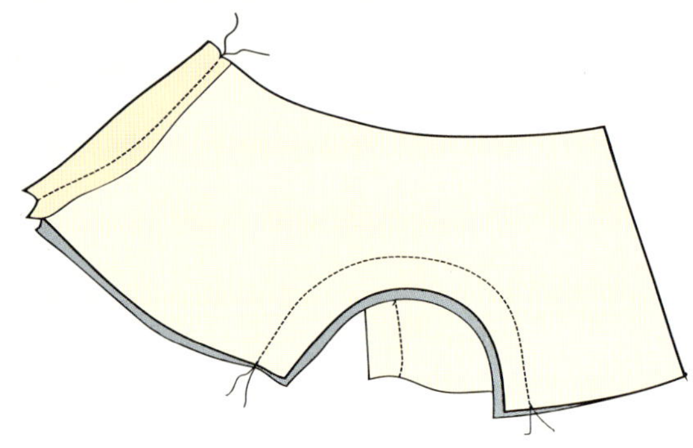

Fig.3

YOU WILL NEED

- 15cm (6in) x 35cm (14in) hessian*
- 15cm (6in) x 20cm (8in) cotton poplin lining fabric
- Small piece of card
- 25cm (10in) of 25mm (1in) wide bias binding
- Basic sewing kit (see Materials)

Use a 0.5cm (¼in) seam allowance, unless a different amount is stated.

* We have used a luxury hessian – this has a tighter weave than the average hessian, so it's a little easier to handle; a rougher hessian will give you a straw-like appearance. Alternatively, use felt or cotton poplin, cut double on the brim.

CUTTING OUT

1 Pin your cut-out pattern pieces (see The Patterns) onto single-thickness hessian using **Fig.1** as a guide. Mark any notches with a water-soluble pen.

2 Cut one band and one crown out of the lining fabric of your choice. Mark any notches with a water-soluble pen.

MAKING UP

Making the Band

1 With right sides together, sew the short ends of the hessian together to form a band (**Fig.2**). Repeat to make a band from the cotton lining. Press seams open and flat.

2 With right sides together, match the hessian and the cotton lining bands together, and sew around the ear cut-outs (**Fig.3**). Carefully snip into the seam allowance, but not too close to the stitching line.

3 Turn through to the right side (i.e. hessian side facing out) and press the curved shape flat. Staystitch or tack (baste) the top edges together, then do the same along the bottom edges in preparation for the next step (**Fig.4**). Now turn the prepared band so that the lining side is facing out.

Sewing the Crown onto the Band

1 Take the hessian crown and sew it onto the prepared band, right sides of the hessian together, using the marked notches to match them up perfectly (**Fig.5**).

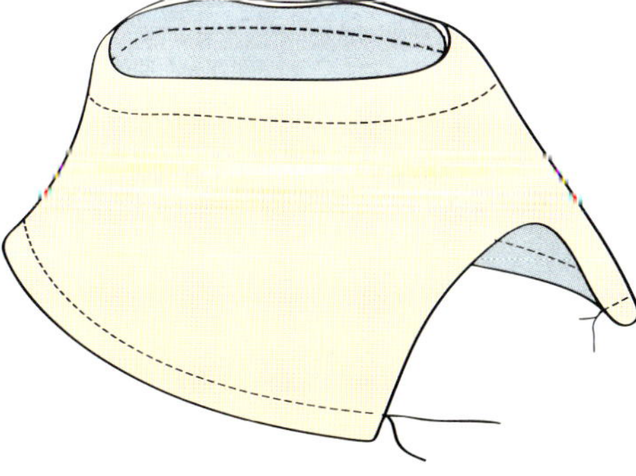

Fig.4

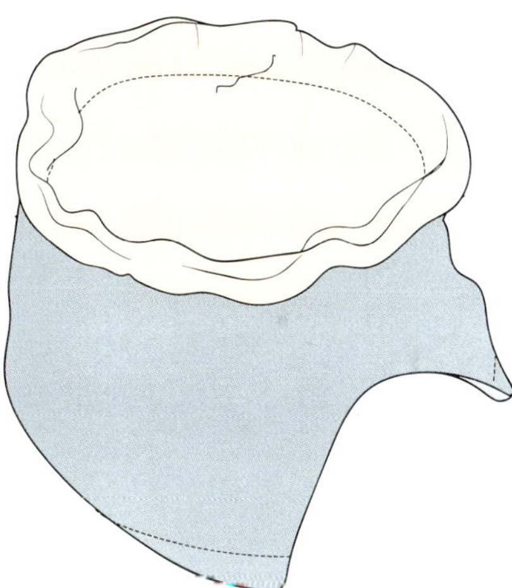

Fig.5

Attaching the Brim to the Band

1 Take the hessian brim and use a short stitch to sew a line of stitching between 0.5cm to 1cm (¼in to ⅜in) away from the outer edge. Note that the deeper you sew, the more the brim will fray. At the inside edge of the brim sew a narrow 0.5cm (¼in) away from the edge to staystitch (**Fig.6**).

2 Attach the prepared brim to the band with right sides together: find the centre front and centre back point, match and pin; then continue to match and pin as you work around the shape, allowing space for the ear gaps (**Fig.7**). Tack (baste) together in preparation to attach the bias binding strip.

3 Prepare the bias binding strip as Figs.11 and 12 of Sidney's Long Johns (i.e. cutting off the extra width and pre-pressing the curve). On the left-hand edge of the prepared bias binding strip, turn 1cm (⅜in) to the wrong side and press (**Fig.8**).

Fig.6

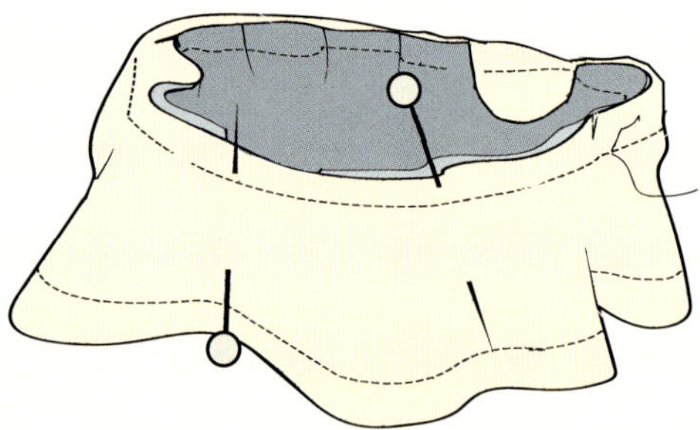

Fig.7

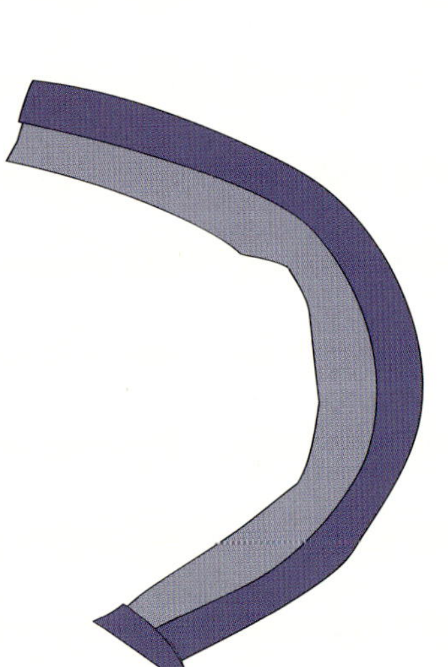

Fig.8

Attaching the Bias Binding Strip

1 This is a fiddly project, but this is undoubtedly the trickiest step of all! Working with the hat lining to the inside, pin the bias on the inside of the hat, with the flat edge of the bias matching the band/brim edge. Start at the centre back with the folded end of the bias and gradually sew in place. Don't stretch the bias as you sew or it will change the shape of the hat – allow the bias to be relaxed. When you have worked all the way around, trim the excess bias about 1cm (⅜in) beyond the folded end of your start point (**Fig.9**).

2 Trim the seam allowance just sewn back to half of its depth. Finger press the bias binding so that it comes over the seam allowance and sits flat on the brim, but making sure that it isn't visible on the right side of the ear gaps. Edgestitch the folded edge of the bias onto the brim of the hat (**Fig.10**).

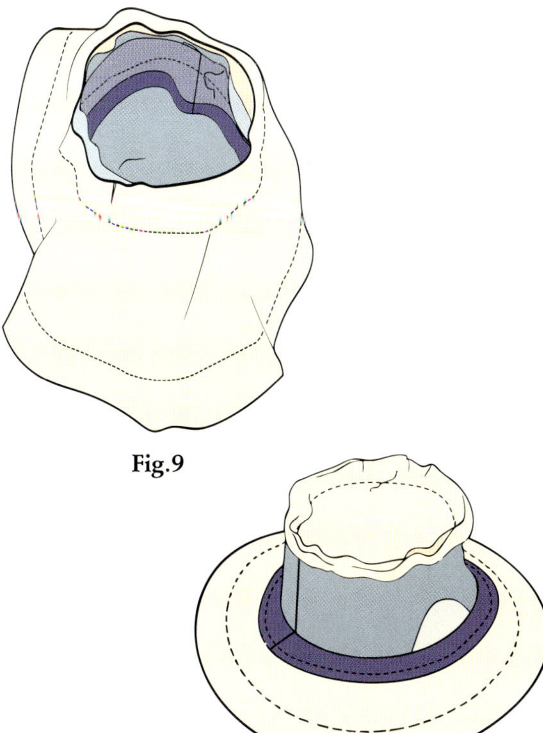

Fig.9

Fig.10

Making the Crown Lining

1 Cut the crown template (see The Patterns) out of card and use this to help to press the seam allowance in on the crown lining (**Fig.11**).

2 Once pressed all the way around, remove the card template. Working on the inside of the hat, pin the pressed crown lining in place over the hessian crown, tucking in the raw seams (**Fig.12**). Slipstitch to secure in place, then push the hat through to the right side.

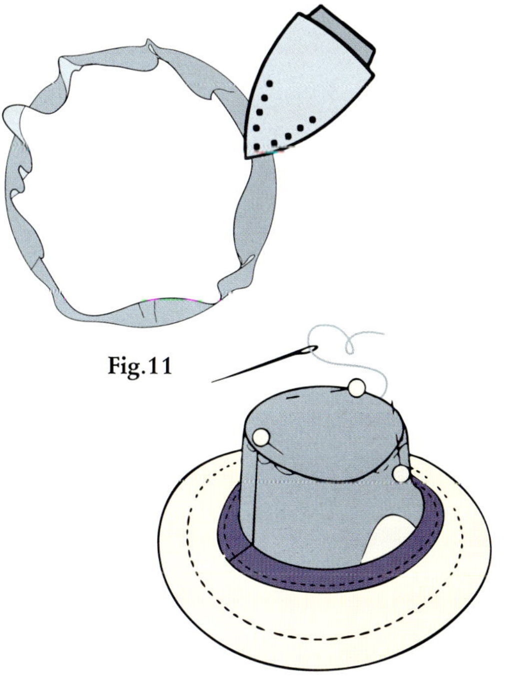

Fig.11

Fig.12

LUNA LAPIN AND THE *Olympian*

Luna Lapin was working on something extraordinary – a gown for Gracie Grenouille (pronounced *Gren-wee!*), the French frog princess. Luna couldn't believe she was making a dress for royalty! The dress was truly magnificent, layer upon layer of the most sublime fabric, fashioned into petals that revealed glimpses of paw-stitched tulle beneath. Just as Luna was trimming the final thread, a knock came at the door.

"Bonjour, Mademoiselle Lapin," Gracie said, her bright eyes twinkling as she flung open the door. Graceful, green, and a whirlwind of energy, Gracie grasped Luna by both hands and kissed her cheeks enthusiastically, knocking a spool of thread on the floor as she did so. Luna didn't mind. There was something utterly charming about this spirited princess.

"Your majesty, it's a pleasure to meet you," Luna said, offering a curtsy. "I've been working on your gown for the royal – "

"Oh, forget the gown!" Gracie interrupted with a laugh, waving the thought away with a webbed hand. "I've come for something much more important. I need you to design my outfit for the Olympics!"

Luna blinked in surprise, setting down her scissors. "The Olympics? But… isn't that against royal tradition?"

"Bah! My father, King Grenouille, insists a princess mustn't compete. It's never been done before!" Gracie puffed out her chest, her frog legs flexing like she was already at the starting line. "But I will compete, Luna. All my life, I have been training. I have learned to swim and dance alongside the best in all of France, and I am confident in my abilities. I want the world to know Gracie Grenouille is a hard worker, and nothing – not even tradition – can stop me!"

There was a fire in Gracie's eyes that Luna recognised. Luna understood determination. After all, she, too, had followed her heart. No one thought a quiet and kind rabbit from the burrows would make a name for herself. But still, she hesitated. "But your father… he seemed so strict when commissioning the gown. I don't want to cause trouble."

Gracie grinned widely, a playful twinkle in her eye. "Bah, he's already displeased! He was born with a complaint in his throat! He thinks a princess should only wear gowns and sip tea. He underestimates me, Luna. I think you know how that feels." Luna nodded.

MERCERIE
MERCERIE

"I want this more badly than I have wanted anything my whole life," Gracie continued. "I want an outfit that speaks of strength, *joie de vivre*, speed! He was right about one thing, Luna. You are the best. You must help me."

Luna loved creating beautiful things, but more than that, she loved helping others follow their dreams. Gracie didn't want just any outfit – she wanted to wear something that symbolised her place in the world. Luna believed in the magic of clothes and that the right outfit could help shape you into the best version of yourself.

"I'll do it," Luna said, a smile dancing across her face. "But promise me one thing."

"Name it!" Gracie said, leaping in the air excitedly.

"That you'll give your all and prove that you can do anything you put your mind to."

Gracie placed a hand over her heart dramatically. "I, Princess Gracie Grenouille, solemnly swear to give it my all!" she said, laughing and twirling on the spot. "We are a perfect match, *mon cherie* Lapin, you'll see!"

Luna began working on Gracie's Olympic outfit. She sketched her ideas, from sequins to latex, and made drawings of them all. Gracie came and went as she pleased, sharing stories of her training – jumping lily pads, swimming through rivers, and even balancing on tree branches to improve her agility. She cast her big green eyes over Luna's work: too many sequins, too heavy, not bright enough. But Luna knew the perfect outfit was somewhere in the tip of her pencil, so she didn't give up even as the Olympics got closer and closer.

One day, Luna woke up to the breaking headline: "Royal Rule Breaker Goes for Gold". Reporters began to show up all over Briar Meadows, hoping to snap a picture of Gracie in training or to catch a sneak preview of Luna's new designs. Luna ignored it all, so much so that she nearly missed the smartly dressed stoat knocking on her front door.

The stoat cleared his throat before beginning to read, "His Majesty King Grenouille, the one true ruler, first of his name, requests you send his daughter, Her Royal Highness Gracie Grenouille, back to the safety of the Palace at once. The power of the Crown insists on your immediate abandonment of this ridiculous project, and you are to see that Gracie returns to her rightful role as heir to the throne. The King demands that you return to making gowns, or it is said you may never work again."

Quiet as she was, Luna did not take kindly to threats and forcefully but apologetically closed the door on the young stoat. Gracie watched on in admiration.

"You believe in me, don't you, Luna?" she said, her usual confidence replaced by doubt.

"Unequivocally!" said a determined little rabbit.

Finally, the day of the Olympics arrived. The arena was filled with folk from all over the world – lean spotted cheetahs, dashing red foxes, hardy-looking goats, the most handsome black horse Luna had ever seen, and even a lone turtle – all eager to join the games. Luna stood proudly by Gracie's side as they approached the royal box. King Grenouille looked stern, but the Queen's eyes twinkled with a hint of pride.

Gracie stepped forward, dressed in Luna's creation – a practical tracksuit in a regal shade of princess pink, with a bold floral "G" on the cosy hoodie and go-faster stripes on the pants. It was an outfit as bold and determined as she was, and so, with a deep breath, she faced the King.

"Father, I know this is not what you expected of me," Gracie began, trying not to let her voice crack under the weight of her proclamation. "My whole life, I have trained hard and worked hard for this moment. Tradition says I shouldn't compete, but I believe our country deserves a princess who can be graceful and strong. Let me prove myself to our people."

The crowd fell silent as King Grenouille studied his daughter. For a long moment, no one spoke. Then, with a heavy sigh, the King nodded. "You are determined, Gracie. Far more than I ever realised. If this is what you wish, then compete. But remember – win or lose, the weight of the Grenouille name is yours to bear."

The games began, and Gracie excelled beyond anyone's expectations. She leapt farther, swam faster, and balanced more gracefully than she had before. After seeing Gracie in action, there was no doubt that it was her hard work, not her reputation, that had earned her a place in the Olympic Games.

In the end, Gracie didn't win gold, but she won something far more important: the pride of her kingdom and the knowledge that she had worked hard at her dreams.

As the sun set on that glorious day, Gracie climbed off the podium, a bronze medal glinting in the fading light as she looked towards her friend. "Thank you for believing in me, Luna," she said, her voice filled with emotion. "I can't wait to do it all again in four years."

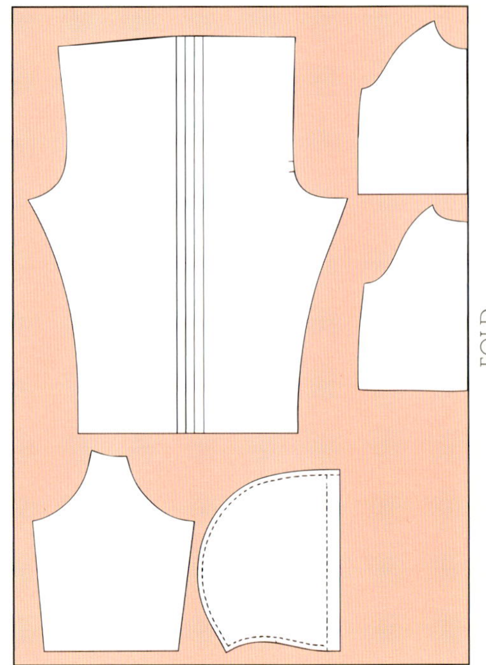

Fig.1

Gracie's Tracksuit

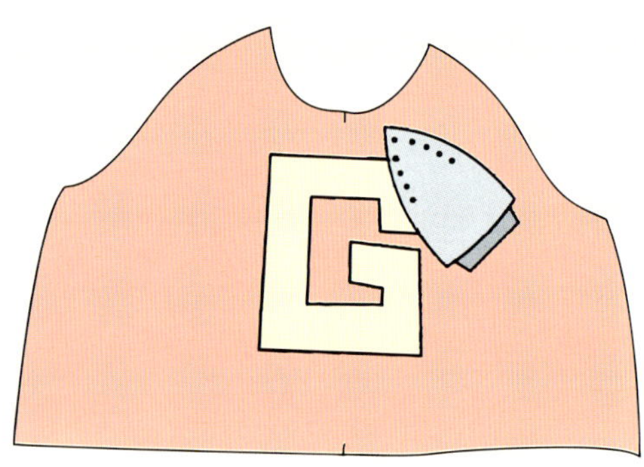

Fig.2

YOU WILL NEED

- 50cm (20in) x 75cm (29½in) sweatshirt fabric
- 28cm (11in) x 5cm (2in) of ribbing to match
- 10cm (4in) square of double-sided fusible webbing
- 10cm (4in) square of fine cotton print fabric
- 2m (78in) of 7mm (approx. ¼in) satin ribbon
- 16cm (6½in) of 1cm (3/8in) elastic
- Basic sewing kit (see Materials)

Use a 0.5cm (¼in) seam allowance, unless a different amount is stated.

CUTTING OUT

1 Fold the sweatshirt fabric in half with wrong sides together. Pin your cut-out pattern pieces (see The Patterns) onto the fabric using **Fig.1** as a guide. Cut all pieces as stated on the pattern. Mark any notches with a chalk pen or by making a small snip into the fabric within the seam allowance. Make an 'on the fold' snip to mark the centre on the front and back pieces of the hoodie.

MAKING UP THE HOODIE

Note: For tips on sewing with knit fabrics, see Materials. Always test your stitch length on a scrap of fabric before sewing for real.

Preparing the Appliqué

1 Reserve a 2cm (¾in) strip from the double-sided fusible webbing for the track pants. Lay the remaining piece of fusible webbing, rough side facing down, onto the wrong side of the cotton print fabric. Cover with a pressing cloth and place a hot iron on the cloth for 8–10 seconds. Allow to cool completely. Cut out the 'G' template from light card (see The Patterns), flip it and draw around it onto the fusible webbing backed fabric, then carefully cut out the reversed letter 'G' shape.

2 Peel the paper backing off the back of the 'G' and position it centrally onto the front panel of the hoodie. Cover with a pressing cloth and press with the iron until fused (**Fig.2**). Unless you intend to wash the hoodie, it is not necessary to sew around the edge of the letter, but you can if you wish.

Attaching the Sleeves to the Front and Back

1 With right sides together, match one side of the front body to one front sleeve seam (**Fig.3**). Sew together with a straight stitch or narrow zigzag. You will notice the curves seem to be working against each other, but they do fit, you just need to continually adjust the shapes to match along the sewing line.

2 Repeat step 1 to sew the remaining sleeve to the other side of the front body (**Fig.4**).

3 Join the back body to the back edge of the sleeves with right sides together, one side at a time (**Fig.5** and **Fig.6**). Press the seams open and flat as far as you can.

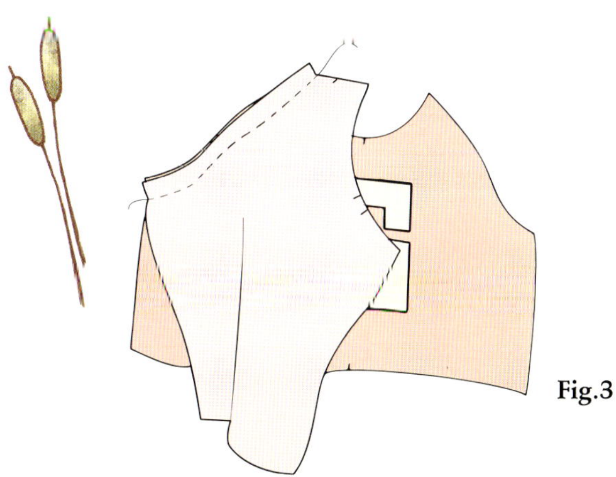

Fig.3

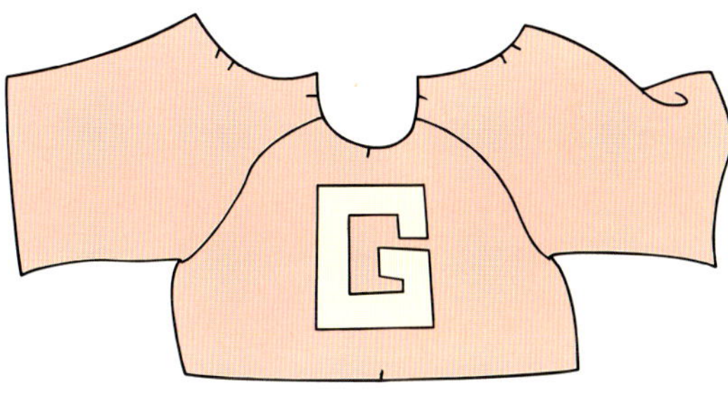

Fig.4

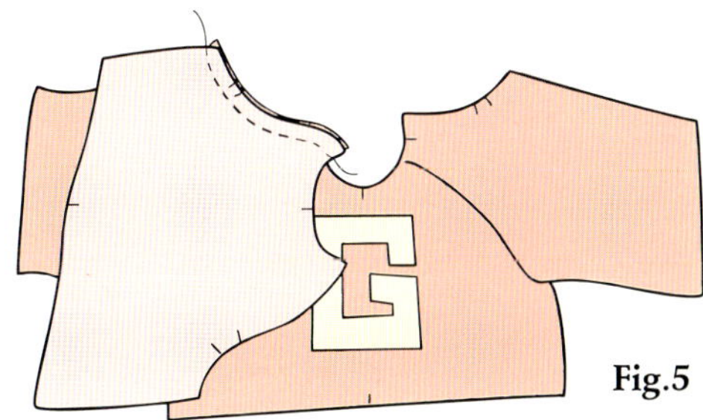

Fig.5

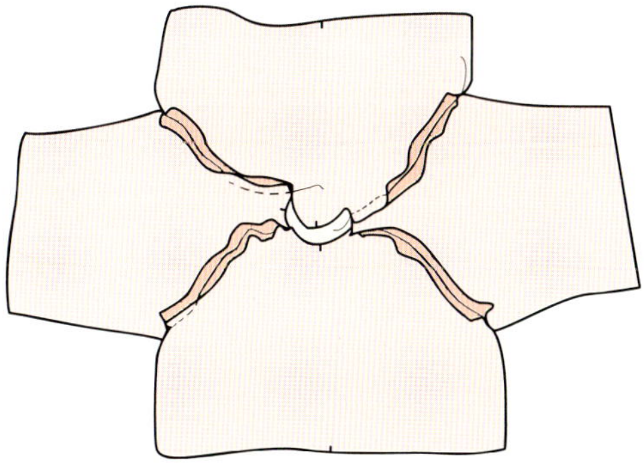

Fig.6

Making and Attaching the Hood

1 With right sides together, match and then sew together the curved edge of the hood pieces using straight stitch or narrow zigzag (**Fig.7**).

2 Press back the front edge of the hood by 1cm (⅜in) for the hem and use a stretch stitch or zigzag to sew in place (**Fig.8**).

3 With right sides together match the bottom edge of the hood onto the neckline, lining up the hood's front edges with the front notch. Tack (baste) in place, then sew to attach (**Fig.9**). It's easier to have the whole project on top of the sewing machine to do this.

Hemming the Sleeves and Sewing the Side Seams

1 Turn a 1cm (⅜in) hem to the wrong side of the sleeves and sew in place with a stretch or zigzag stitch.

2 With right sides together, match the underarms and side seams, and sew using straight stitch or narrow zigzag (**Fig.10**).

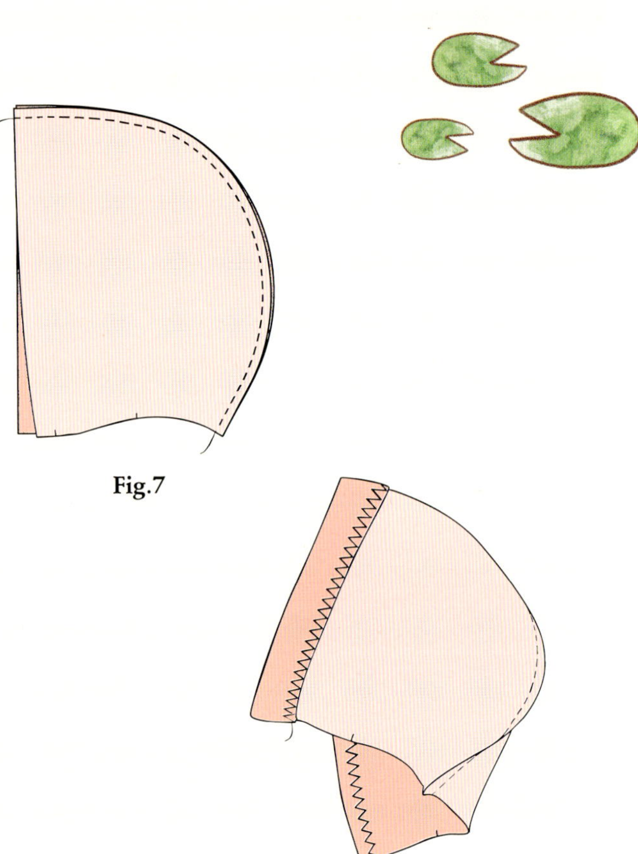

Fig.7

Fig.8

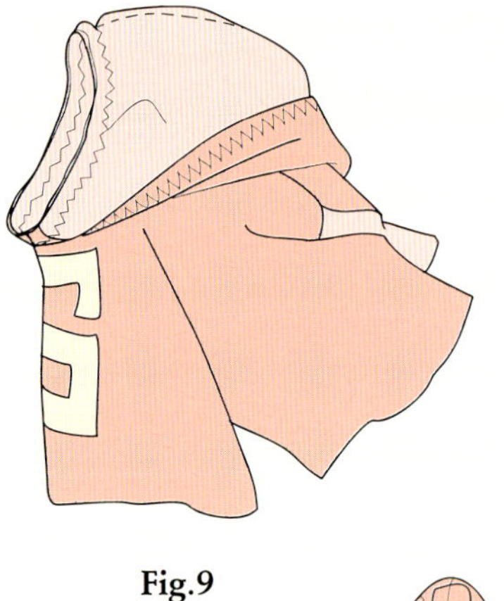

Fig.9

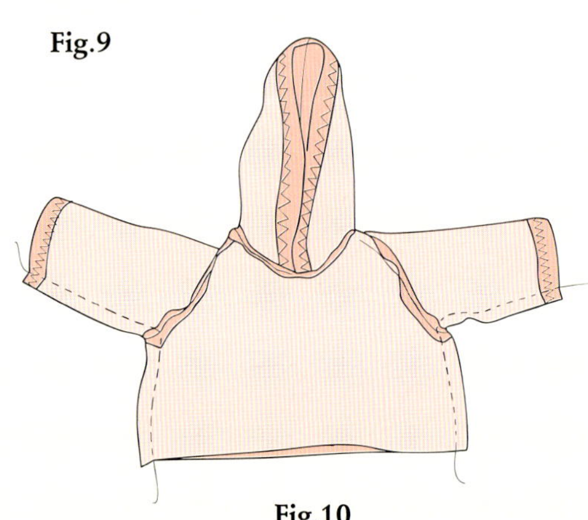

Fig.10

Note: At this point, you could choose to turn up a 1cm (⅜in) hem on the bottom edge of the hoodie and stretch-stitch through the layers to finish. However, for a more authentic look, proceed as follows.

Attaching the Ribbing Band Hem

1 Take the band of ribbing fabric that measures 28cm x 5cm (11in x 2in) and, with right sides together match the two short edges and sew to make a loop (**Fig.11**). Fold the loop in half so the seam allowance is hidden inside and the long edges match. Fold to find the half and quarter points, and mark these with pins.

2 With right sides together, match the raw edge of the doubled hem band to the bottom edge of the hoodie at the four marked points. The sewn seam on the band will match up to one side seam. Sew the band on, stretching the band onto the main body, using a wide stretch stitch or overlock stitch (**Fig.12**).

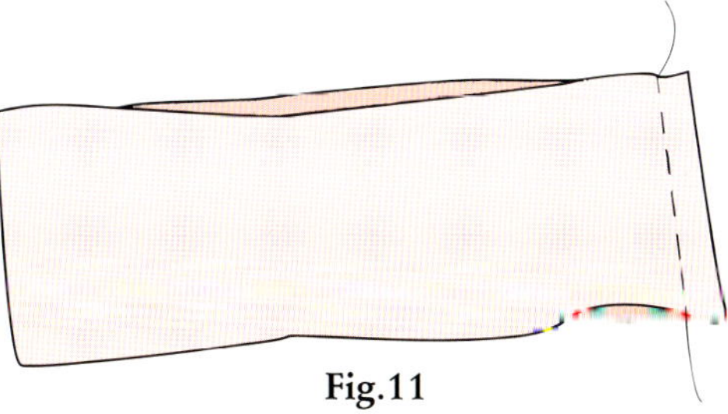

Fig.11

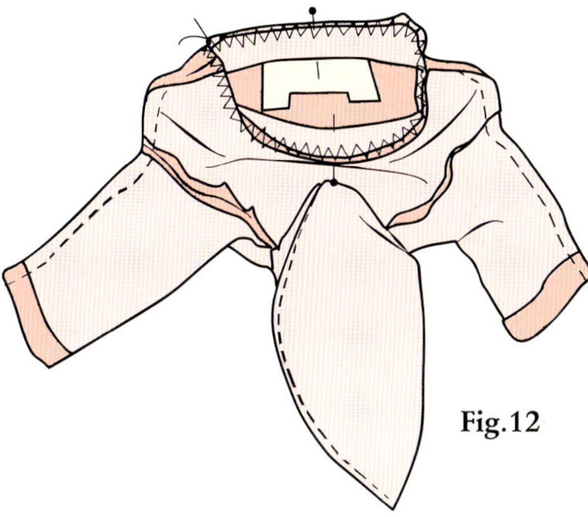

Fig.12

MAKING UP THE TRACK PANTS

Attaching the Side Stripes to the Legs

1 Cut four pieces of ribbon a little longer than the length of the leg pieces. Lay the leg pieces right side facing up and, on each leg in turn, position the satin ribbon carefully to form the first stripe following the guide on the pattern. You could use tiny strips of fusible webbing to help you to accurately position the stripe before sewing, or tack (baste) in place.

2 Once you are happy with the stripe position, edgestitch along each side with a relaxed stitch length.

3 Position and sew the second stripe on each leg piece in the same way, then trim any excess ribbon (**Fig.13**).

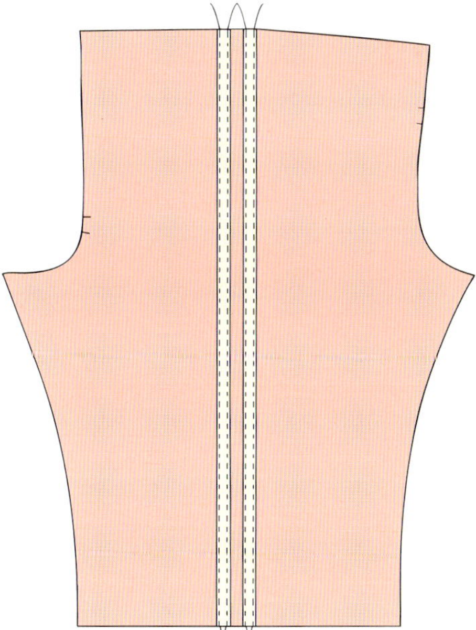

Fig.13

Sewing the Front Rise

1 Place the legs right sides together, matching the front rises. Pin then sew the front rise, leaving an opening between the notches in the front seam for the drawcord opening (**Fig.14**). Press the seams open and flat near the opening, and edgestitch around the opening to hold back the seam allowance (**Fig.15**).

Sewing the Back Rise

1 Press 2.5cm (1in) to the wrong side all the way around the waist of your joined leg pieces (**Fig.16**).

2 Opening up the pressed waist at the back, match the back rises with wrong sides together and pin in place. Sew the back rise (**Fig.17**). Gracie has no tail, but if you are making these for an animal that has a tail, don't forget to leave a back tail opening too. Press the seams open and flat.

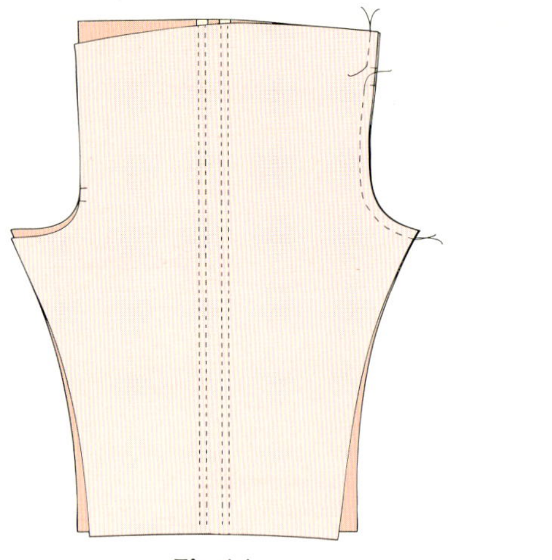

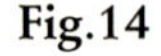

Fig.14

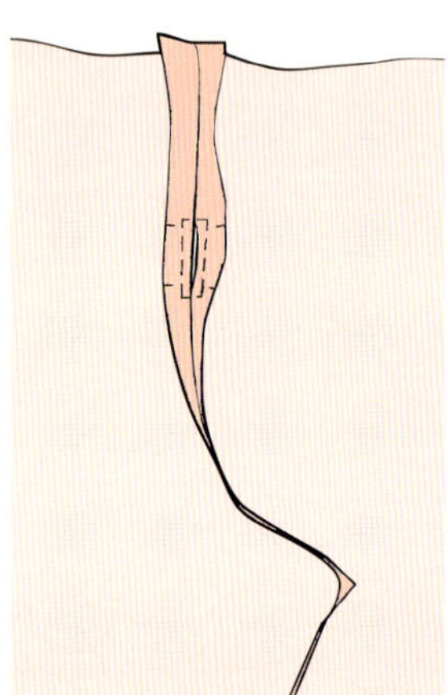

Fig.15

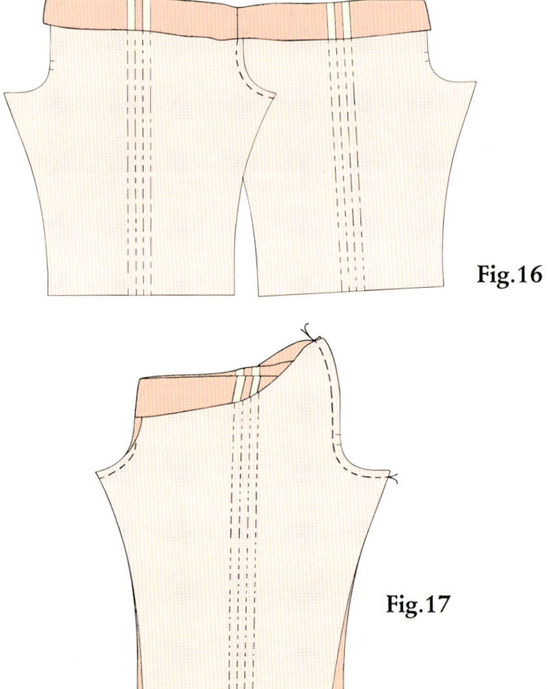

Fig.16

Fig.17

Sewing the Waist Casing

1 Refold the waist at the back, then edgestitch close to the folded edge. Then sew a second line of stitching 1.5cm (⅝in) away from the folded edge to create a casing (**Fig.18**).

Sewing the Hems and Inside Legs

1 Turn 1cm (⅜in) to the wrong side of the leg hems and sew through all layers with a stretch or zigzag stitch.

2 With right sides together, match and pin the inside legs – front to back – making sure the rise seams match. Sew with straight stitch or narrow zigzag (**Fig.19**).

FINISHING OFF

1 To create a drawcord for the track pants, attach a length of ribbon to each end of the elastic with a zigzag stitch (**Fig.20**). Use a safety pin to thread the drawcord through the casing (**Fig. 21**). Pull the ends to be even, trimming any excess ribbon as necessary, then knot each end twice.

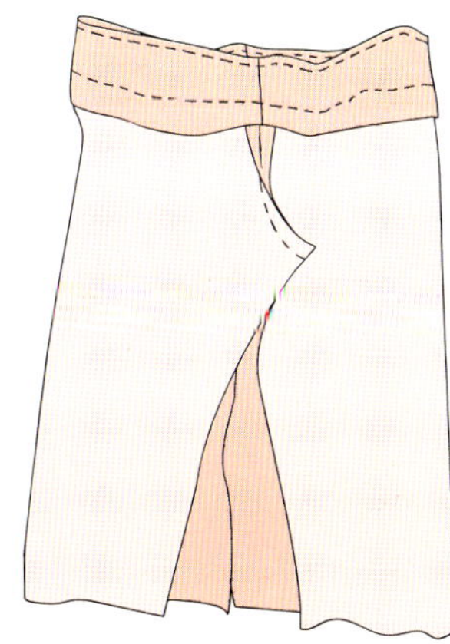

Fig.18

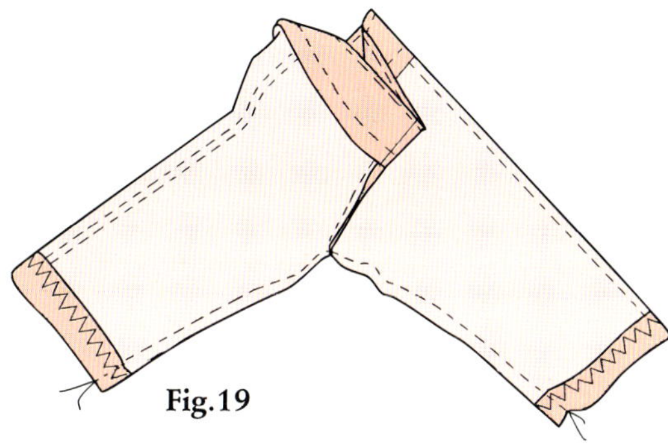

Fig.19

Fig.20

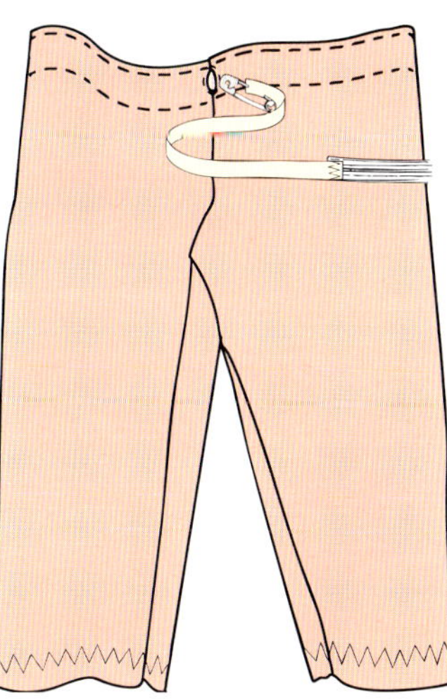

Fig.21

LUNA LAPIN AND THE *Big Mess*

It was a crisp autumn morning in the sleepy woodland village where Luna Lapin lived. The trees were beginning to shed their golden leaves, and Luna was preparing for a day of stitching and drinking tea in her usual gentle way. The month of October reached out to Luna like an old friend, wrapping her up in the warmth of a first fireside evening and the scent of cashmere and wet earth. Luna always found this time of year inspirational, which meant she had so much work to do, but first, she needed to nip to the bakery and pick up a loaf of bread. If she got to Earth Works Bakery as it opened, the sourdough would still be warm from the oven. Luna liked to tear off a corner as she walked and eat it as the incoming cold nipped at her nose. Her friend, the robin, often perched on her shoulder, waiting for his share.

When Luna arrived, the bakery lights were turned off, and the pretty blue door was wide open. Inside was quite the mess – leaves and twigs scattered across the checkerboard floor blown in overnight. At the centre of it all was Maurice the mole, fast asleep and snoring quietly. His flour-speckled baker's smock crumpled all around him. His velvety head rested under large pink paws on the table, coffee cup upturned next to him. The air in the bakery was usually thick with the smell of cinnamon and icing sugar, but today, there was the unmistakable smell of burning bread.

Luna's first instinct was kindness. "Oh goodness," she said softly, straightening the tangle of the smock. Flour fluffed up in clouds from where it had gathered in the honeycomb-patterned stitching. "The poor mole must be exhausted."

But just as she leaned closer, Maurice's eyes flashed open. He jumped up in a huff, nearly tripping over his own feet. "What have you done now?" he snapped, eyes blinking as if the daylight itself were an unwelcome guest.

"Good morning, Maurice," Luna said, her voice unmoved by his abruptness. "I didn't mean to wake you. It looks like you've had quite a rough night."

Maurice scowled, rubbing his eyes. "Rough? Of course it's rough! I can't stay awake, but I can't seem to sleep either. There's too much to do, too many things to worry about." It was at that moment that the fire alarm began to cry out.

Luna raced to the kitchen, looking around at the mess that Maurice had made in his tired stupor. It was unlike him to be so rude; normally he was as sweet as his almond croissants. His fur was ruffled, and his dressing gown lopsided and covered in flour.

Maurice opened the oven to a cloud of black smoke; there was flour everywhere, egg shells littered the countertop and the washing up was piled precariously in the sink. His normally pristine kitchen showed signs of weariness.

"I'm too busy for this!" Maurice grumbled. "I can't stop! Always baking, always working. But it's never enough. I'm so tired… and everything just keeps going wrong."

Luna thought for a moment. "It sounds to me like what you need isn't more baking, Maurice. What you need is a proper rest. When was the last time you had a day off?"

Maurice glared at her, but there was a flicker of knowing behind his tired eyes. "Rest? Who has time for that?" he said, before he began to choke on the smoke.

Luna, always wise and gentle, led Maurice to her cosy cottage. She brewed him some calming chamomile tea and handed him her favourite blanket. Maurice slumped into one of Luna's soft chairs. His shoulders relaxed as he sipped his tea.

"Sometimes rest is the most important work we can do. Without it, everything becomes a mess, inside and out," said Luna quietly.

Maurice blinked, his eyelids heavy. "But…if I rest, who will do all the baking?"

Luna smiled warmly. "The world will still be here when you wake. Bread can't rise without giving itself time. You, of all folk should know that. Everything will be much better after a good sleep. Rest is revolutionary, Maurice. It gives us the strength to be kind and to do our best."

Now tucked up in the blanket, Maurice let out a long sigh. "Maybe you're right… Five minutes wouldn't hurt, just whilst the smoke clears."

Before he knew it, Maurice was fast asleep. Luna watched over him momentarily, ensuring he was comfortable, and then quietly returned to her stitching. Soon, he was in a deep enough sleep that even the hum of Luna's sewing machine wouldn't wake him. The mess could wait – Maurice had finally found peace in sleep, and the village would just have to wait for their perfectly baked loaves and famous egg custards.

Hours later, Maurice woke up feeling better than he had in weeks. The autumn sun shone as they walked back down the main street to the Earth Works Bakery. When they arrived, the cafe was full of folk, and the mess was almost gone (with Freddie the Badger's quiet help), and for the first time in a long while, Maurice wasn't grumbling.

"Thank you all," he said softly, grasping Freddie by the paw.

"When Luna didn't stop by with the morning's loaf, I knew something was going on," Freddie explained. "There was quite a queue when I arrived. We can't have you doing it all yourself, Maurice; you'll burn out, and where else would I get a perfectly flaky cheese and onion roll?"

Luna beamed. "Sometimes, the bravest thing we can do is rest. How about you get a little more? The bakery will still be here in the morning. We will finish this off," she said.

The next morning, when Luna walked down to buy her loaf of bread, she was greeted by a handwritten sign on the door: "New opening times – Closed Sundays and Mondays to catch up on rest." Luna chuckled to herself. Maybe tomorrow, she would treat herself to a blackberry tart

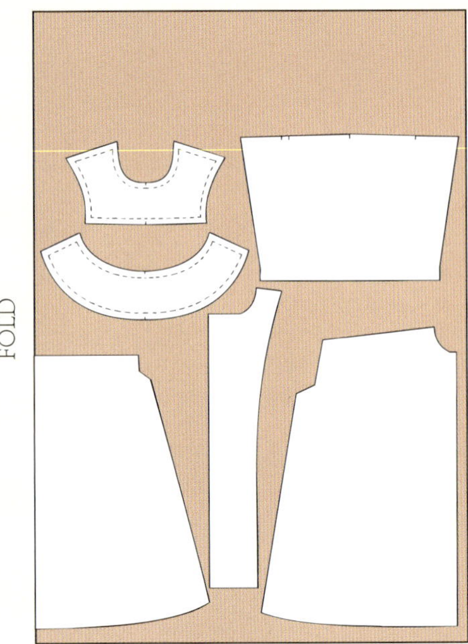

Fig.1

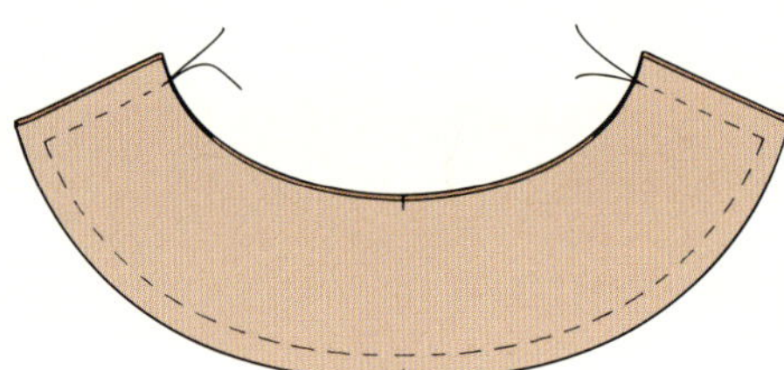

Fig.2

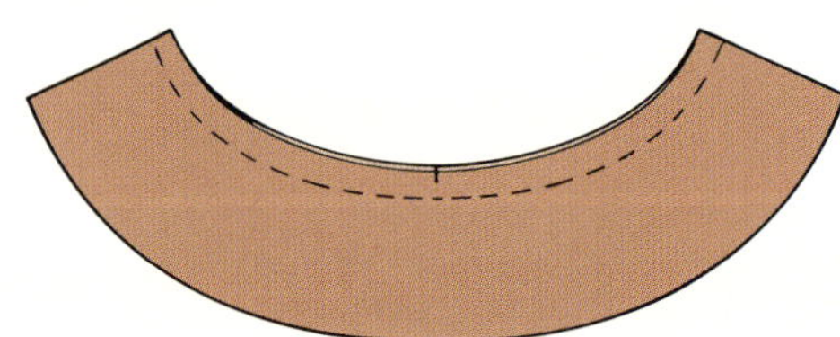

Fig.3

Maurice's Baker's Smock

YOU WILL NEED

- 50cm (19½in) x 70cm (27½in) lightweight linen fabric
- 2m (78in) of wool embroidery thread in contrasting colour
- Four 8mm (3/8in) pearly buttons
- Four press stud fasteners
- 16cm (6½in) of 1cm (3/8in) elastic
- Basic sewing kit (see Materials)

Use a 0.5cm (¼in) seam allowance, unless a different amount is stated.

CUTTING OUT

1 Fold the fabric in half with right sides together. Pin your cut-out pattern pieces (see The Patterns) onto the fabric using **Fig.1** as a guide (the smocking guides are not cut out of fabric and should be set aside for now). Cut all pieces as stated on the pattern. Mark any notches with a tiny snip, including an 'on the fold' snip to mark the centre of the back. Transfer any other pattern markings to the fabric.

2 To use the smocking guides I have provided, first use a chunky bodkin or needle to make a hole through the dots marked on each of the guides. Now transfer the markings for the smocking to the relevant pieces of fabric. Place the guide over the shape of one of the front fabric pieces, pin in place and then use a water-soluble marker to mark through each hole on the guide. Flip the guide over to transfer the markings to the second front piece. For the back, line the guide up to the centre back, pin in place and mark in the same way.

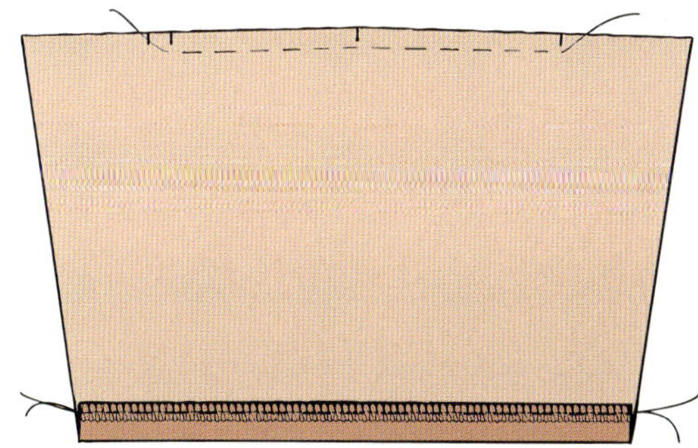

Fig.4

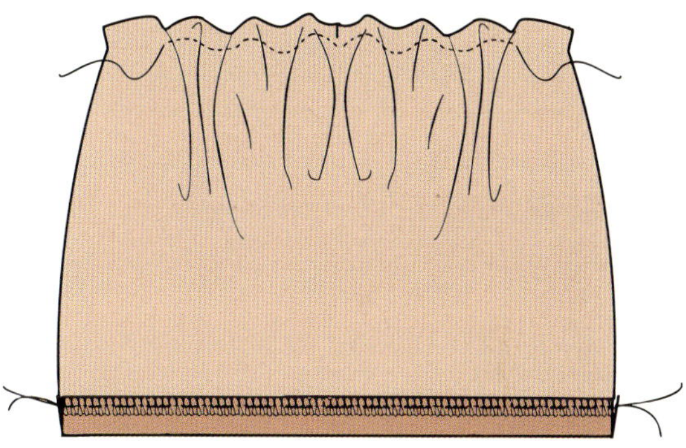

Fig.5

MAKING UP

Making the Collar

1 Place the collar pieces right sides together and sew around the outside curve (**Fig.2**).

2 Trim off the excess seam allowance and turn through to the right side. Press flat, ensuring the seam is to the edge and that the shape is nicely rounded and the corners pushed out. Tack (baste) the raw edges together (**Fig.3**), then set aside.

Preparing the Sleeves

1 First finish the raw edge of the sleeve hem using an overlock or zigzag stitch. Then hem the sleeves by turning 1cm (⅜in) to the wrong side. Press and edgestitch through all layers close to the hem edge.

2 To create the distinctive full sleeves of the finished smock, you need to work some gathering stitching between the outer notches marked on the top edge of the sleeves. Change your machine stitch to be at its longest, or to the gathering setting, and sew 0.5cm (¼in) in from the edge (**Fig.4**). Take the top thread from one end and firmly but steadily pull the thread so the material moves along and gathers, to measure roughly 6cm (2¼in) (**Fig.5**) along the gathered area.

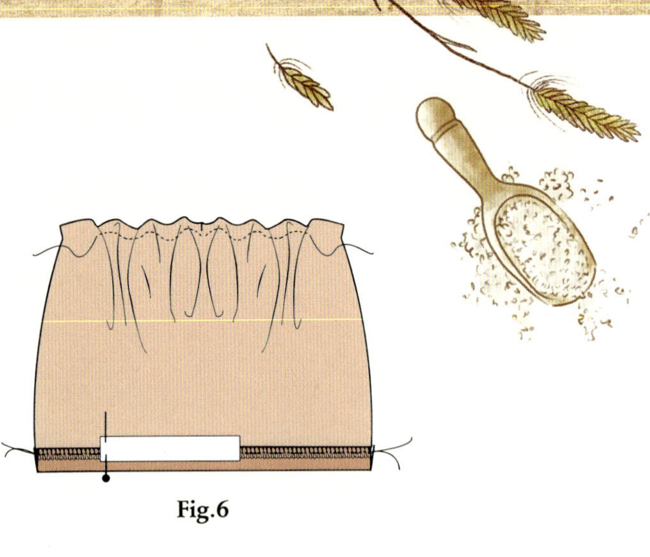

Fig.6

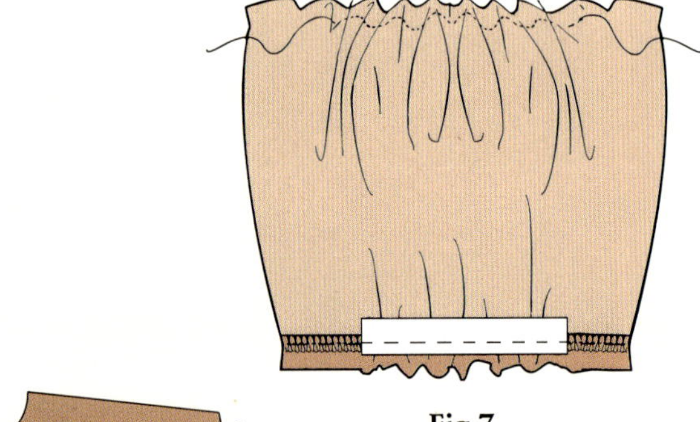

Fig.7

Fig.8

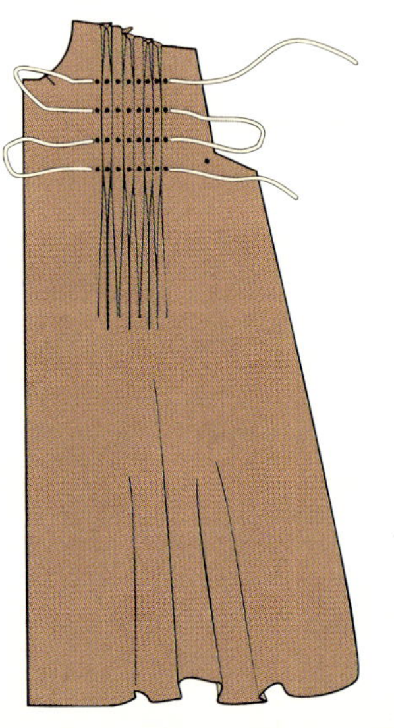

Fig.9

Gathering the Cuffs

1 For the gathered cuffs, start by cutting the elastic into two pieces, each measuring 8cm (3¼in). Working on each sleeve in turn, take a piece of elastic and pin one end 3cm (1⅛in) in from the side, at the level of the hem stitching (**Fig.6**); then pin the elastic 6cm (2½in) along its length, 3cm (1⅛in) in from the other side. This leaves a 2cm (¾in) tail of elastic for you to hold onto as you sew (although for clarity, this tail is not shown in the diagram).

2 Secure by reverse stitching at one end, then stretch the elastic as you sew to the opposite end and reverse to secure. Trim away the excess 2cm (¾in) tail (**Fig.7**).

Preparing for the Honeycomb Smocking

1 Take the left-hand front piece as worn and place right side facing up. Following the transferred marks and using a double tacking (basting) thread, sew a line of running stitch: starting at the outer edge, bring the needle down through the fabric about 0.2cm (1⁄16in) before the first marked dot and back up through the fabric about 0.2cm (1⁄16in) from the other side of the dot. Continue stitching, leaving 0.2cm (1⁄16in) spaces between your stitches and the marked dots. When you reach the end of the first row, continue to stitch the next row, leaving a loop of thread as you turn. Repeat to complete four rows of stitching as seen in **Fig.8**.

2 Pull the threads to draw in the fabric, creating 'tubes' – I like to pull the threads very tight, to pinch the pleats I've made, and then relax everything a little so I can see either side of each 'tube' (**Fig.9**). Tie off the threads before moving on.

3 Repeat steps 1 and 2 on the right-hand front piece as worn in preparation for smocking (note the mirroring of the pattern), and on the back piece too, but here you have only three rows of smocking to prepare for.

Sewing the Honeycomb Smocking

1 Thread your needle with the wool embroidery thread and knot one end. Referring to **Fig.10**, bring your needle out through the back of the fabric at the bottom left of your smocking area, marked A. *Take the needle over two tubes to bring it out at the start position to form a stitch, and repeat to form a second stitch. Put the needle through the middle of the two tubes* and head inside the second tube to row 2, to position B. Bring the needle out on the right-hand side of the second tube on row 2. Repeat from * to * with the second and third tubes on row 2. Then put the needle through the middle of the tubes and head inside the third tube to come down to the right-hand side of the third tube on row 1 at position C. Follow this pattern to complete the smock stitching across rows 1 and 2.

2 Repeat the stitching method described in step 1 on rows 3 and 4 to complete the honeycomb smocking pattern. Remove the tacking (basting) threads, which will allow the smocking to relax outwards.

3 Repeat to complete the smocking on the right-hand front piece as worn, mirroring the pattern (**Fig.11**), and on the back piece too, where you have only three rows of smocking to complete (**Fig.12**).

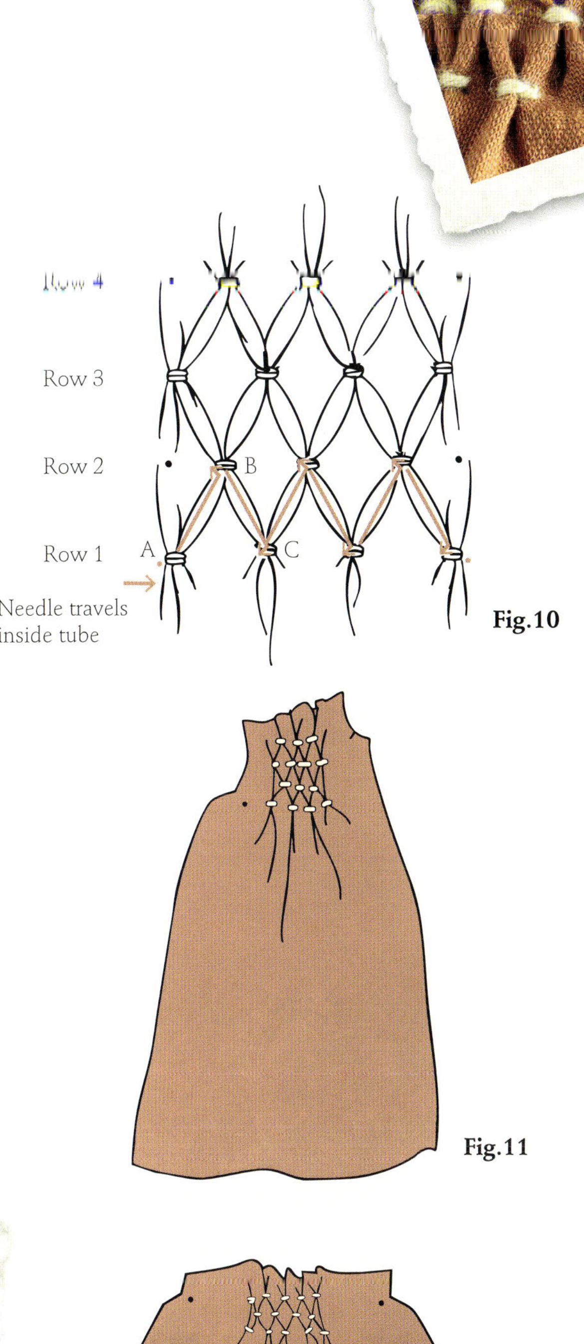

Fig.10

Fig.11

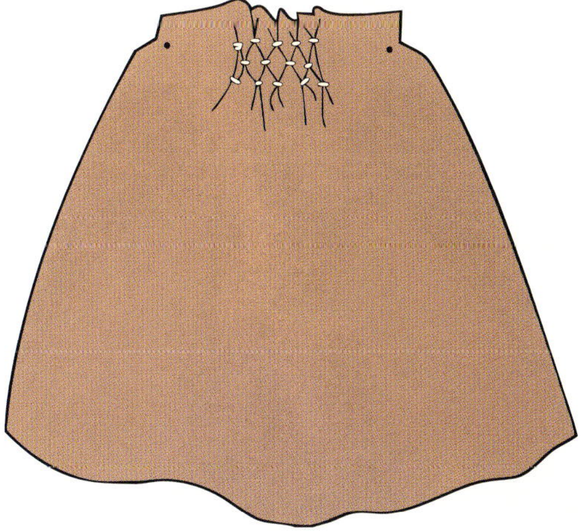

Fig.12

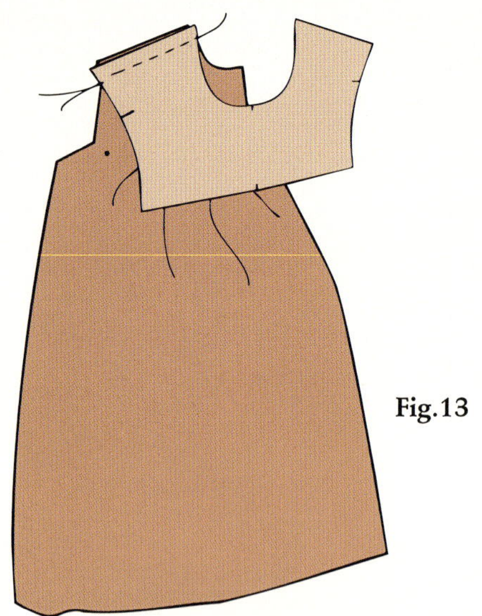
Fig.13

Attaching the Outer Yoke to the Fronts and Back

Note: As the method used in traditional shirt making, there are two yokes used in this construction. The inner yoke is attached at a later stage to enclose the raw edges of the seams made by attaching the outer yoke to the front, back and collar.

1 With right sides together, match one of the front shoulder seams to a front yoke seam, and sew together. It will feel as if you are bunching up the area above the smocking and you probably are, but that's okay – just make it fit the yoke measurement (**Fig.13**). Repeat on the other side, then press seams towards the yoke.

2 With right sides together, match the edge of the gathered back to the straight edge of the outer yoke and sew together (**Fig.14**). Press the seam towards the yoke.

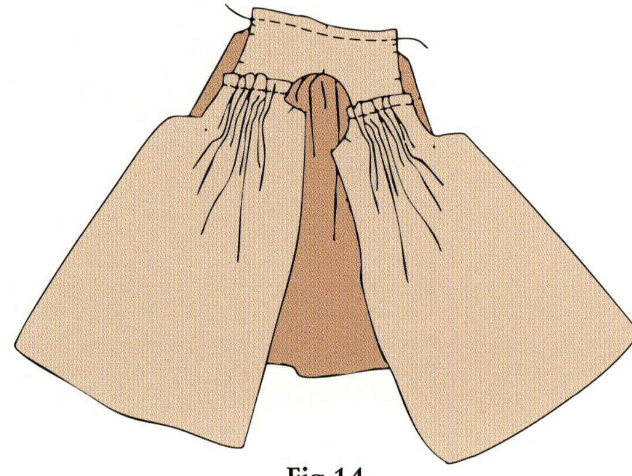
Fig.14

Attaching the Front Facings

1 With right sides together, sew a front facing to each front (**Fig.15**). Press the seam towards the facing. Finish the curved edge with an overlock or zigzag stitch (as seen on **Fig 16**).

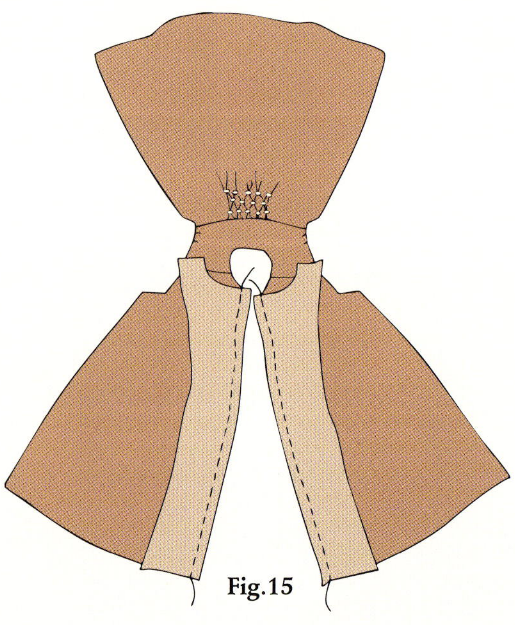
Fig.15

Attaching the Collar

1 Pin the collar into position on the right side of the smock, matching up edges and using the notch at the centre back to guide you. The collar front edges should finish at the notch, about 0.5cm (¼in) from the front facing seam. Staystitch or tack (baste) in place using a tiny (slightly less than 0.5cm/¼in) seam allowance (**Fig.16**).

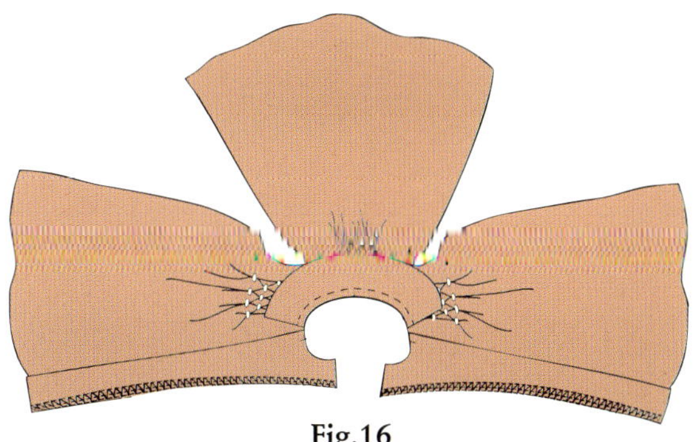

Fig.16

Attaching the Inner Yoke

1 Press the seam allowances to the wrong side of the inner yoke (**Fig.17**). With right sides together, match and pin the inner yoke around the neckline, sandwiching the collar and matching the folded front yoke edges to the existing stitching line (**Fig.18**).

2 Fold each front facing back at the notch, so that it matches the curve of the neckline and overlaps the raw turned-back edges of the inner yoke. Sew through all layers 0.5cm (¼in) away from the edge of the neckline (**Fig.19**).

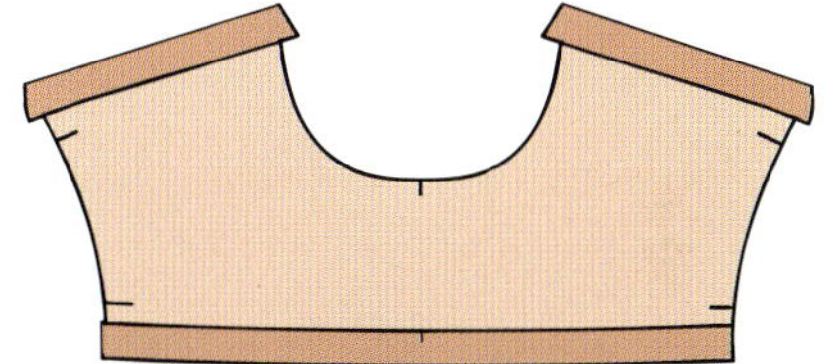

Fig.17

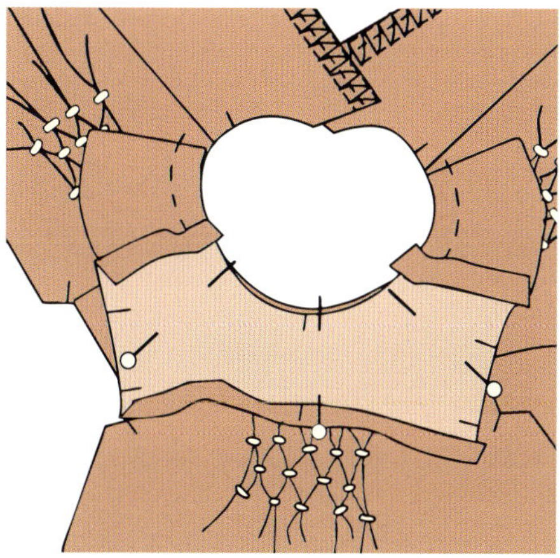

Fig.18

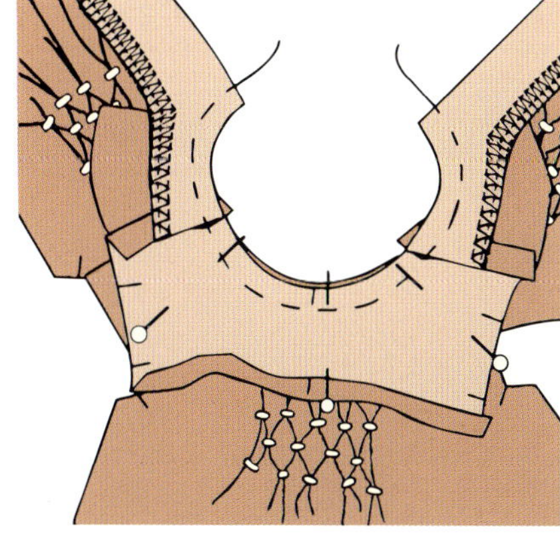

Fig.19

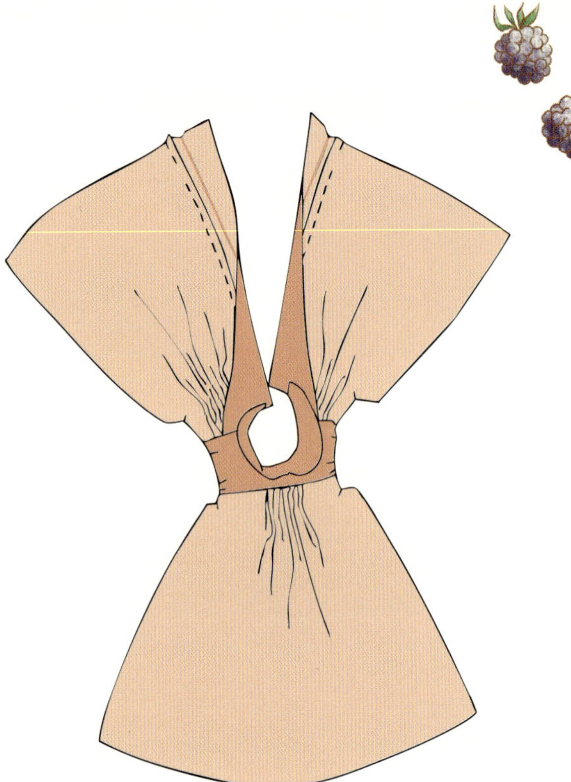

Fig.20

3 Trim the corners to reduce the bulk, snip into the seam allowance in the curved parts and trim the neck seam allowance to 0.3cm (⅛in), then turn through. Push the front corners out, then press the body away from the collar. Press the front facing so that the seam width is consistent all the way down to create a 1cm (⅜in) button band. Then, on the wrong side of the garment, line up the folded edges of the inner yoke with the stitched lines of the outer yoke and slipstitch in place. Snip into the dots on the fronts and the back that mark the armhole, in preparation for the next step (**Fig.20**).

Attaching the Sleeves

1 Working on each side in turn, pin a sleeve to the main body with right sides together. Match up the notches for correct positioning and adjust the gathering on the sleeve head to be even, and use the snips made in the previous step to open up the body armhole to accommodate the sleeve. Sew in place (**Fig.21**).

2 Overlock or zigzag stitch the seams to finish, then press towards the sleeves.

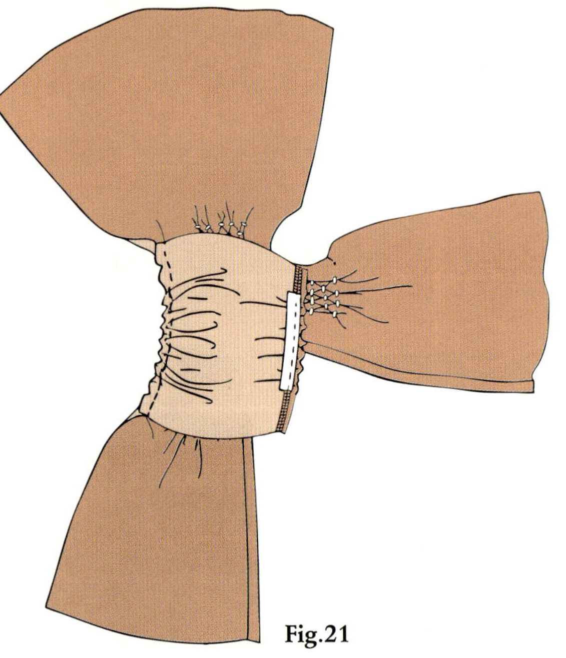

Fig.21

Sewing the Side Seams

1 With right sides together, match up the sleeve hems, underarms and lower edges. Sew, pivoting at the armhole seam (**Fig.22**). Snip into the seam at the armhole before finishing the seam allowance with overlock or zigzag stitch. Press the seam towards the back as far as you can.

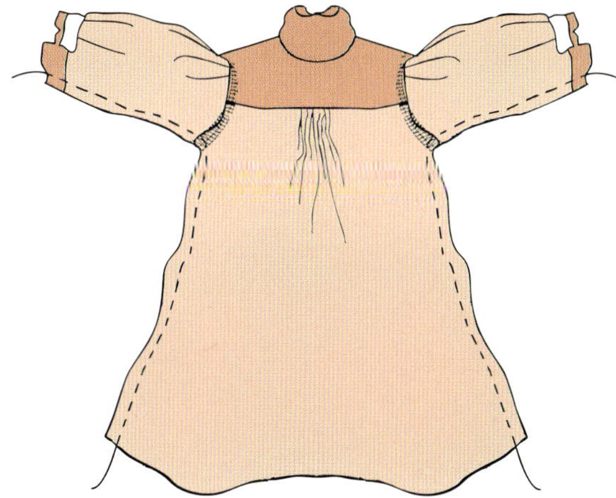

Fig.22

Sewing the Hems

1 Fold the front facing back to the wrong side at the hem, at the level of the notch, to sew at a depth of 1cm (⅜in) (**Fig.23**). Then, before turning back through, finish the raw edge of the whole hem using an overlock or zigzag stitch. Trim the front corners to reduce the bulk before you push the front corners out.

2 Turn 1cm (⅜in) to the wrong side around the hem. Press and edgestitch through all layers close to the finished edge, starting and finishing at the button band (**Fig.24**).

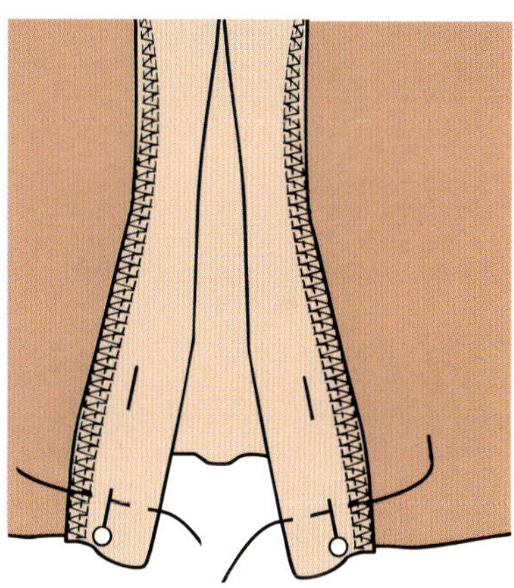

Fig.23

FINISHING OFF

1 Sew the buttons on the left-hand side as worn through both layers of the front facing using the pattern piece as your guide. Position one half of a press stud under each button and sew in place. Then sew the other half of each press stud onto the right-hand side as worn.

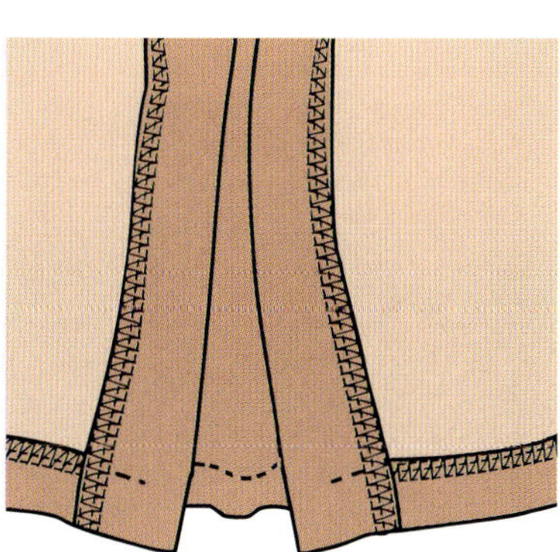

Fig.24

LUNA LAPIN AND THE *Northern Lights*

Erik Eriksen was a special kind of bear. He always knew what was going to happen just before it did. Erik couldn't see the future, but he was one of those rare folks who truly listened and took notice, and that carried its own kind of magic. Erik belonged to the land he grew up in. The sea, salt, and snow flowed through his veins and into his heart. The dark winter nights and long summer days of the Arctic were part of him.

On one long, dark midwinter day, Erik Eriksen sat listening to the low magnetic hum of the northern wilds. Not everyone can hear the quiet music of the Arctic, but on that day, the snow sang just for him. Something wasn't right on the ice.

Erik stood, patted down his check trousers, sending specks of snow spiralling away, and headed back to the nearby town. It was Christmas Eve, and Longyearbear was preparing for its annual feast. Erik loved Christmas. The town sparkled with fairy lights, and a great Nordic spruce twinkled in the town square. The townsfolk were busy preparing for the evening's festivities; delicious scents drifted from the homes of Arctic foxes, and grey seals flopped along the streets, gathering firewood on little sleighs to help keep the bonfires burning.

Meanwhile, somewhere in the tundra, Luna Lapin, Ottoline, and Hugh were beginning to lose hope of ever seeing the Northern Lights. Their paws ached with cold despite their mittens, and the world around them was nothing but miles of shadow and snow. The vast emptiness felt overwhelming. Luna had never been anywhere that looked so lonely. Every sound shattered the silence in an ear-splitting crack.

Earlier that morning, Hugh the Hound looked at himself in the mirror and caught the echo of age in his muzzle. Outside, he could hear Ottoline humming to herself. Hugh wished he had told her sooner how much he loved her. He thought about the lifetime of adventures they could have shared. Age was cruel, but no matter. They had each other now. Luna knocked on the door, and Hugh shook off his worry. This was their last expedition together.

Luna Lapin kept kindness where other creatures had lungs. Though she wouldn't say it out loud, part of her was worried about her old friends being alone on the Svalbard Archipelago. If she was being completely honest (which she almost always was), she would have rather been making mince pies in Granny's kitchen. But Granny had insisted that either Luna make her way to the Arctic Circle or she would go herself. And so Luna

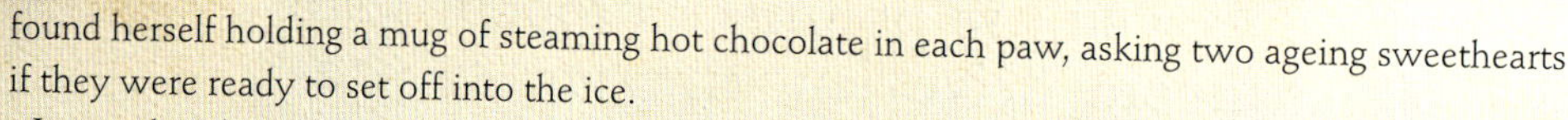

found herself holding a mug of steaming hot chocolate in each paw, asking two ageing sweethearts if they were ready to set off into the ice.

It was their last day in Svalbard, a remote settlement off the coast of Norway, populated mainly by scientists and fishermen. They had taken three ferries to reach Longyearbear, where the cheery red of the old church glowed in the never-ending night. The three of them had spent almost every waking moment hoping to glimpse the Northern Lights.

Luna had never experienced anything like polar night. From October to February, the entire archipelago was plunged into a blue-black darkness, with the only light coming from the warm glow of the little houses, the silver of moon and stars, or the flicker of an explorer's lantern as they searched for the magical, dancing Aurora Borealis.

The three friends had searched and searched for the Northern Lights, but not even a flicker appeared in the endless night.

Neither hope nor hot cocoa could lift their spirits from hours of trudging through the cold. Walking through the deep snow was far more difficult than Luna had imagined. The darkness seemed to roll on forever, and Luna couldn't help but wonder if the lights would even be worth the bone-deep chill that stretched from her paws to the tips of her long ears.

Their pace slowed to a crawl, each step heavier than the last. Luna's brow furrowed – she knew they should have turned back miles ago. The darkness was swallowing them, and the cold gnawed at their bones. Hugh was struggling – Luna could see it in the way he walked, his head low, shoulders hunched against the biting wind. His age weighed him down more with every gust. The icy air seemed to slice through his fur, cutting deep into his joints, making his bones ache in a way he had never felt before. He swore he could feel icicles forming on his snout, sharp as daggers.

Ottoline walked ahead, her eyes filled with hope and determination, her gaze fixed on the horizon. Hugh knew that she wanted so badly to show him the magic of the skies, so he clenched his fists, steeled himself, and forced another slow, shaky step. But with each breath, the air grew colder, and the weight of exhaustion pressed down on him. His legs wobbled beneath him, the world spinning as a wave of dizziness washed over him.

The snow underfoot suddenly felt like quicksand, pulling him down. Hugh gasped for breath, but the air froze in his chest, sharp and unforgiving. He clutched at his heart as a searing cold ripped through him, stealing his voice, his strength. Darkness swallowed him whole. His knees buckled, and he fell hard into the snow, his body stiffening as the cold claimed him. He had become part of the ice, the snow, the endless bitter wind.

And then, there was silence. Time seemed to stop. The vast emptiness of the Arctic night smothered him in its frozen grip. Hugh's vision blurred, the world fading into a haze of swirling white. He was slipping away, the cold tightening its hold, dragging him deeper into the ice.

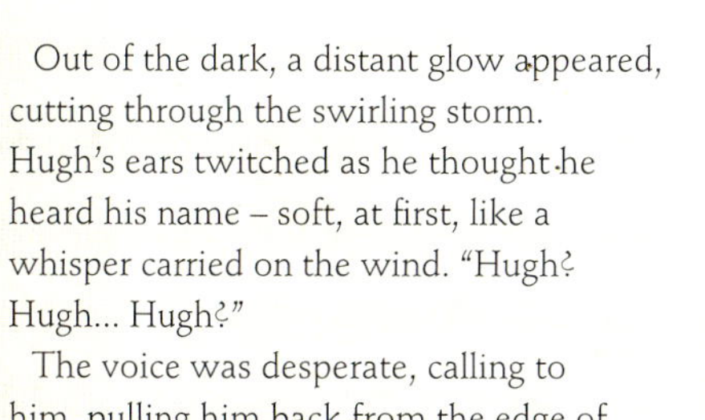

Out of the dark, a distant glow appeared, cutting through the swirling storm. Hugh's ears twitched as he thought he heard his name – soft, at first, like a whisper carried on the wind. "Hugh? Hugh... Hugh?"

The voice was desperate, calling to him, pulling him back from the edge of the abyss. He could barely make out the figures moving towards him, shadowy forms against the snow. The light glowed brighter, and he felt something warm touch his paw, thawing the ice that had begun to claim him. It was Ottoline – her voice, her touch, her tears frozen to her fur as she clung to him.

"Hugh, please!" she cried, her voice breaking through the silence. The sound of her desperation was louder than the storm, more real than the cold that had taken hold of him.

The light hovered above him, a soft, jolly glow that began to push the darkness away. Hugh's eyes flickered open. He was being pulled, or perhaps carried, through the snow. He could make out the soft outline of Ottoline, her worried face turned towards him. Even in the darkness, he saw her exactly as she was. Ahead, leading them, was a tall figure in a yellow coat, with a slow, lyrical voice that seemed to rise and fall like the wind itself.

"Come with me," the voice urged, calm and steady. "It's not too far now."

Hugh's breath hitched. "The lights…" he murmured, barely able to form the words.

The figure chuckled gently. "Don't you worry, friend. You'll see them. I can promise you that."

And as they trudged forward, Hugh thought he saw a glimmer of green flicker in the sky, just at the edge of the horizon.

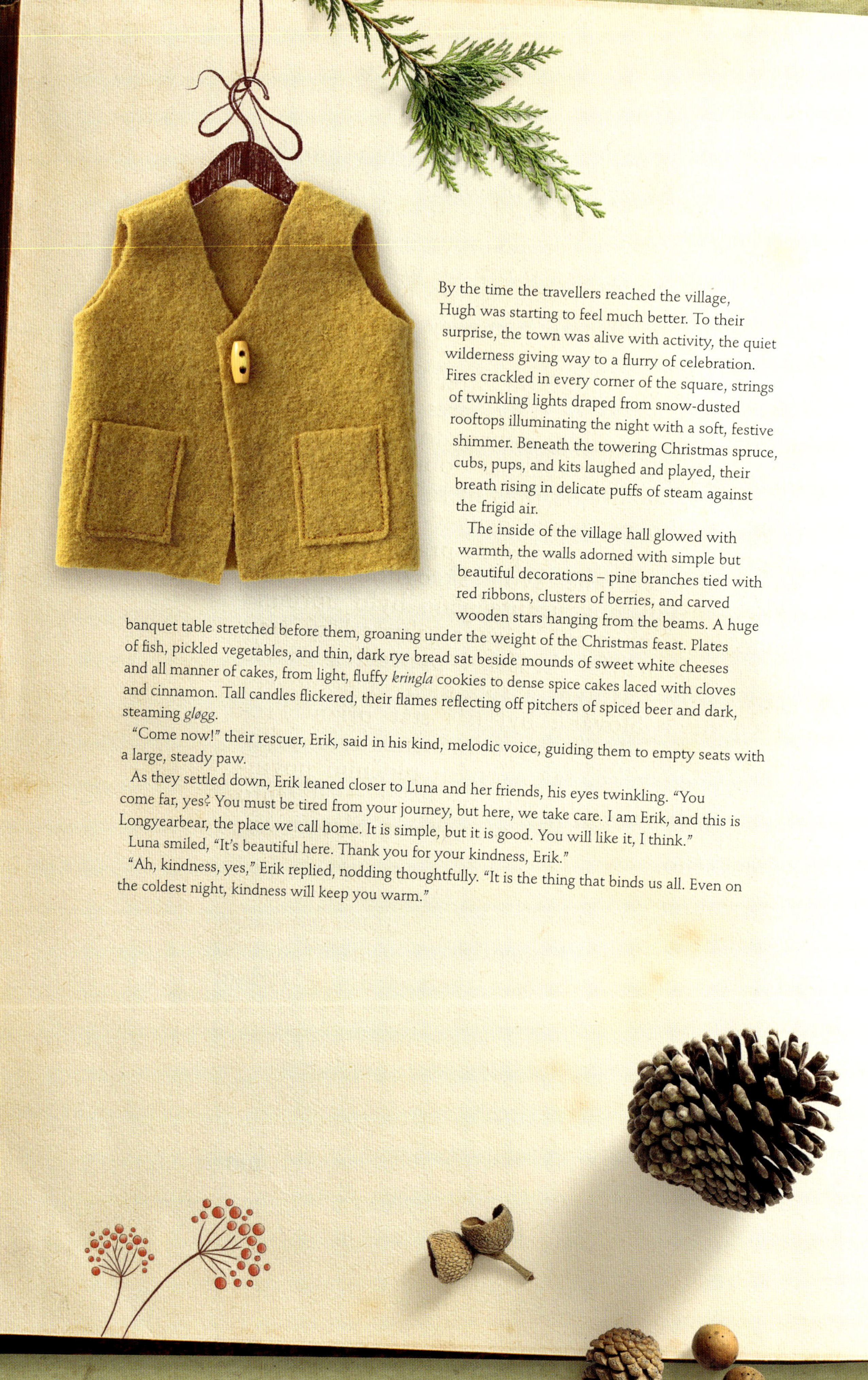

By the time the travellers reached the village, Hugh was starting to feel much better. To their surprise, the town was alive with activity, the quiet wilderness giving way to a flurry of celebration. Fires crackled in every corner of the square, strings of twinkling lights draped from snow-dusted rooftops illuminating the night with a soft, festive shimmer. Beneath the towering Christmas spruce, cubs, pups, and kits laughed and played, their breath rising in delicate puffs of steam against the frigid air.

The inside of the village hall glowed with warmth, the walls adorned with simple but beautiful decorations – pine branches tied with red ribbons, clusters of berries, and carved wooden stars hanging from the beams. A huge banquet table stretched before them, groaning under the weight of the Christmas feast. Plates of fish, pickled vegetables, and thin, dark rye bread sat beside mounds of sweet white cheeses and all manner of cakes, from light, fluffy *kringla* cookies to dense spice cakes laced with cloves and cinnamon. Tall candles flickered, their flames reflecting off pitchers of spiced beer and dark, steaming *gløgg*.

"Come now!" their rescuer, Erik, said in his kind, melodic voice, guiding them to empty seats with a large, steady paw.

As they settled down, Erik leaned closer to Luna and her friends, his eyes twinkling. "You come far, yes? You must be tired from your journey, but here, we take care. I am Erik, and this is Longyearbear, the place we call home. It is simple, but it is good. You will like it, I think."

Luna smiled, "It's beautiful here. Thank you for your kindness, Erik."

"Ah, kindness, yes," Erik replied, nodding thoughtfully. "It is the thing that binds us all. Even on the coldest night, kindness will keep you warm."

They spent the evening feasting and drinking, the spiced beer warming them. Luna couldn't stop nibbling on the *Julekake,* a soft white bread filled with colourful candied fruit and cardamom's sweet, earthy scent.

When the meal finally ended, and the last of the cakes had been eaten, the group drifted outside into the crisp, frosty air. Lanterns lined the streets, casting long shadows across the snow. Erik stood in the square, his breath steaming in the cold night. Slowly, he began to sing a low, haunting tune that rose and fell like the waves of the sea. The music entranced Luna, its deep resonance seeming to come from beneath the snow. The song felt like it was as old as the glaciers themselves.

The sky above them began to stir. The snow-dusted horizon met the luminous, shifting lights of the Aurora Borealis. Luna gasped, her heart swelling with awe. The lights flared and danced, rippling across the heavens in green, lilac, and soft grey waves. The sky was alive with movement, twisting and soaring with Erik's song.

The beauty of the lights was more than Luna could have ever imagined. Underneath the colours of the sky, the world suddenly felt so full of goodness.

Erik had stopped singing, his breath rising and falling in time with the lights as if they were part of the same ancient, quiet magic.

"It's like it moves just for you," Luna whispered.

Erik chuckled softly, his voice warm and slow. "The world, it moves for us all. But you must learn to listen. Sit with it. Love it. And then, it will dance for you, too."

By the soft glow of the firelight, Luna could see Ottoline and Hugh nestled together under a shared blanket, Ottoline's head resting gently on Hugh's shoulder. They stayed silent and content, watching the sky dance above them for a very long time.

Erik's Svalbardian Waistcoat

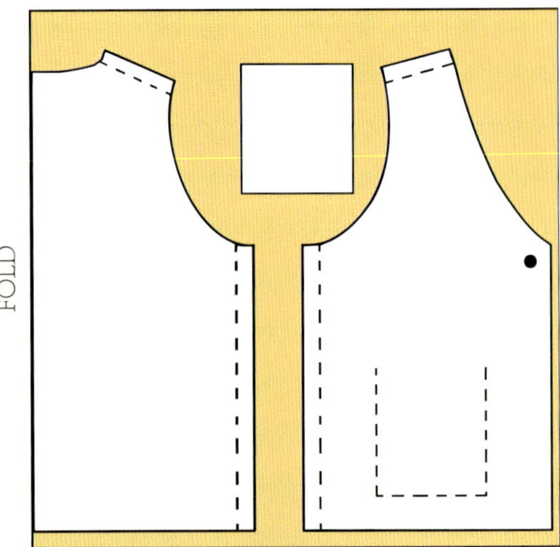

Fig.1

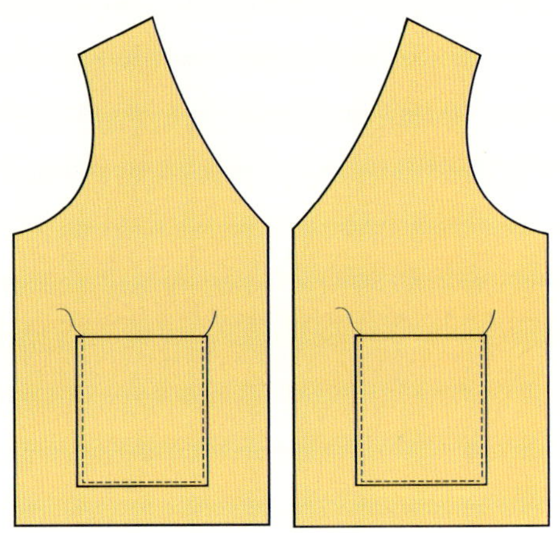

Fig.2

YOU WILL NEED

- **17cm (7in) x 34cm (14in) boiled wool fabric***
- **One 1cm (3/8in) long wooden toggle**
- **Basic sewing kit (see Materials)**

Use a 0.5cm (¼in) seam allowance, unless a different amount is stated.

*Alternatively, you could choose to use any fabric that doesn't fray, such as bouclé or felt.

CUTTING OUT

1 Fold the fabric in half with wrong sides together. Pin your cut-out pattern pieces (see The Patterns) onto the fabric using **Fig.1** as a guide. Cut all pieces as stated on the pattern. Transfer the pocket positions to the fabric.

MAKING UP

Attaching the Pockets to the Fronts

1 Position the pockets onto the right side of the fronts. Pin in place, then sew using an edgestitch (about 0.2cm/1⁄16in from the edge), leaving the top edge open (**Fig.2**). Secure your stitching well at the start and finish, and turn corners crisply (see Techniques: Machine Sewing Techniques).

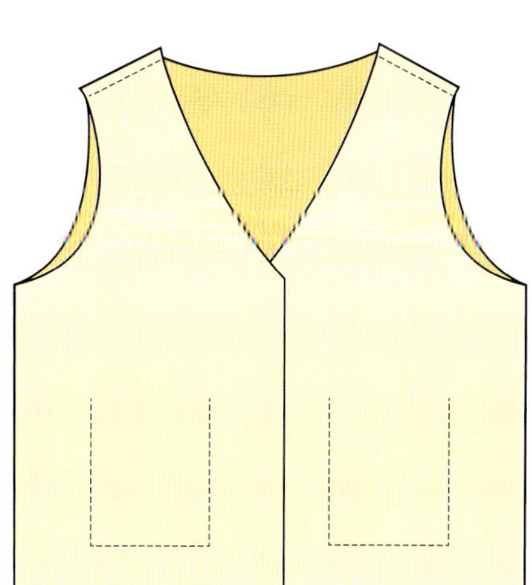

Fig.3

Sewing the Shoulder Seams

1 With right sides together, match one front shoulder seam to one back shoulder seam, taking care, as this is a raw edge garment, to match the seams at the level of the sewing line not the edges of the seam allowance, and sew together. Then repeat to join the remaining front to the back at the shoulder seam (**Fig.3**).

2 Press the seams open and flat. If you find that you do have any unevenness on the outside or neck edges, just trim back to the shorter seam edge.

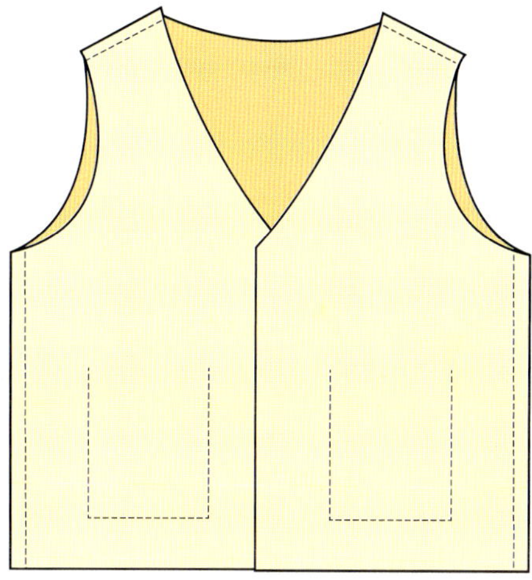

Fig.4

Sewing the Side Seams

1 With right sides together, match the fronts to the back at the sides, taking care that the armhole levels are perfect, then sew the side seams (**Fig.4**). Press the seams open and flat using plenty of steam in your iron.

FINISHING OFF

1 Cut a small snip (approx. 3mm–4mm/⅛in) for the buttonhole on the left-hand side as worn, as marked on the pattern. On the right-hand side as worn, sew the toggle in place (**Fig.5**).

Fig.5

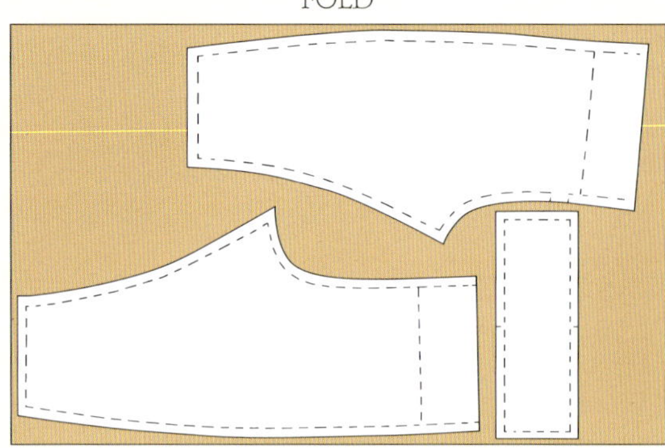

Fig.1

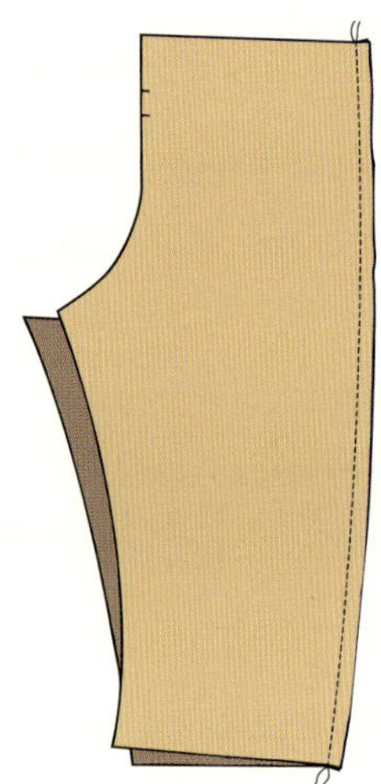

Fig.2

Fig.3

Erik's Barrel Leg Trousers

YOU WILL NEED

- 40cm (16in) x 50cm (20in) peached cotton check fabric*
- 80cm (31½in) of 4mm (⅛in) narrow elastic
- Basic sewing kit (see Materials)

Use a 0.5cm (¼in) seam allowance, unless a different amount is stated.

*Alternative fabric choices include cotton poplin, cord, and lightweight tweed.

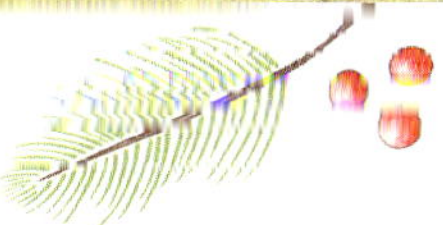

CUTTING OUT

1 Fold the fabric in half with wrong sides together, ensuring your check lines in the doubled fabric are running level. Pin your cut-out pattern pieces (see The Patterns) onto the fabric using **Fig.1** as a guide and paying attention to the straight grain arrows. Take care to place the back leg hem and the front leg hem at a similar level on the check design. Cut all pieces as stated on the pattern. Mark any notches with a tiny snip.

Fig.4

Fig.5

MAKING UP

Attaching the Front Legs to the Back Legs

1 With right sides together, match one front leg to one back leg along the sides. Sew together (**Fig.2**).

2 Press the seam allowance towards the back leg, then edgestitch through all layers about 0.2cm (1/16in) from the seam (**Fig.3**).

3 Repeat steps 1 and 2 to join the remaining front leg to the remaining back leg, making a mirror image.

Attaching the Cuffs to the Trouser Legs

1 With wrong sides together, press each cuff piece in half so the long edges match (**Fig.4**).

2 Taking one cuff, match its doubled raw edge to the bottom edge of one of the trouser legs, with right sides facing, and sew together (**Fig.5**). Repeat to sew the remaining cuff to the other trouser leg. Press seam allowance towards the legs (**Fig.6**).

Sewing the Inside Leg Seams

1 Working on each trouser leg in turn, match the front to the back along the inside leg (right sides together), taking care to match up the cuff seams, and sew together (**Fig.7**).

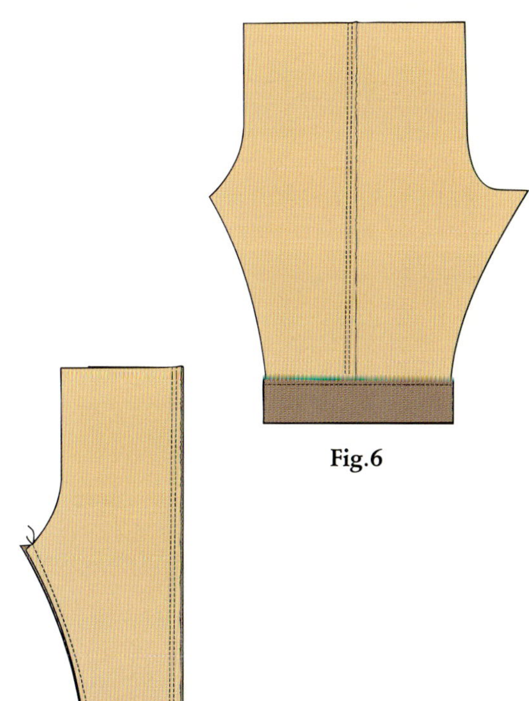

Fig.6

Fig.7

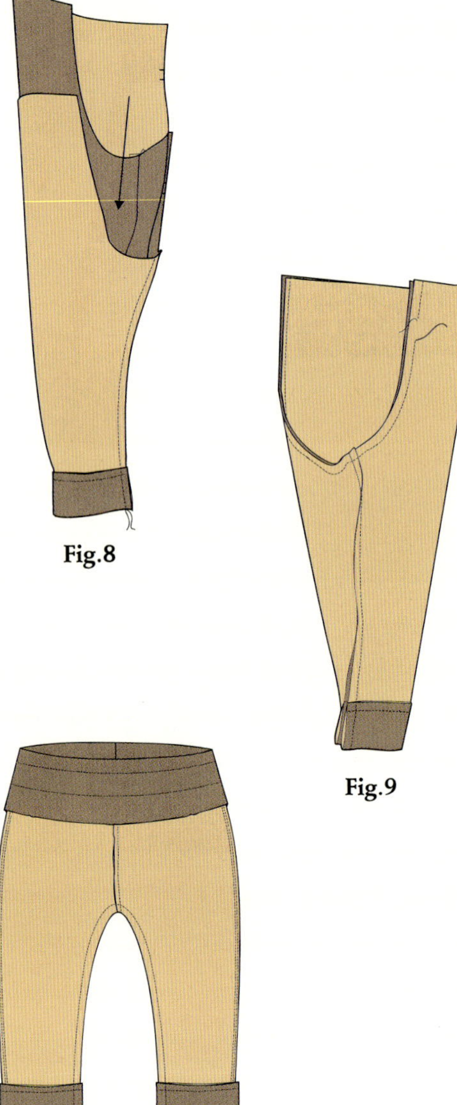

Fig.8

Fig.9

Fig.10

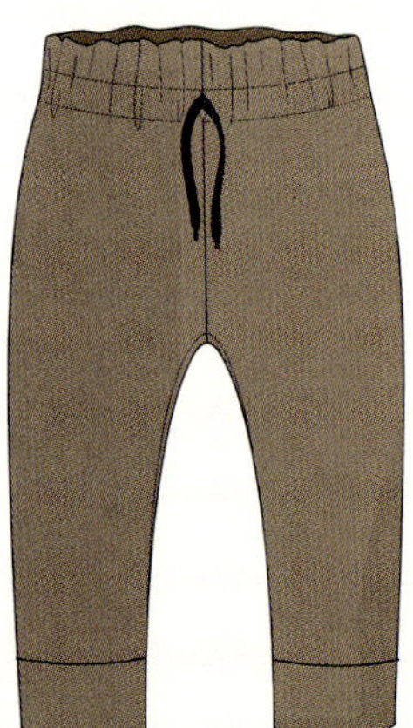

Fig.11

Joining the Legs

1 Leaving one leg wrong side out, turn the other leg right side out. Slide the right-side out leg inside the wrong-side out leg (**Fig.8**). Carefully matching edges and notches and inside leg seams, pin and sew the rise to join the legs, leaving an opening in the front seam (as marked with the notches) for the drawcord opening (**Fig.9**). Press the seams open and flat.

Sewing the Waist Casing

1 Finish around the edge of the waist with an overlock or zigzag stitch. Then press 3.5cm (1⅜in) to the wrong side all the way around.

2 Sew a line of stitching 0.5cm (¼in) away from the folded edge all the way around, then sew a second line of stitching 1.5cm (⅝in) away from the folded edge to create a casing (**Fig.10**).

FINISHING OFF

1 Use a safety pin to thread the length of the elastic through the casing. Pull the ends to be even, knot each end twice, and trim off any excess (**Fig.11**).

Erik's Duffle Coat

YOU WILL NEED

- **22.5cm (9in) x 90cm (36in) felt (mellow yellow)**
- **12cm (4¾in) x 18cm (7in) of contrast cotton for yoke lining**
- **8cm (3½in) x 10cm (4in) of stripey cotton for the pocket fish**
- **Three 1cm (⅜in) long wooden toggles**
- **70cm (27½in) of 1mm waxed cord**
- **5cm (2in) square of pleather (faux leather)**
- **Basic sewing kit (see Materials)**

Use a 0.5cm (¼in) seam allowance, unless a different amount is stated.

CUTTING OUT

Note: Remember, felt has no wrong side or right side, though you may notice there is a slight colour difference from one way to the other. Just pick the one you like most to be your right side.

1 With the wrong side of the fabric facing up, fold in the short edges to give you two folded edges, with about three-quarters of the fabric to one side and one-quarter of the fabric to the other so that the right side of the fabric is now facing up. Pin your cut-out pattern pieces (see The Patterns) onto the fabric using **Fig.1** as a guide. Cut all pieces as stated on the pattern. Mark any notches with a tiny snip, including an 'on the fold' snip to mark the centre of the back and the yoke. Transfer any other pattern markings to the fabric.

2 Fold the lining fabric in half, wrong sides together, and pin the yoke pattern piece in place on the folded edge, following the markings on the pattern. Cut out; mark any notches with a tiny snip, including an 'on the fold' snip.

Fig.1

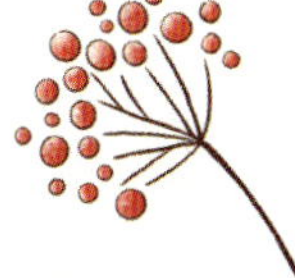

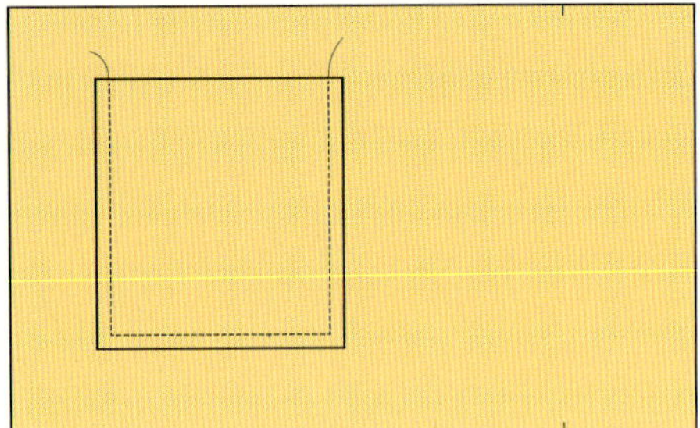

Fig.2

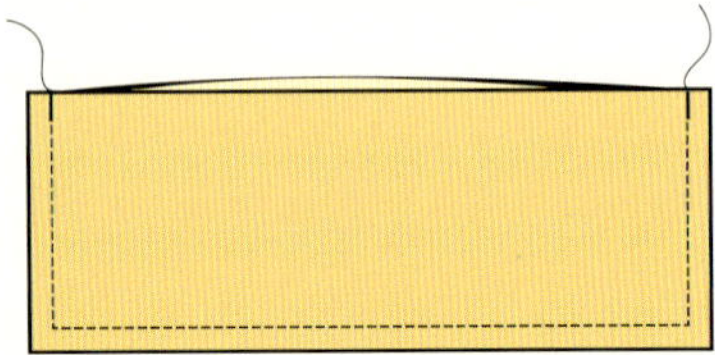

Fig.3

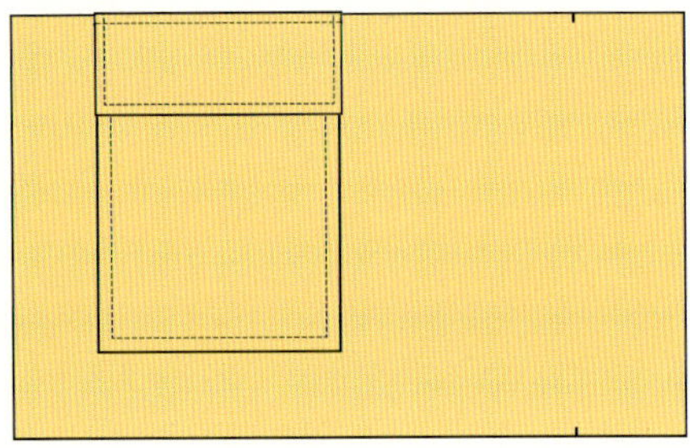

Fig.4

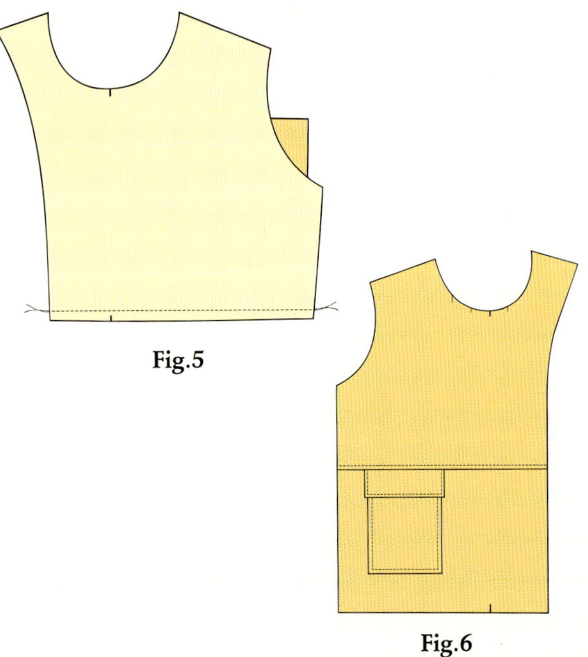

Fig.5

Fig.6

MAKING UP

Sewing the Pockets to the Lower Fronts

1 Position the pockets onto the right side of the lower fronts. Pin in place, then sew using an edgestitch (about 0.2cm/1⁄16in from the edge), leaving the top edge open (**Fig.2**). Secure your stitching well at the start and finish, and turn corners crisply (see Techniques: Machine Sewing Techniques).

2 With wrong sides together, press each pocket flap in half so the long edges meet. Edgestitch around the two short edges and the folded edge (**Fig.3**).

3 Position the pocket flaps onto the top edge of the lower fronts so that they line up perfectly over the pockets (**Fig.4**). Staystitch or tack (baste) in place along the upper edge in preparation for the next step.

Sewing the Lower Fronts to the Upper Fronts

1 With right sides together, match one upper front to one lower front, sandwiching the pocket flap in between, and sew together (**Fig.5**). Press the seam allowance upwards, then edgestitch through all layers on the upper front (**Fig.6**). Repeat to attach the remaining upper front to the remaining lower front, making sure that you have a mirror image.

Sewing the Shoulder Seams
1 With right sides together, match one front shoulder seam to one back shoulder seam. Sew together. Repeat to join the remaining front to the back at the shoulder seam (**Fig.7**).

Sewing the Front Sleeves to the Back Sleeves
1 With right sides together, join the front sleeve to the back sleeve (**Fig.8**). Press the seam allowance towards the front sleeve and edgestitch through all layers. Repeat with the remaining front and back sleeve pieces to make a mirror image.

2 Hem the sleeves by turning 1cm (⅜in) to the wrong side of the sleeve. Press and sew in place through all layers (**Fig.9**).

Attaching the Sleeves
1 With right sides together, set one sleeve to the armhole, matching the notch to the shoulder seam (**Fig.10**). Work around, matching and pinning the head of the sleeve armhole in place, then sew together (**Fig.11**). Repeat to attach the other sleeve to the remaining armhole. Press seam allowances towards the sleeves.

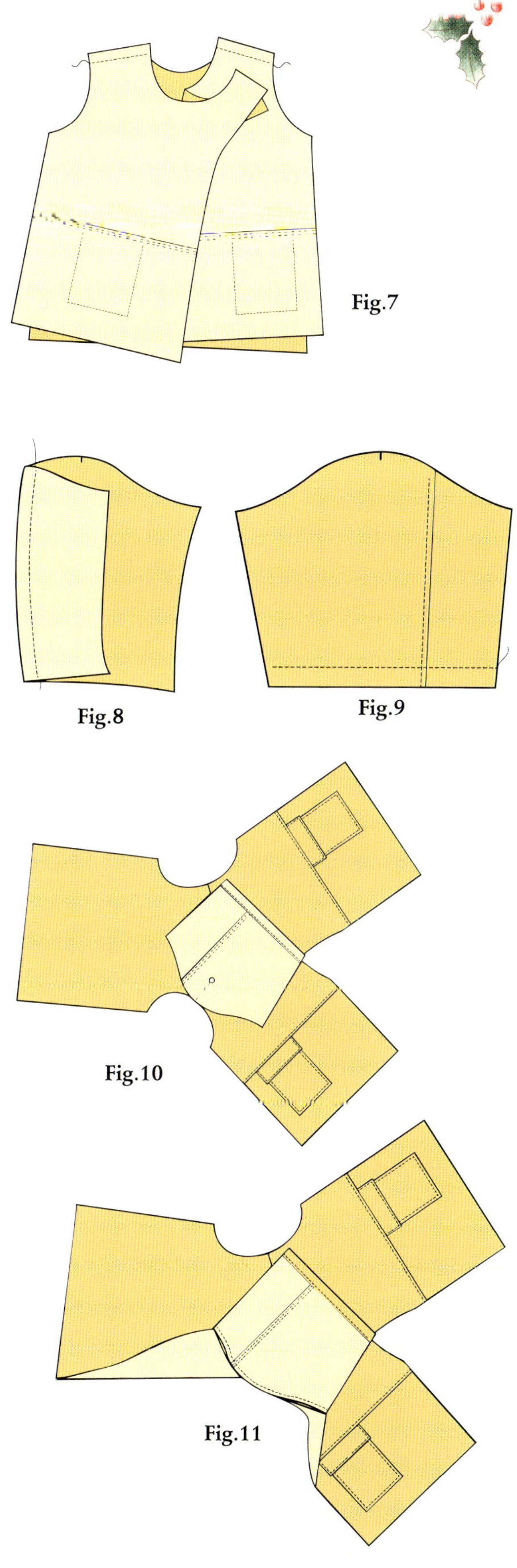
Fig.7
Fig.8
Fig.9
Fig.10
Fig.11

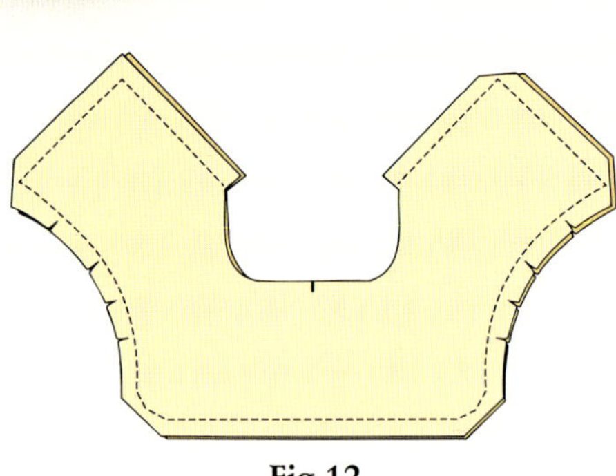
Fig.12

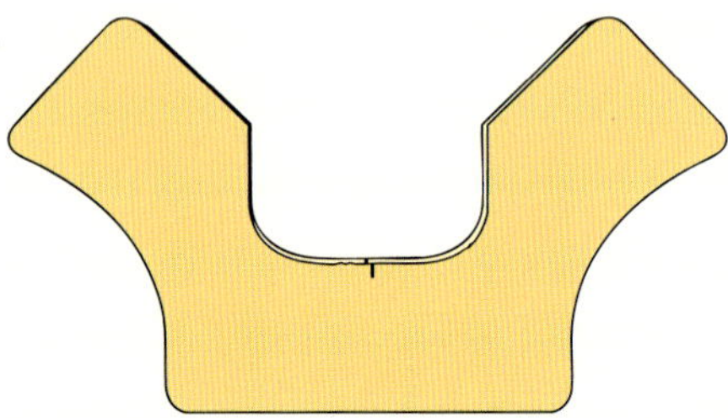
Fig.13

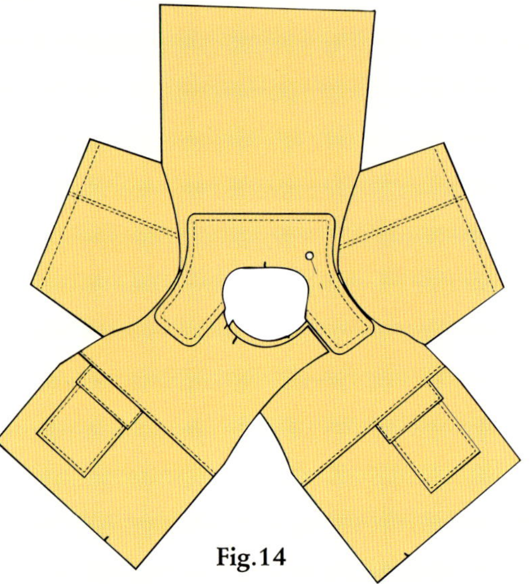
Fig.14

Sewing the Yoke

1 With right sides together, match the yokes (one felt, one cotton lining), then sew together around the short edges and the outside edges, leaving the neck edge unsewn. To change direction at the corners, leave your needle down in the fabric, lift the presser foot, and turn before continuing. Trim excess seam allowance from the corners and snip into the seam allowance on the curved edges (**Fig.12**).

2 Turn the yoke through to the right side, pushing the corners out to be nice and crisp. Use your fingers and thumb to roll the seam right onto the edge and press flat. If there is extra lining fabric at the neck edge, trim it back to the original shape of the felt (**Fig.13**).

3 Position the yoke, lining side facing down, onto the main body, matching around the neck edge, and to the notches in the neckline. Smooth the shape so that it echoes the armhole shape. Tack (baste) into position, then carefully edgestitch the yoke onto the main body (**Fig.14**).

4 Tack (baste) the neck edge layers together in preparation for the next step.

Sewing and Attaching the Hood

1 With right sides together, match and then sew together the curved edge of the hood (**Fig.15**).

2 Press back the front edge of the hood by 1cm (3/8in) for the hem and sew in place (**Fig.16**).

3 With right sides together match the bottom edge of the hood onto the neckline, lining up the hood's front edge with the notches. Tack (baste) in place (**Fig.17**).

4 Fold the front facing back to sandwich the hood and pin in place, then sew in place around the neckline from one front edge to the other (**Fig.18**).

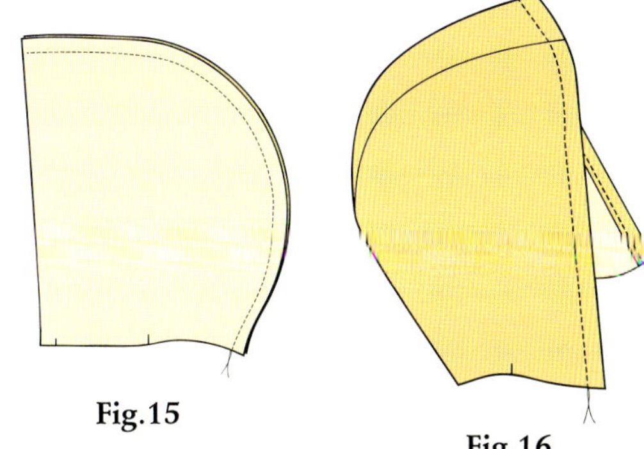

Fig.15

Fig.16

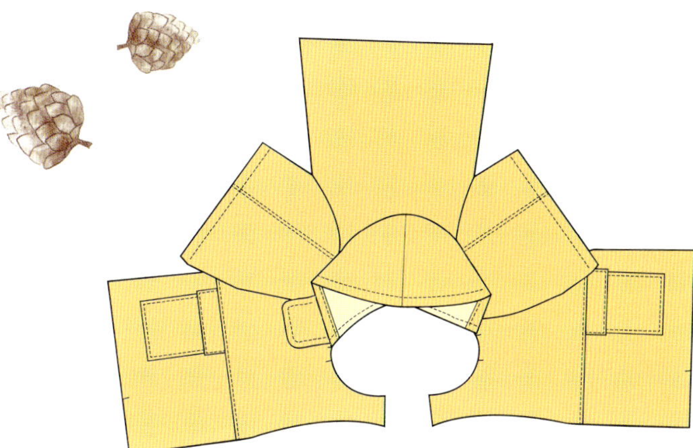

Fig.17

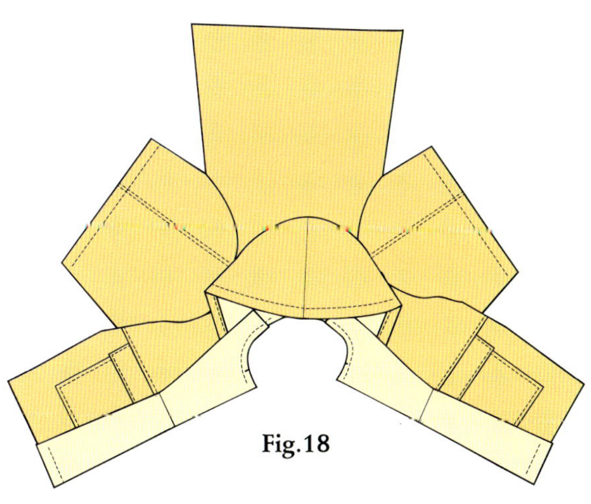

Fig.18

5 Sew the front facing back at the hem to a depth of 1.5cm (5/8in). Trim the excess off the corners and trim the facing layer of the hem away. Trim the neck seam allowance down to 0.3cm (1/8in) all around (**Fig.19**).

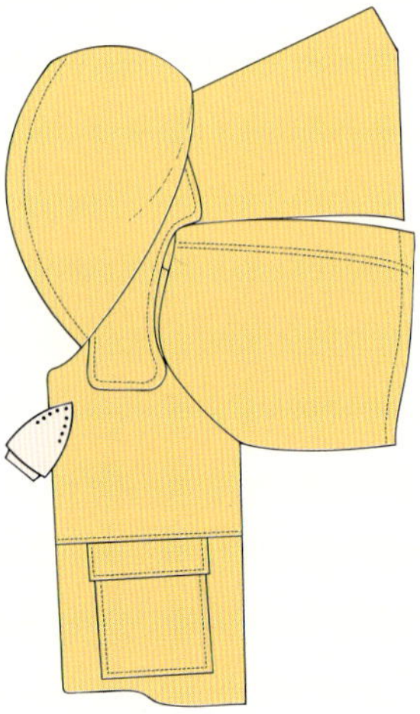

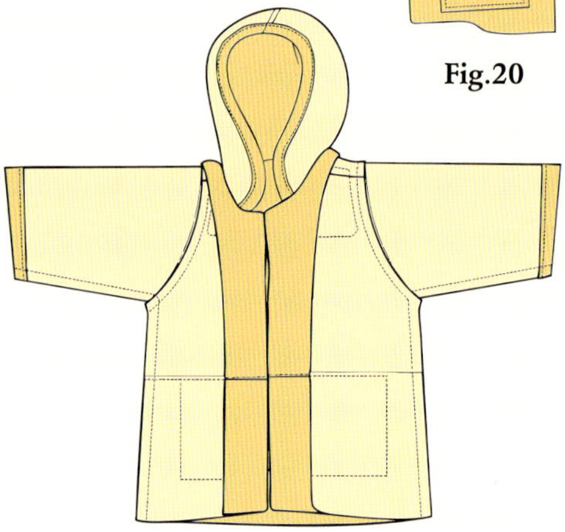

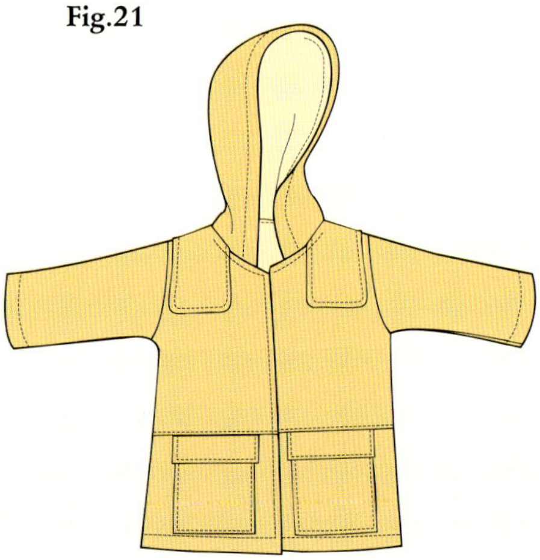

6 Now push the corners back through at the front and press the front fold down between the corners (**Fig.20**).

Fig.19

Fig.20

Sewing the Side and Sleeve Seams

1 With right sides together, match the underarm and side seams and sew together (**Fig.21**).

2 Press up a 1cm (3/8in) hem allowance all the way around the bottom edge of the coat. Then, starting at the front neck on one side of the coat, holding back the facing, edgestitch all the way down the front, pivoting at about 0.6cm (1/4in) from the bottom edge to sew across the hem, just below the pockets. Continue to sew all the way around the hem then back up the front edge on the opposite side of the coat to finish at the neck edge (**Fig.22**).

Fig.21

Fig.22

Attaching the Toggle Buttons and Loops

1 Make three toggle buttons and three loops (see Techniques: Making a Toggle Button and Loop).

2 Position the toggle buttons onto the right-hand side of the coat as worn, using the pattern markings to find the fastening levels (the toggle should sit just inside the edgestitch). Position the loops to the left-hand side of the coat as worn, making sure the edge of the loop sits against the folded edge of the front of the coat. Stick the tail ends down with tape to hold them in place as you sew; reverse sew over the tail ends to ensure the threads are securely caught (**Fig.23**). Trim the tail ends and remove the tape.

3 The tail ends of the toggle buttons and loops are covered with triangular tabs of pleather. Use the front pattern pieces as a guide to cutting the pleather pieces and secure them in place over the tail ends using tape (or quilter's glue). Carefully edgestitch around the pleather triangles, using your handwheel if necessary, then remove the tape (**Fig.24**).

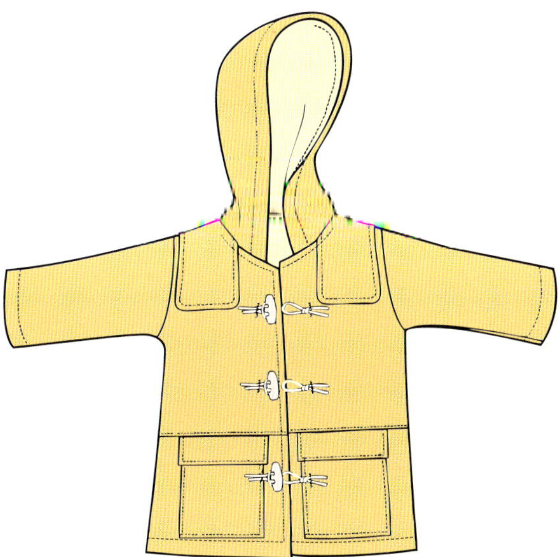

Fig.23

Fig.24

Making the Pocket Fish

1 Make the pocket fish using the stripey cotton. Cut out the pattern (see The Patterns) from doubled fabric.

2 Match the two pieces with right sides together and sew around the shape, leaving a small opening. Turn through and stuff, then slip stitch the opening closed.

3 Sew on a tiny button for the eye, or work a French knot if you prefer.

HOW TO SEW *Luna and friends*

In this section we cover how to sew the animal bodies. Although there is still a lot of hand sewing, we have more machine sewing in this edition – including Maurice and the donkeys, Sidney and Sol, who are primarily machined. These different approaches are noted where appropriate. You will find that Luna and Sidney and Sol have different body constructions to Gracie, Maurice, and Erik who share a similar body construction, but again there are variations to each one. Luna, Gracie, and Sidney and Sol are roughly 40.6cm (16in) tall when finished, whereas Maurice is about 5cm (2in) smaller as he has a shorter leg, and Erik is a little taller by 3.5cm (1½in) with a longer leg. Once you are familiar with Luna and her friends, you could easily switch body constructions to your favourite make. Erik's barrel leg trousers are about 3.5cm (1½in) longer to fit his legs, so remember to make these shorter if you want to make them for a smaller friend.

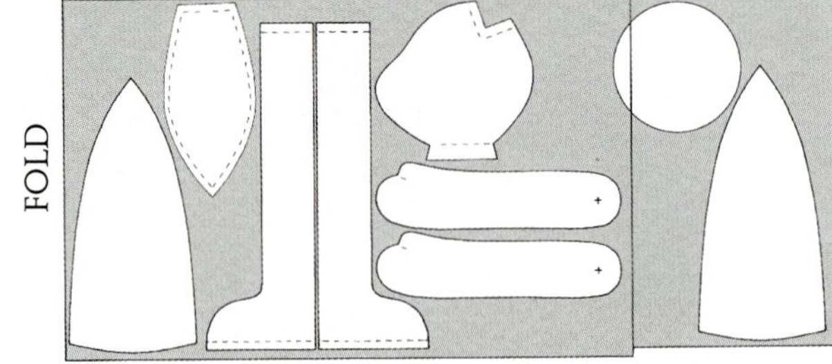

Fig.1

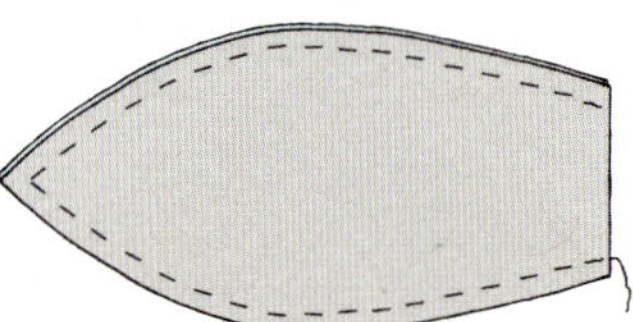

Fig.2

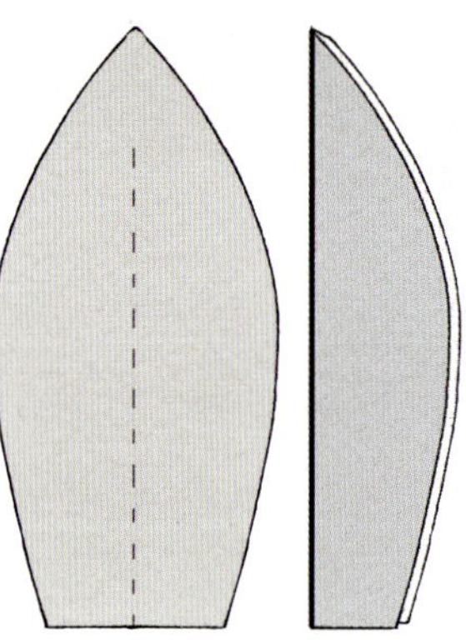

Fig.3

How to Make Luna

YOU WILL NEED

- **23cm (9in) x 92cm (36¼in) wide light grey felt**
- **15cm (6in) x 20cm (8in) cotton lawn fabric**
- **13cm (5in) x 13cm (5in) mid-weight fusible interfacing**
- **Two 10mm (⅜in) buttons for eyes and two 15mm (⅝in) buttons for arm joints**
- **Wool yarn for tail (optional)**
- **Toy stuffing about 120gm (4½oz)**
- **Six-stranded embroidery cotton (floss) in brown for facial features**
- **Basic sewing kit (see Materials)**

Use a 0.5cm (¼in) seam allowance, unless a different amount is stated.

CUTTING OUT

1 Pin the cut-out pattern pieces (see The Patterns) onto the partially folded felt, using the layout in **Fig.1** as a guide. Cut the pieces out and mark any triangles or notches with a tiny snip in the felt. Transfer all other pattern markings using tailor's tacks or a water-soluble pen.

2 Cut out a pair of ears and a pair of footpads from the lawn fabric. Cut out a pair of ears from interfacing. Mark the notches as before. Transfer all other pattern markings using tailor's tacks or a water-soluble pen.

MAKING UP

Making the Ears

1 Using an iron, fuse the interfacing to the wrong side of the cotton lawn ears. Place the right side of a cotton lawn ear onto a felt ear, matching edges, and sew around the curved edges, leaving the straight edge open (**Fig.2**). You can machine sew or use a hand-sewn backstitch (see Techniques: Hand Sewing Stitches). Repeat to make the second ear.

2 Trim the seam allowance off at the points and then turn each ear through to the right side. Use a knitting needle or similar tool to carefully push the shape out. Roll the seams out to the edge between your fingers and press flat with a warm iron.

3 Sew through the ear layers to hold them together on a central line, aiming for invisible stitches on the felt side. Finish about two-thirds of the way up. Fold each ear in half to enclose the lawn fabric (**Fig.3**), and pin in place.

Making the Head

1 Line up the bottom of an ear with the straight edge of a head piece, making sure the open edges of the ear are facing the nose. Fold the head piece over to cover the ear as in **Fig.4**. Make sure that the ear is tucked right up to the fold point. Sew through all layers on the marked sewing line. Repeat to join the other ear to the other head piece, to create a mirror image of the first one.

2 Turn the head pieces out to the right side and pin the centre front seams together so that the edges are level and the ear seams match up. Oversew the two pieces together, leaving the neck opening free (**Fig.5**).

3 Stuff the head through the neck opening using small pieces of stuffing to build up the shape (**Fig.6**). Tuck the neck seam allowance up into the head.

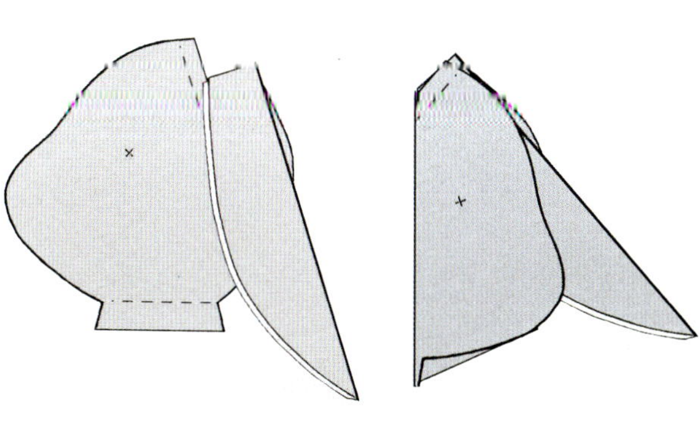

Fig.4

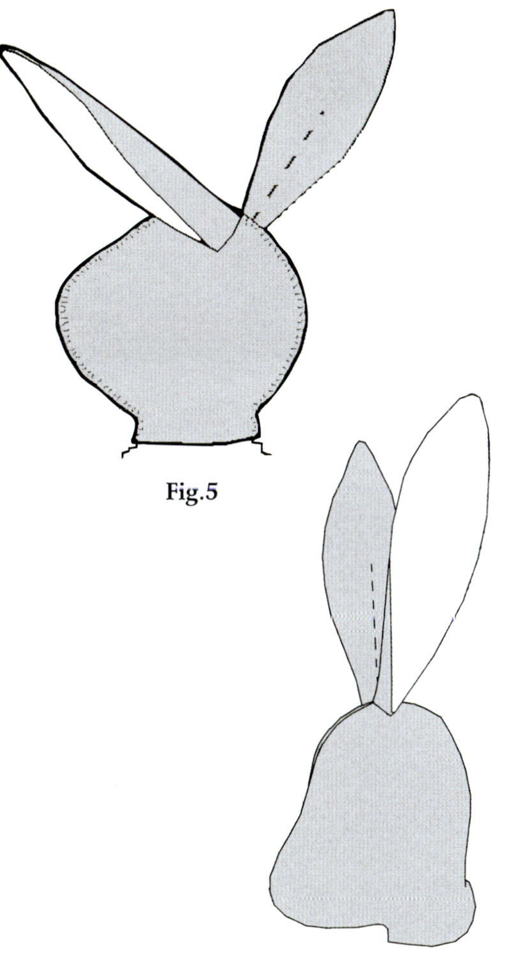

Fig.5

Fig.6

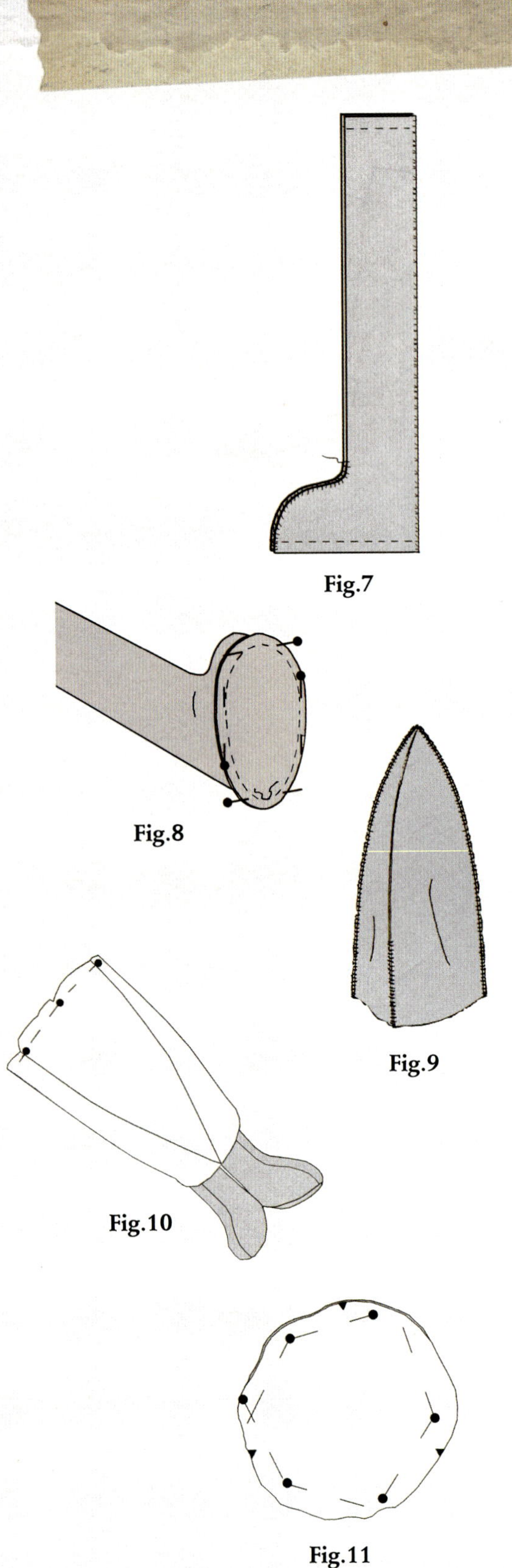

Fig.7

Fig.8

Fig.9

Fig.10

Fig.11

Making the Legs

1 Oversew two leg pieces together down the long back seam. Starting from the foot, sew the front seam up to just over the foot (**Fig.7**).

2 Now turn the leg so that these seams are to the inside and pin the footpad in place, using the notches on the footpad to match up with the seams you have just sewn. Ease the footpad in place and pin to hold (I use just four pins: first, I stretch the felt slightly, then with the pad facing me, I pin wide and long to hold the felt flat at the back). Sew all the way around using a backstitch (**Fig.8**). Turn the foot back to be right side out with the raw edges enclosed and stuff the foot firmly. Resume oversewing the front leg seam, stuffing the leg firmly as you go. Leave about 1cm (⅜in) at the top with no stuffing. The legs should be the firmest stuffed part of the bunny (and the same length). At the top, fold the leg so that the front and back seams are in line with one another and either pin or sew together to close the opening. Repeat steps 1 and 2 to make a second, matching leg.

Making the Body and Attaching the Legs

1 Take two of the body pieces and oversew down one edge. Sew the third body piece onto one of the free sides, then join the remaining two unsewn edges together, starting at the lower edge of the body and finishing after about 5cm (2in) before fastening off (**Fig.9**). Turn inside out, so that the seams are to the inside ready for the next stage.

2 Push the legs inside the turned body. Feed them in through the opening in the body seam left in the previous step. Position the flattened top of each leg level with one of the lower edges of the body so that the outside edge of each flattened leg is in line with a tummy seam and the toes are facing up towards the tummy. Sew in place using a backstitch or tacking (basting) stitch (**Fig.10**).

3 Take the circular base and match up the three notches to the three seams of the body; enclose the raw edges of the legs and, using backstitch, sew through all layers of the tummy, legs and base with a 0.75cm (5⁄16in) seam allowance (**Fig.11**). A double thread is better when sewing through four thicknesses of felt. Complete the sewing around the circle.

4 Turn the body back out so that the legs are dangling. Stuff the body and sew down the opening, starting from the top and meeting up with where you had previously sewn. Make sure that you use enough stuffing for the body to be firm.

5 Check you have enough stuffing in the head, but still a gap for the point of the body cone. Push the point of the body cone into the head and pin in place (**Fig.12**). Using double thread and a medium-size darner needle, sew the head to the body using slip stitch and ensuring it is well attached by going around the neck at least twice.

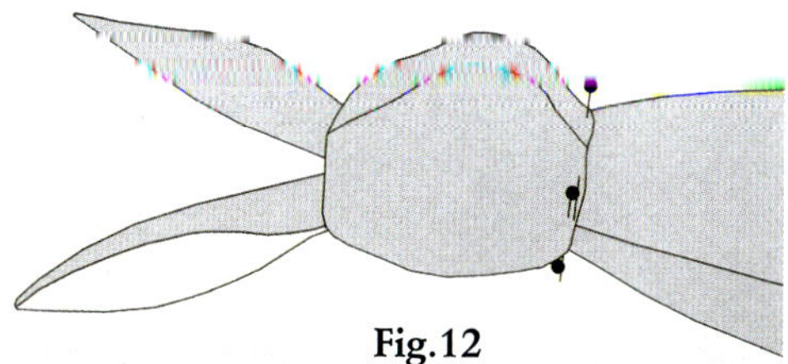

Fig.12

Making the Arms

1 Match two arm pieces and sew together starting at the back of the arm. Oversew over the arm top, down the front and down to the hand (**Fig.13**). Use a deeper stitch to define the thumb and then oversew until you are 4cm (1½in) away from where you started.

2 Stuff the arm firmly and then close the opening. Repeat this process to make a second arm.

3 Stitch the arms onto the body so that the top of the arm matches the level of the neck seam. Check you have the thumbs facing forwards. Position the buttons on the arms using the pattern piece as a guide and pin in place (**Fig.14**). Use a double thread and a large needle to sew the arms onto the body, going through the whole body and passing through the buttons on each side (**Fig.15**). Don't pull the arms in so tight that they change the shape of the body, but just enough to pull the arms in snug to the body. Secure by passing the needle through at least fifteen times – this needs to be secure as you will be moving the arms frequently to dress Luna.

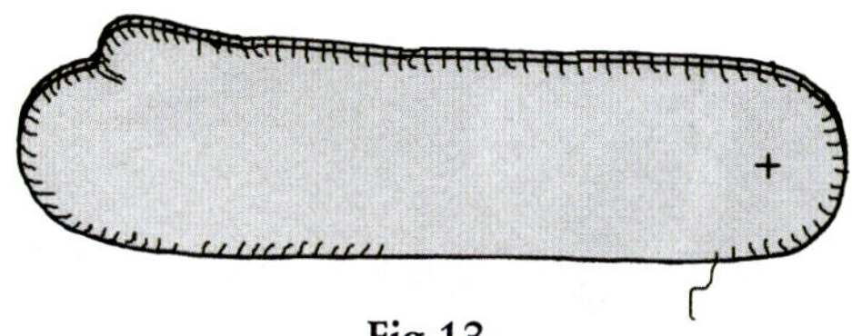

Fig.13

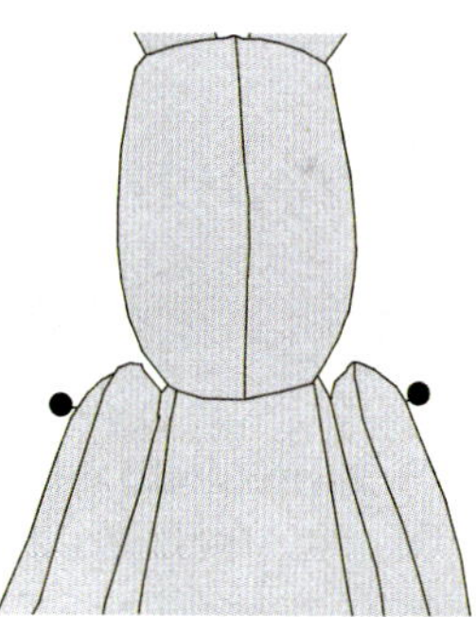

Fig.14

FINISHING OFF

1 Using three strands of embroidery thread, sew on buttons for eyes (see pattern piece for positioning). Add both eyes at the same time, sewing through the face, pulling in slightly to indent the face a little.

2 Using three strands of embroidery thread, satin stitch a triangular nose (see Techniques: Hand Sewing Stitches). The top of the nose should measure 6.5cm (2½in) from the ear/head seam. The nose should be about 1cm (⅜in) wide at its widest point. Keep your stitches relaxed to avoid creating a pinched beak! Alternatively, a Y-shaped nose created with long stitches works, too.

3 Adding a pompom tail is optional. Using the wool, make a pompom by winding it around a credit card or piece of stiff card. Snip down both edges and bind the centre with a remnant of wool. Shape and fluff up the wool, then trim with scissors to be about 2cm (¾in) in diameter. Sew the tail onto the back seam of the body just above the base. Luna is now ready to be loved and dressed.

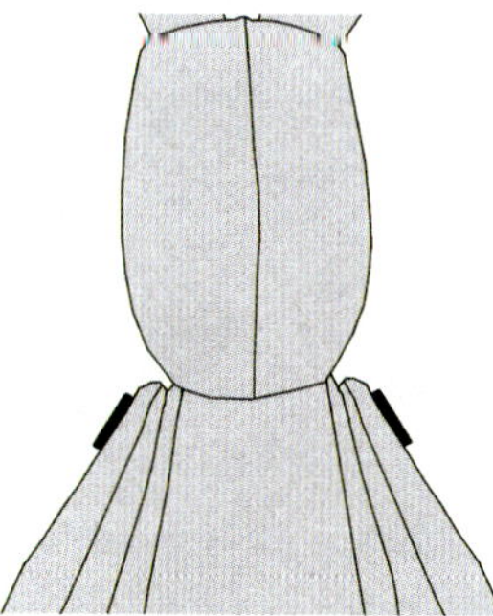

Fig.15

How to Make Sidney & Sol

YOU WILL NEED

- 21cm (8½in) x 90cm (36in) wide main felt (peanut for Sol; chocolate for Sidney)
- 5cm (2in) square contrast felt (white for Sol; peanut for Sidney)
- 20cm (8in) x 30cm (12in) snow white bouclé
- 4.5cm (1¾in) x 18cm (7in) faux fur fabric with a pile of around 2cm (¾in)
- Two 10mm (⅜in) buttons for eyes
- Three 15mm (⅝in) buttons for arm joints and tail, and two 23mm (⅞in) buttons for leg joints
- Toy stuffing about 120gm (4½oz)
- Basic sewing kit (see Materials)

Use a 0.5cm (¼in) seam allowance, unless a different amount is stated.

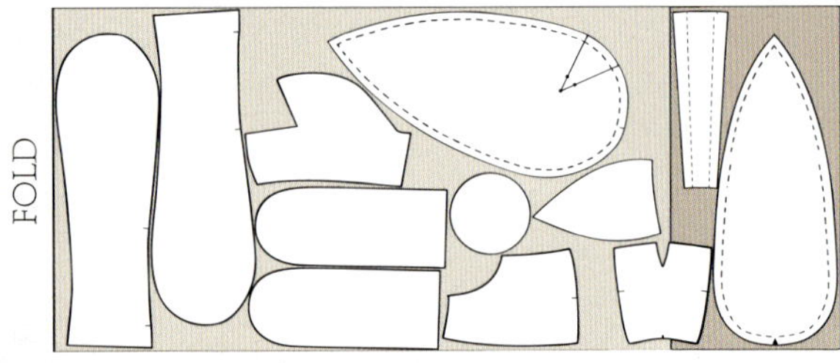

Fig.1

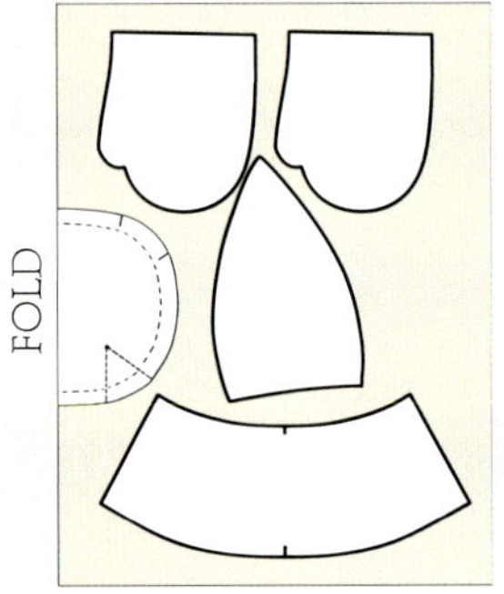

Fig.2

Fig.3

CUTTING OUT

1 Pin the cut-out pattern pieces (see The Patterns) onto the partially folded main felt, using the layout in **Fig 1** as a guide and noting which pieces should be cut in which colour and material. Pin the relevant pieces onto the bouclé fabric, folded in half with right sides together, using **Fig.2** as a guide. Cut the pieces out and mark notches with a tiny snip in the edge, including the 'on the fold' snip to mark the muzzle centre fold. Transfer all other markings using a water-soluble marker pen or tailor's tacks.

2 Pin the tail tuft and mane pieces onto the wrong side of the faux fur fabric, matching arrows on pattern with direction of pile (**Fig.3**), and cut out (see Materials for advice on working with faux fur). Finally cut the two eye backs from the contrast felt.

MAKING UP

Note: Sidney and Sol are mainly machine sewn with some hand sewing for small scale areas and assembly.

Making the Ears

1 Match one outer (main felt) ear piece to an inner (bouclé) ear piece with right sides together; machine sew along the curved edges (easiest with felt piece on top), pivoting at the top point (**Fig.4**). Trim excess seam allowance, especially at the point. Repeat to make a second ear, a mirror image of the first.

2 Turn ears through to the right side; use a knitting needle or similar to push the tips out gently. Pleat the bouclé at the base of the ear so that the felt is visible at the front, then tack (baste) in place (**Fig.5**).

Making the Back of the Head

1 Placing side back head pieces with right sides facing up and front edges facing each other, position an ear on each, bouclé side facing down, so that the bottom of the ear sits tight to the cut-out corner of the dart and the edge of the base of the ear aligns with the felt (**Fig.6**). There should still be 0.75cm (5/16in) visible above the ear to allow for the head seam allowance. Tack (baste) in place.

2 Fold the side back head piece over to enclose the ear and match up the edges of the dart. Sew through all layers 0.5cm (1/4in) from the edge, continuing to the marked dart end. You can use a handsewn backstitch here but machine sewing is easier (**Fig.7**). Push the ear darts out to the right side (**Fig.8**).

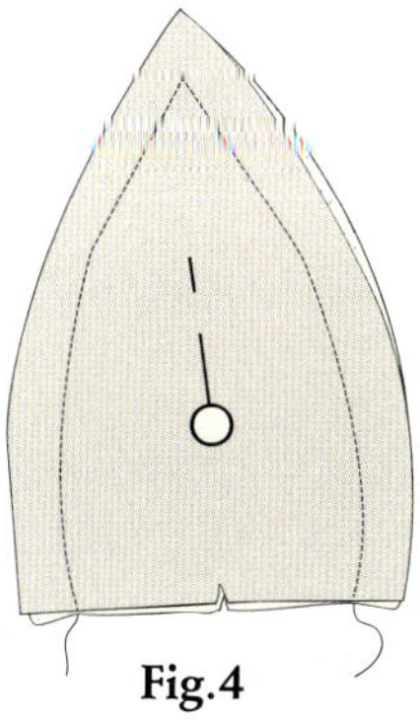

Fig.4

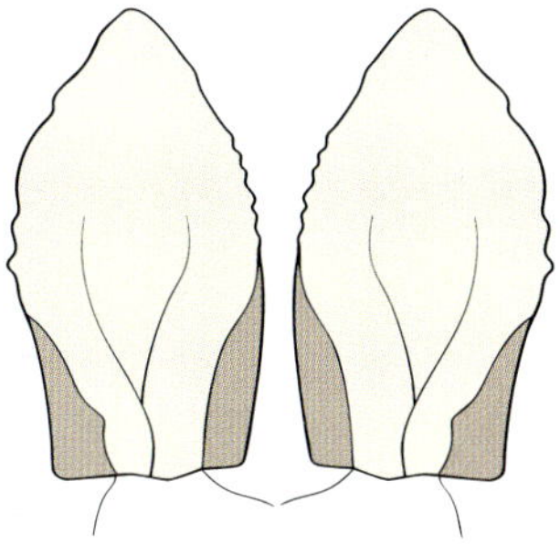

Fig.5

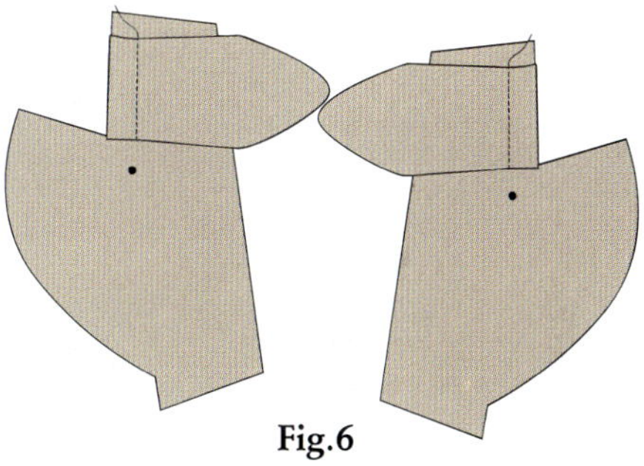

Fig.6

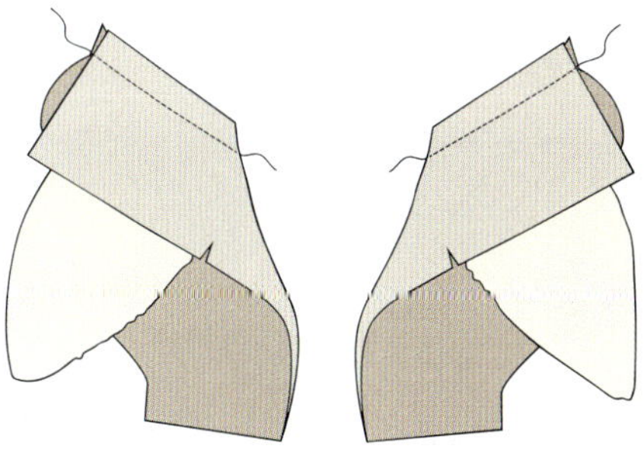

Fig.7

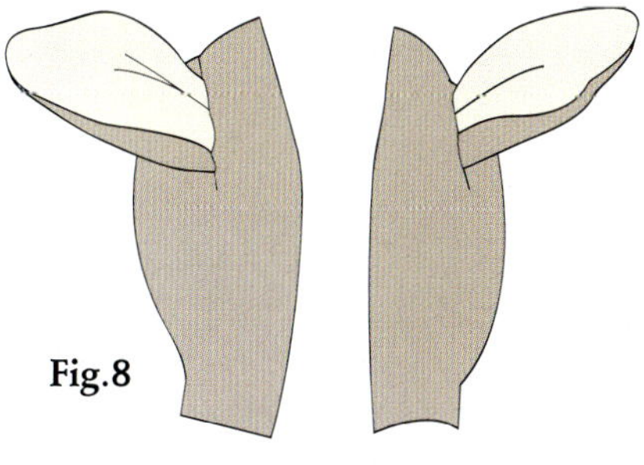

Fig.8

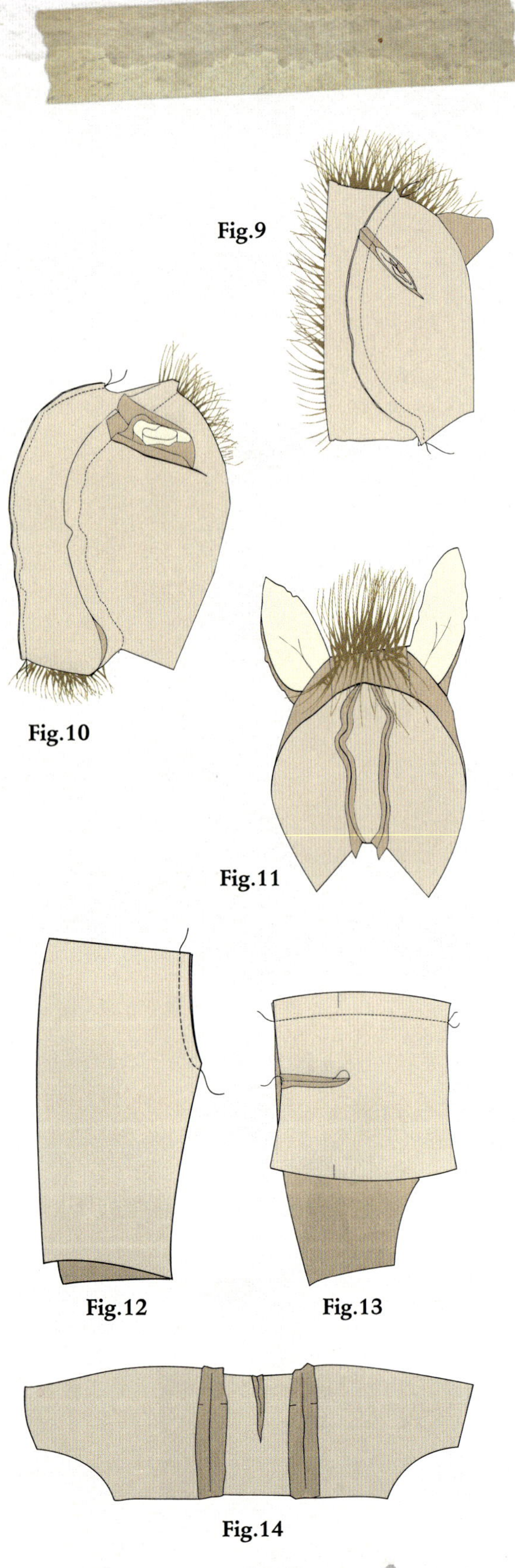

3 You will now use the strip of faux fur fabric, which forms the mane, to join the side back head pieces together. The mane should sweep forward so the pile is running to the bottom of the back neck. With right sides together and keeping the ear out of the way, match one long edge of the fur strip to the rounded shape of the side back head, pushing the pile to the inside and away from the raw edge, then sew together (**Fig.9**).

4 Repeat to attach the other side back head to the other long edge of the fur strip to complete the back of the head (**Fig.10**) – the first side will feel easier to attach than the second! Turn out to the right side and carefully trim any extra length from the fur strip to form the mane (**Fig.11**).

Making the Front of the Head

1 Fold the nose bridge piece in half and edgestitch (or oversew if hand sewing) the small dart on the wrong side of the felt approx. 0.2cm (1/16in) away (**Fig.12**). You now have a wrong side with visible stitching.

2 With right sides together, match and pin one long edge of the bridge to one of the side front heads, making sure to match the notches, then sew together (**Fig.13**). Repeat to join the other side front head to the other edge of the nose bridge.

3 Press the seam allowances open and flat to complete what will now be called the front head panel (**Fig.14**).

Joining the Back of the Head to the Front Head Panel

1 Smoothing the mane fur backwards, match and pin the mid-point of the back of the head to the centre of the front head panel, right sides together (**Fig.15**). Continue to match and pin all the way round to meet at the neck edges, tucking in the bulk of the back of the head panel as you go. Sew together: start at the centre front, sew around one side to the neck edge, then return to start position to sew around the other side (**Fig.16**).

2 With right sides together, match and sew the throat curve to complete this stage of making the head (**Fig.17**), then set aside.

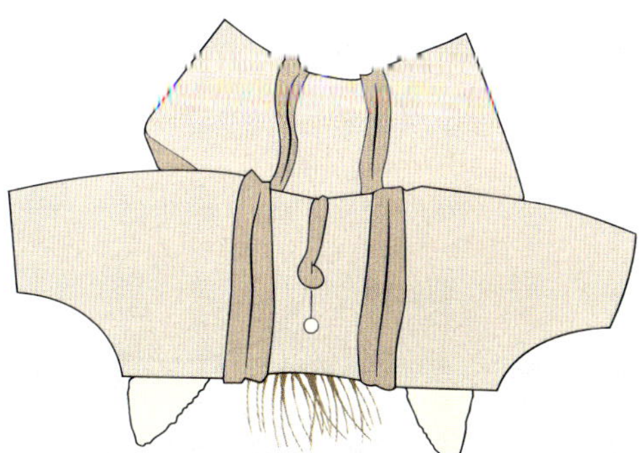

Fig.15

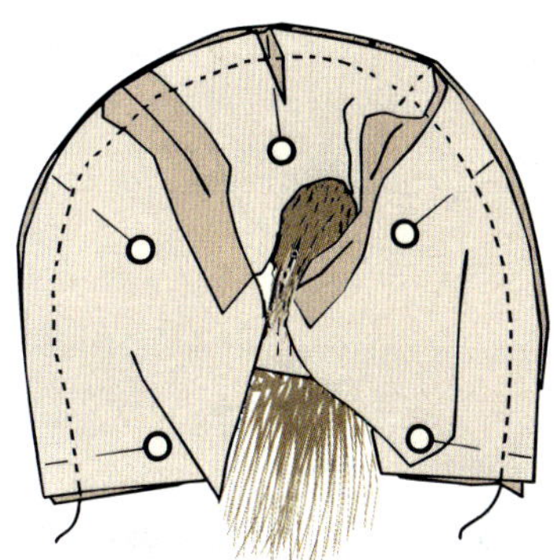

Fig.16

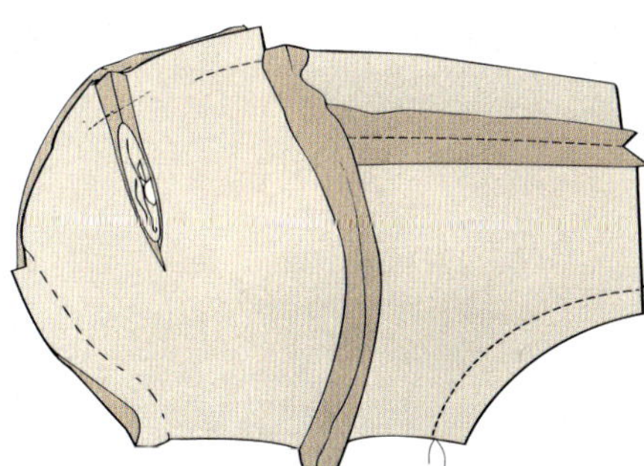

Fig.17

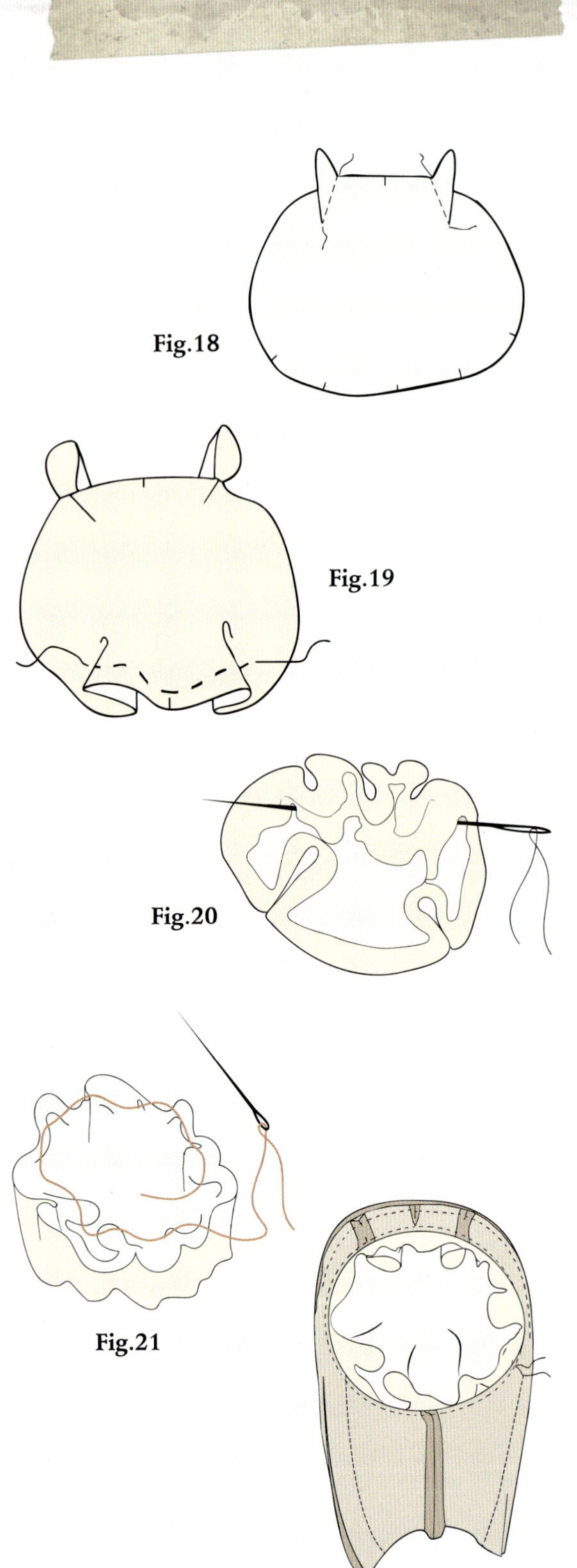

Fig.18

Fig.19

Fig.20

Fig.21

Fig.22

Making the Muzzle

1 Cut the muzzle stitch guide (see The Patterns) from folded paper and use to draw the darts (triangular markings) and tuck positions (marked with letters A and B) on the wrong side of the bouclé fabric muzzle piece, so that the marks mirror each other.

2 Using the triangular markings, pin each dart with right sides together, and sew along the marked line (**Fig.18**).This creates the shaping at the lower edge of the muzzle.

3 On each side, bring mark A down to meet mark B, creating a soft tuck. Tack (baste) through the pleat 0.5cm (¼in) from the edge to keep the tuck in position. This creates the nostrils which will be at the top of the muzzle (**Fig.19**).

4 Now use a double thread and a long stitch to sew around the edge of the muzzle to gather it in slightly. Start and finish on the wrong side of the bouclé, keeping the ends loose so you can still draw or release the threads to fit the nose gap as necessary (**Figs.20** and **21**).

5 With the head wrong sides facing out, open up the nose gap and stretch slightly so it is easier for you to insert the muzzle. Put the muzzle into the hole, right sides together, matching the nostril folds to the bridge seams and making the darts equally distant from the throat seam. It will feel as if the muzzle is slightly bigger than the outer piece, but this fullness will help the end result. Use a hand-sewn backstitch to sew in place all the way around (**Fig.22**).

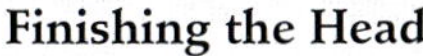

Finishing the Head

1 Pull the ears out of the open neck edge and push the whole head through (**Fig.23**). Check your stitching isn't starting to show too much around the muzzle, if it is, turn back through and backstitch over the seam you just made.

2 Once you are happy, begin to stuff the head, building up the shape to be full and round. Don't overfill the muzzle or the bouclé might stretch and distort the shape. You may need to add more stuffing later, when attaching the head to the body.

3 Position the eye backs onto the head according to the side head pattern and oversew around the shape (note that **Fig.32** shows the position well). Sew on the eye buttons with a slightly lighter colour, passing from one side to the other, without pulling the head shape in.

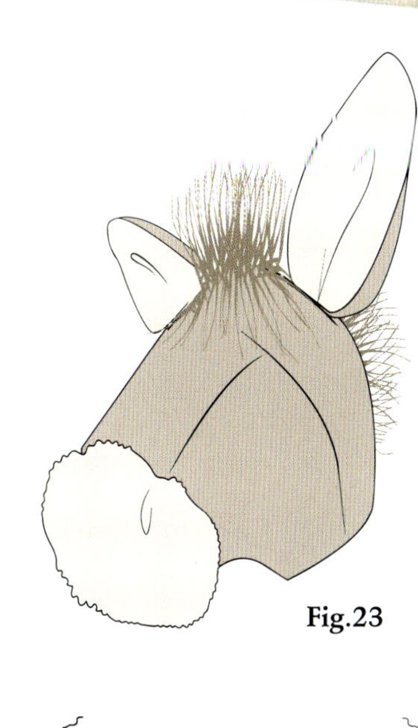

Fig.23

Making the Body

1 Take one side body piece at a time and, with right sides together, match up the notches and fold along to the dart point. Backstitch by hand or machine stitch from the matched notches to the dart point, then trim away the excess seam allowance (**Fig.24**).

2 Match the two side body pieces with right sides together, making sure the side body darts are lining up. On the opposite edge, sew down from the top point to the upper side notch and fasten off. Then sew up from the bottom notch to the lower side notch, leaving a large unstitched gap in between (**Fig.25**).

3 With right sides together, match and pin one edge of the tummy panel to one of the unstitched side body pieces, sewing all the way from the point to where the notches meet. Repeat to join the remaining tummy panel/side body seam (**Fig.26**). Turn through, so the right side is on the outside.

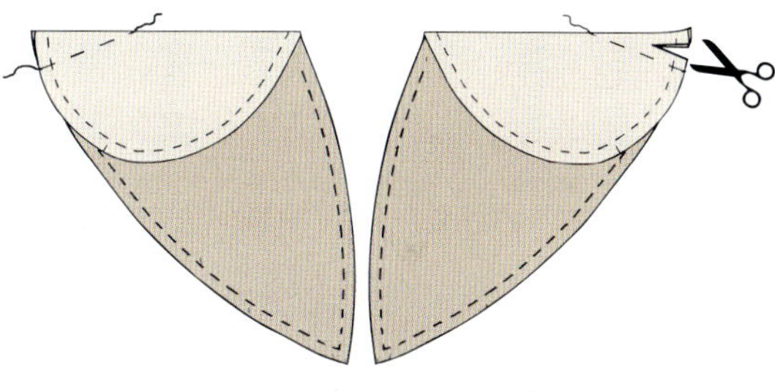

Fig.24

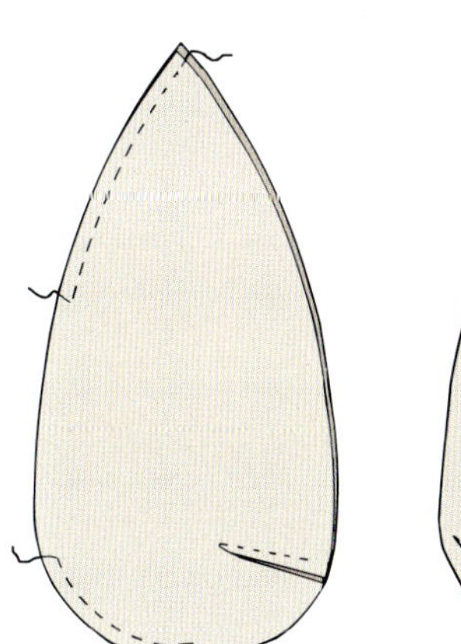

Fig.25

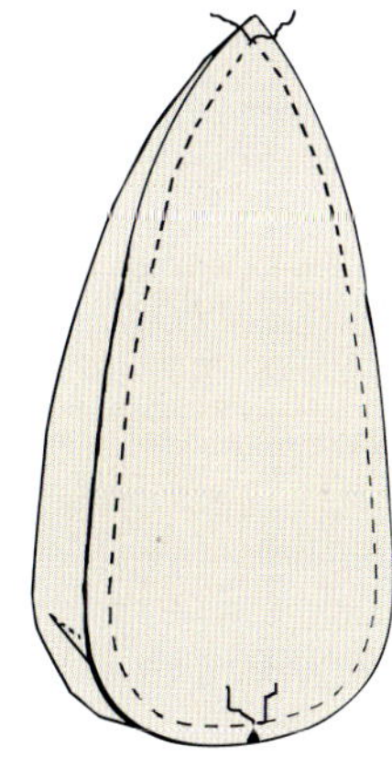

Fig.26

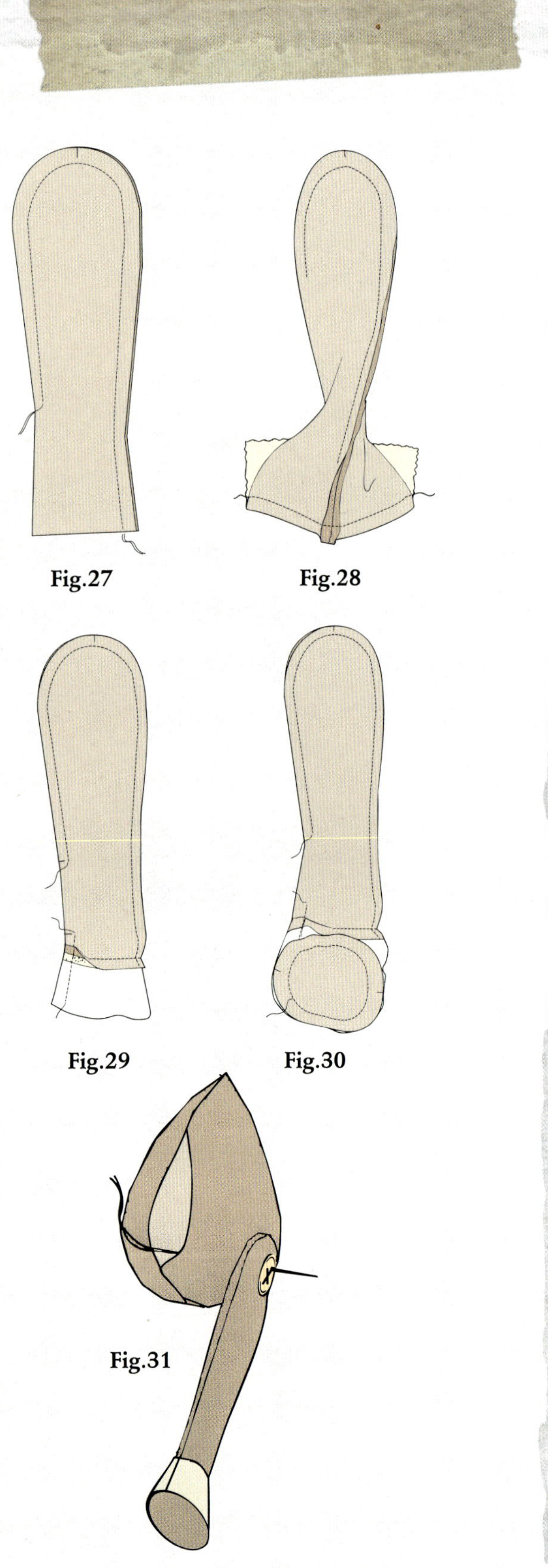
Fig.27
Fig.28
Fig.29
Fig.30
Fig.31

Making the Legs

1 With right sides together, match two leg pieces and sew together, starting at the back notch as seen in **Fig.27**.

2 Flatten out the seam allowance at the bottom edge of the leg. Pin a bouclé hoof piece along its shorter top edge to the leg, right sides together, matching its notch to the leg seam. Sew together (**Fig.28**).

3 Match the short edges of the attached hoof along the back leg seam (still right sides together) and sew to about 1.5cm (⅝in) beyond the leg/hoof seam (**Fig.29**), leaving a gap for turning through.

4 With right sides together, pin a felt footpad to the bottom edge of each bouclé hoof, matching notches and seams, then sew together (this is easier by hand!) **(Fig.30)**.

5 Turn the legs through to the right side and begin stuffing. Stuff the upper haunch less firmly for the first 4cm (1½in) or so, then continue to stuff firmly. Massage the legs as you go to ensure a smooth outer appearance, then sew the opening closed by hand.

Attaching the Legs

1 The legs are attached to the body before the body is stuffed. Measure 1cm (⅜in) from one of the side body darts towards the front for the exact position to sew the top of the leg. Check you have the hoof facing forwards (the hoof seam should be at the back) and position the button on the leg using the pattern piece as a guide. Using a long double thread and a doll needle, go through the opening in the back, then out through the leg and the button. Take the needle back through the button, through the leg, through the body fabric, and repeat until both leg and button are secured (**Fig.31**). Repeat to attach the remaining leg on the other side.

2 Now stuff the base of the body firmly, filling up to the back opening. At this point, you can use a long double thread to sew through the whole body and, passing through the buttons at each side, gently pull the legs in snug to the body. Cut the thread near the eye of the needle and use a smaller needle to fasten off invisibly between the leg and the body. Continue to stuff the body, pushing stuffing up into the cone at the top, then oversew the back opening to close.

Attaching the Head to the Body

1 Turn the 1cm (⅜in) neck seam allowance up inside the head (you might want to trim away some of the mane at the base of the head to make it easier to sew the head on). Push the point of the body cone into the head, lining up at the back first. Using double thread and a medium-size darner needle, sew the head to the body with slip stitch. Ensure it is well attached by going around the neck at least twice. I tend to go around fairly loosely on round one and then tighten up in rounds two and three. The head should sit about 2.5cm (1in) down from the point of the body (**Fig.32**).

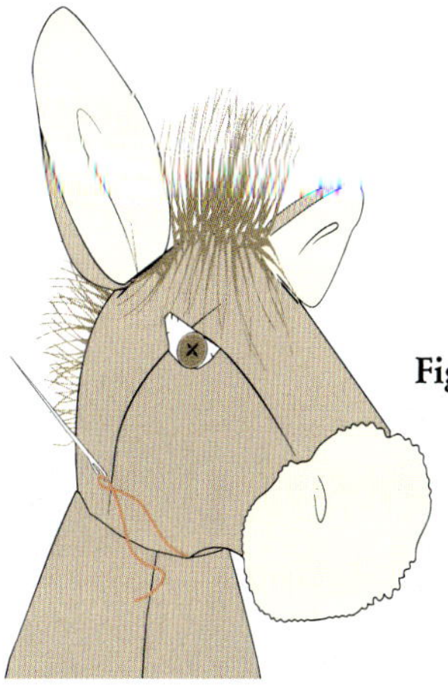

Fig.32

Making the Arms

1 With right sides together, match and pin a bouclé hand piece to the end of a felt arm piece (note the thumb shaping must be on the opposite side to the notches on the arm). Repeat to make a second (mirrored) arm (**Fig.33**). Then make another pair of arm pieces in the same way. Press seams open.

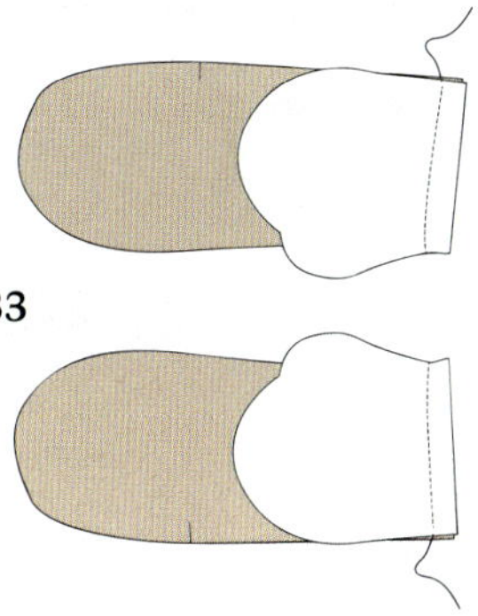

2 With right sides together, match two arm pieces and sew together, starting at the top notch at the back of the arm and working your way around the top of the arm to the hand (changing threads to match the lighter bouclé if you wish). Take your time around the hand curve and pivot at the thumb shaping, and continue to finish at the bottom notch on the arm piece (**Fig.34**). Snip into the seam allowance at the thumb pivot, then turn through to the right side. Stuff the arm firmly, then sew the opening closed. Repeat to make a second arm.

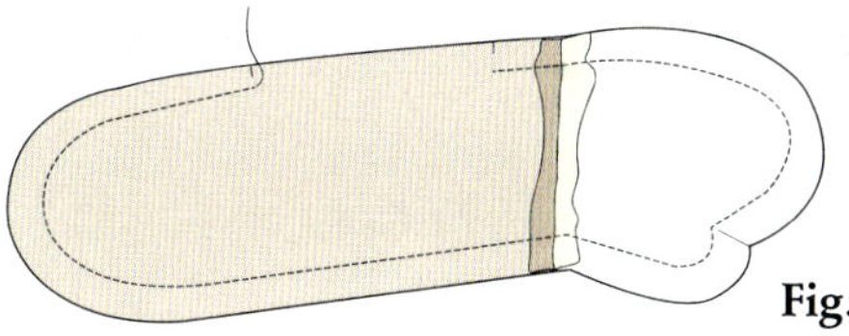

3 To attach the arms to the body, follow the instructions in How to Make Luna, Making the Arms, step 3.

Fig.33

Fig.34

Making the Tail

1 Fold the tail piece in half lengthways and slip stitch the raw edges together. Then press the tail flat so the seam runs centrally down the back. Wrap the faux fur tail tuft around the end of the tail and sew it in place, making sure that the fur pile is running from top to bottom (**Fig.35**).

2 Sew the tail onto the centre back seam at around the level of the leg buttons, stitching a button at the joining point for decoration.

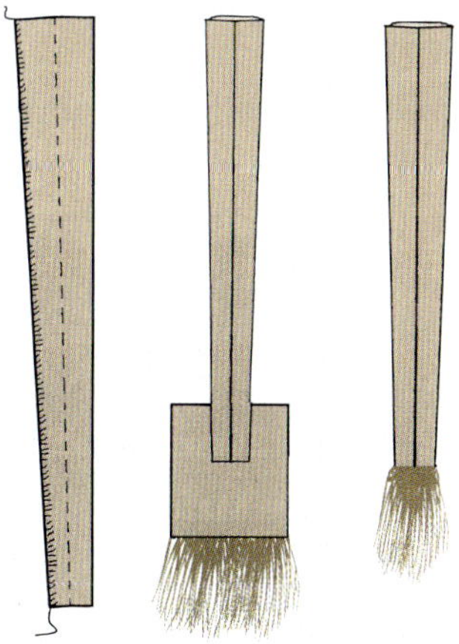

Fig.35

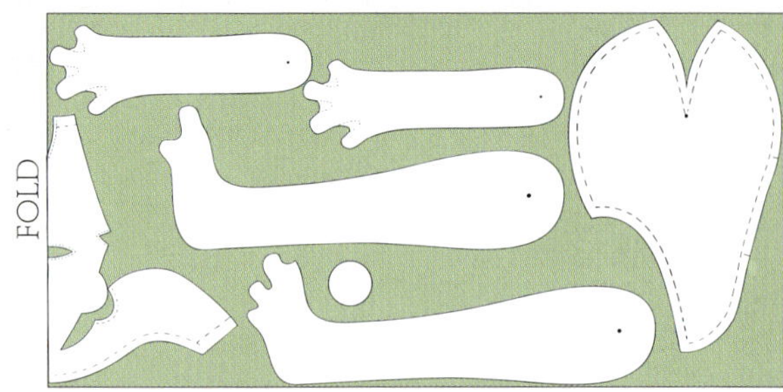

Fig.1

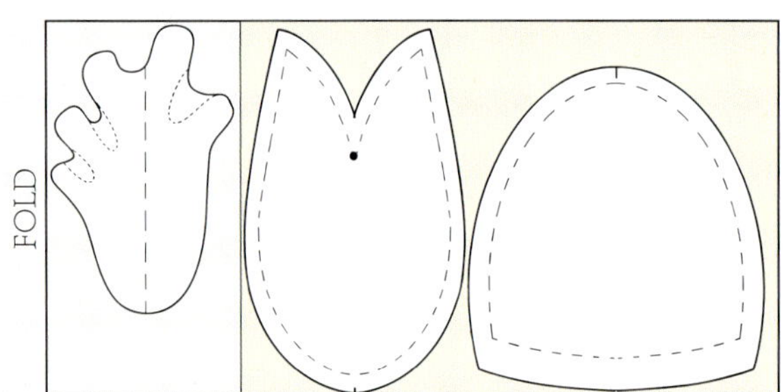

Fig.2

How to Make Gracie

YOU WILL NEED

- 22.5cm (9in) x 90cm (36in) wide main felt (reets relish)
- 11.5cm (4½in) x 30cm (12in) contrast felt (antique white)
- Two 21mm (¾in) cat-style safety eyes
- Two 15mm (⅝in) buttons for arm joints and two 23mm (⅞in) buttons for leg joints
- Toy stuffing about 120gm (4½oz)
- Basic sewing kit (see Materials)

Use a 0.5cm (¼in) seam allowance, unless a different amount is stated.

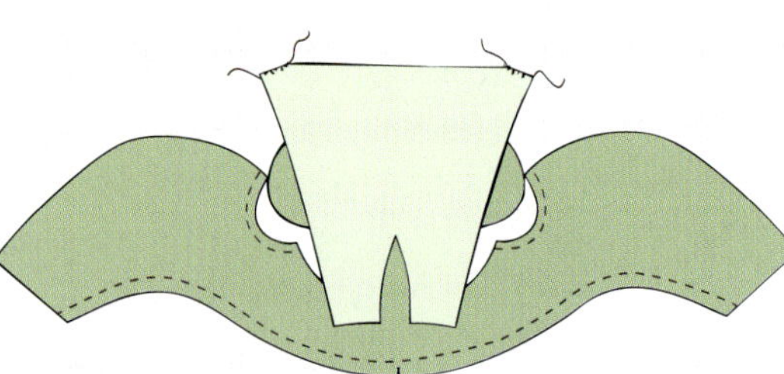

Fig.3

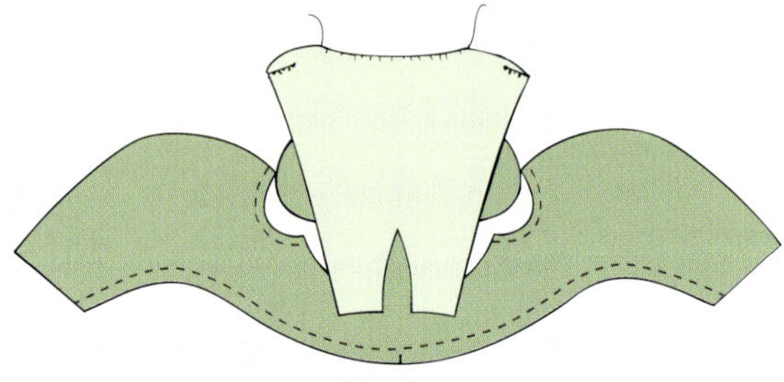

Fig.4

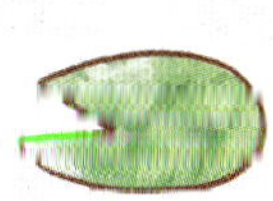

BEFORE YOU BEGIN

Gracie is made with a combination of hand and machine sewing. The head and limbs have no seam allowance and are sewn with oversewing and backstitch. The body has seam allowance so can be sewn on the machine, or by hand sewing with backstitch; or trim the seam allowance off and follow an oversew method.

CUTTING OUT

1 Fold the main (reets relish) felt in half with short ends together and pin the cut-out pattern pieces (see The Patterns) in place, using the layout in **Fig.1** as a guide and noting which pieces should be cut in which colour and material. Pin the relevant pieces onto the partially folded contrast (antique white) felt, using **Fig.2** as a guide. Cut the pieces out and mark any notches with a tiny snip in the edge of the felt, including an 'on the fold' snip on the upper head to mark the centre fold. Transfer all other markings using a water-soluble marker pen.

MAKING UP

Making the Head

Note: The unusual shape of the upper head pattern allows for it to be joined as one piece.

1 First make the upper head darts, starting with the small triangles to each side. Working on one triangle at a time, match the edges and oversew by 0.2cm (1/16in) (**Fig.3**). Now move on to fold, then oversew the pointed oval-shaped dart (**Fig.4**). Finally, fold and then oversew the centre back neck dart (**Fig.5**). This now becomes the wrong side of the head. Trim threads and turn to the right side.

2 Now join the upper head seams. Working on one side, and with wrong sides together, fold the upper head to match the two inner edges. Fastening on at the point, oversew the edges together, stretching the upper edge length to match, and fasten off at the upper semi-circle (**Fig. 6**). Note that the lower semi-circle should be underlapping by about 0.3cm (1/8n) as seen in **Fig.7**. Resume sewing on the other side of the upper semi-circle (again, there will be about a 0.3cm/1/8in underlap on the lower semi-circle) (as also seen in **Fig.7**). Continue sewing along the head, oversewing and adjusting to join the two edges until you reach the back neck edge (**Fig.8**). Then repeat to join the seams on the other side (**Fig.9**).

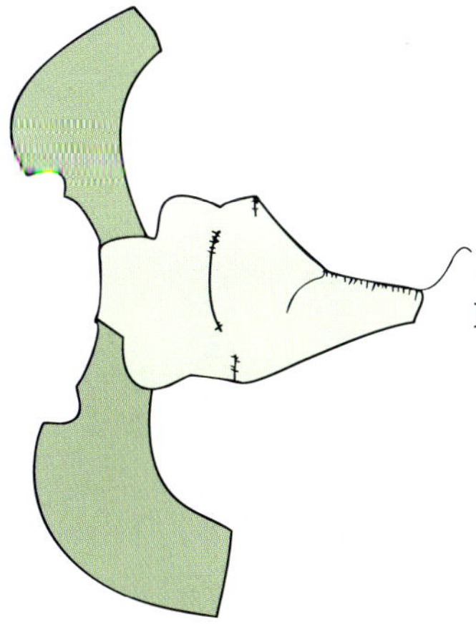

Fig.5

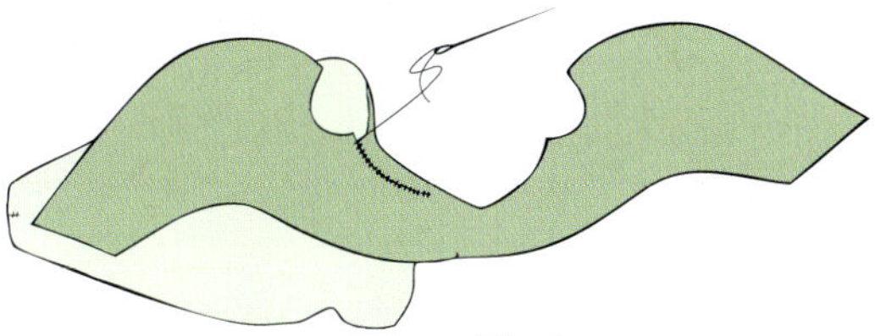

Fig.6

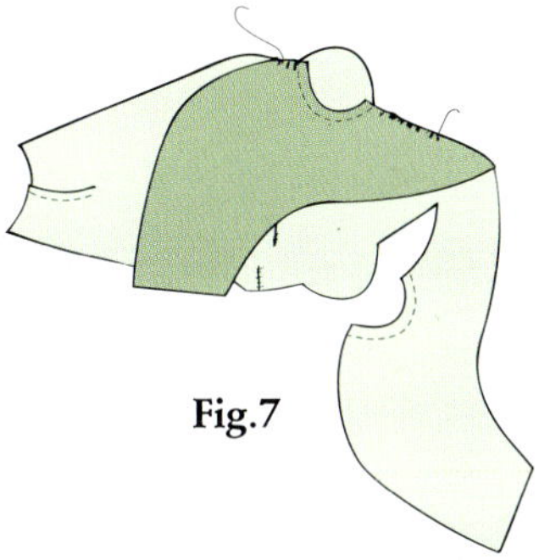

Fig.7

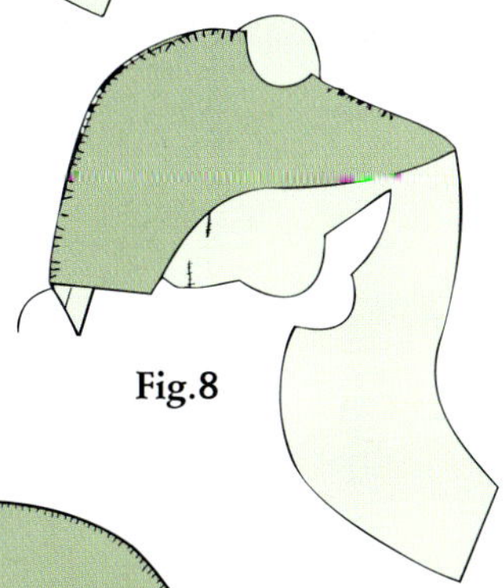

Fig.8

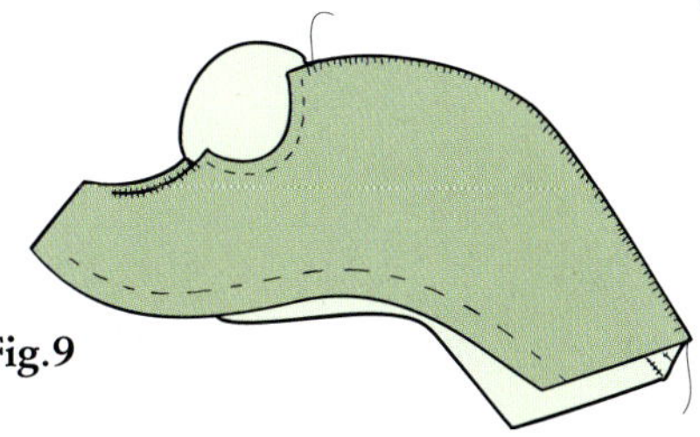

Fig.9

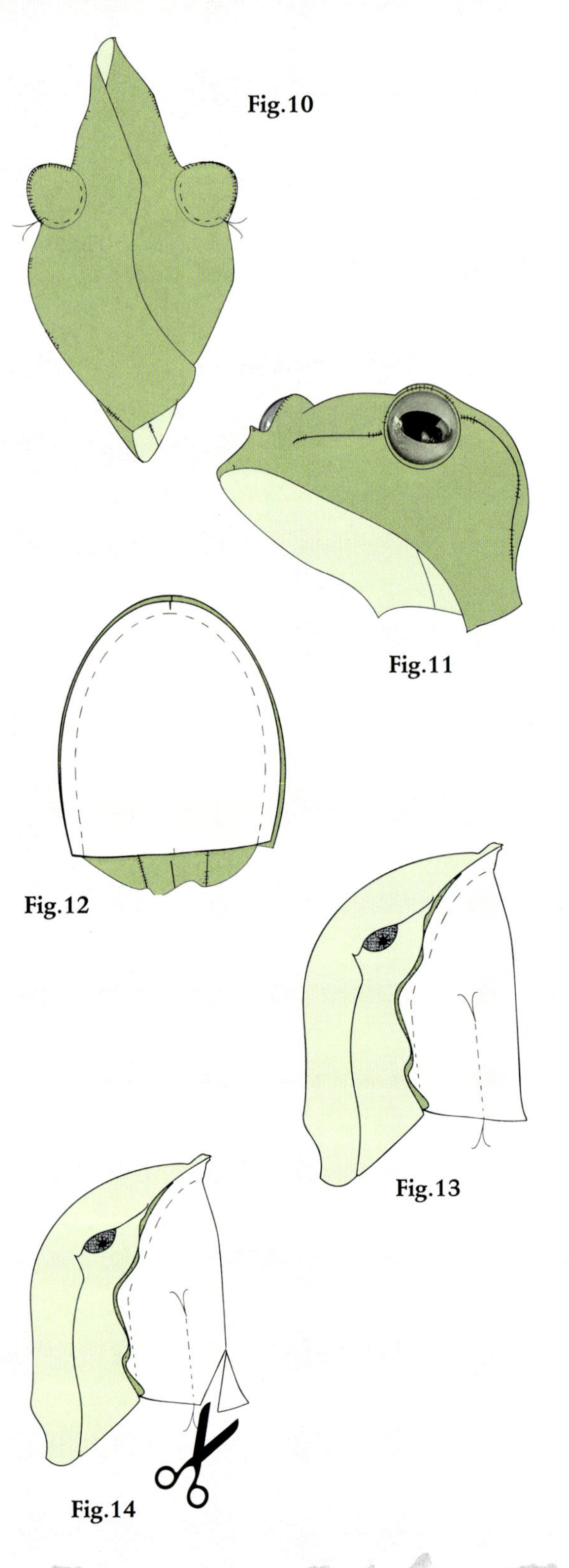
Fig.10
Fig.11
Fig.12
Fig.13
Fig.14

3 Take one of the eye back circles and match it to the upper semi-circle and pop a pin across the top edge. Bring the lower edge of the eye back circle down to match up with the lower semi-circle – the eye back circle should sit with a 0.3cm (⅛in) overlap. Oversew around the outer edge of the circle, then change to a small running stitch on the inner edge of the circle. Repeat to sew the remaining eye back circle on the other side (**Fig.10**).

4 Now add the safety eyes. To do this make a small snip or hole at the centre of the felt circle and push the eye stalk through from the right side to the wrong side. Turn the eye so that the iris is correctly angled (roughly horizontal), then force the plastic washer onto the stalk and press until the washer is tight to the felt (**Fig.11**).

5 Turn the upper head wrong side out, and place it in front of you so that the mouth curve is pointing upwards. Lay the upper throat piece on top, matching the centre point notches. Continue to match around the rest of the seam and sew together by hand or machine (**Fig.12**). Still working on the wrong side, create the centre-front neck tuck. To do this fold the upper throat in half at the neck edge to create a 'mountain-fold', and sew through both layers about 1.5cm (⅝in) from the folded edge, sewing up by about 3cm (1⅛in) from the neck edge to create a pleat (**Fig.13**). Trim the excess off at the neck edge and then flatten the pleat down at the inner end (**Fig.14**).

6 Turn the head right side out (it's easiest to push the nose into the head, then fish it out through the neck). Push and smooth the mouth seam outwards before starting to stuff.

7 Stuff the head, filling the mouth first and then building up the main shape to be full, trying if you can to get a little stuffing around the safety eye stalk. Check that you have a nice symmetrical shape (**Fig.15**).

Making the Body

1 Start by sewing the body darts. Take one body piece and fold with right sides together so the curved dart edges match. Sew from the edge, following the curve to the dot, which marks the dart end (**Fig.16**). Repeat with the remaining body piece to make a mirror image.

2 With right sides together, match the two sides of the body together and sew, starting at the tummy and stopping at the first (lower) notch on the back (**Fig.17**).

3 With right sides together, match the centre notch at the bottom of the lower throat to the body tummy seam and sew around the shape. You are working with two opposing curve shapes, so at times it will feel awkward, but the length of the sewing line is the same, and it fits (**Fig.18**).

4 Now match the back of the body and the curve of the dart at the top of the lower throat and sew together from the upper notch on the back, around the curve at the top of the back and continuing to follow the curve on the lower throat, finishing at the dot, which marks the end of the lower throat dart (**Fig.19**).

5 Turn the body through to the right side through the opening in the back seam. Stuff the shape well, then turn the seam allowance in before oversewing the turning gap closed.

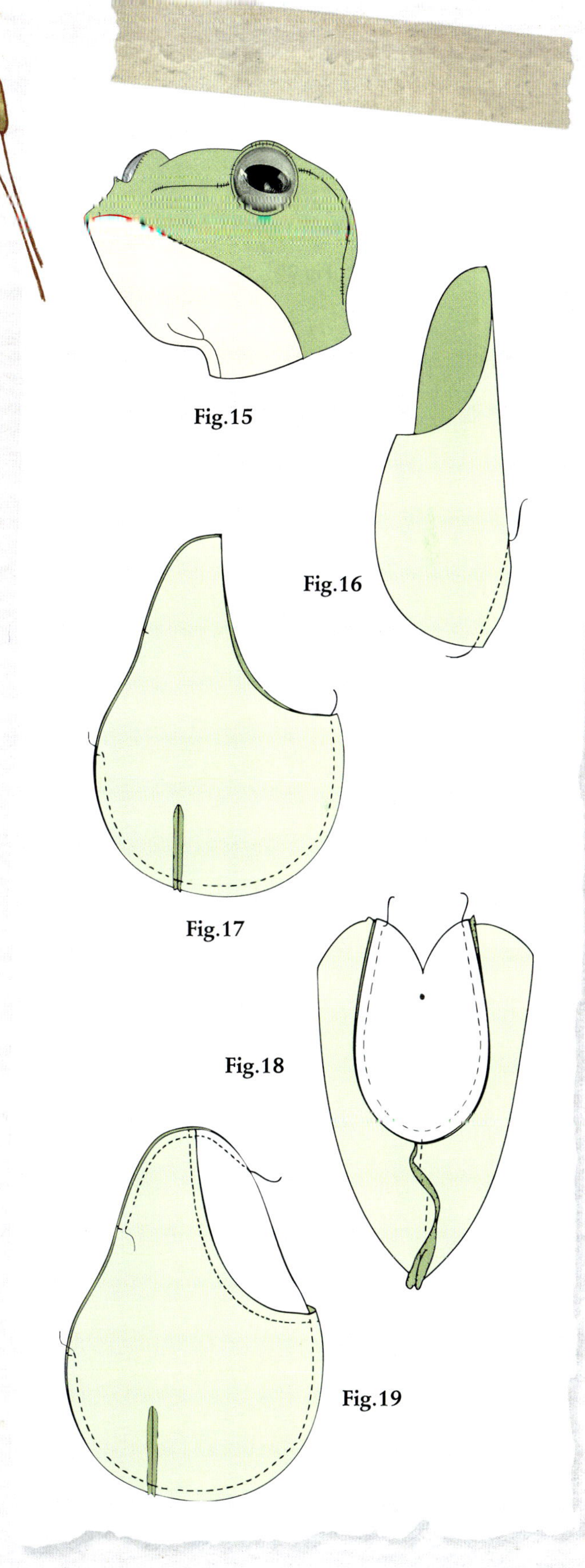

Fig.15

Fig.16

Fig.17

Fig.18

Fig.19

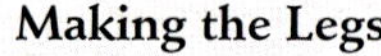

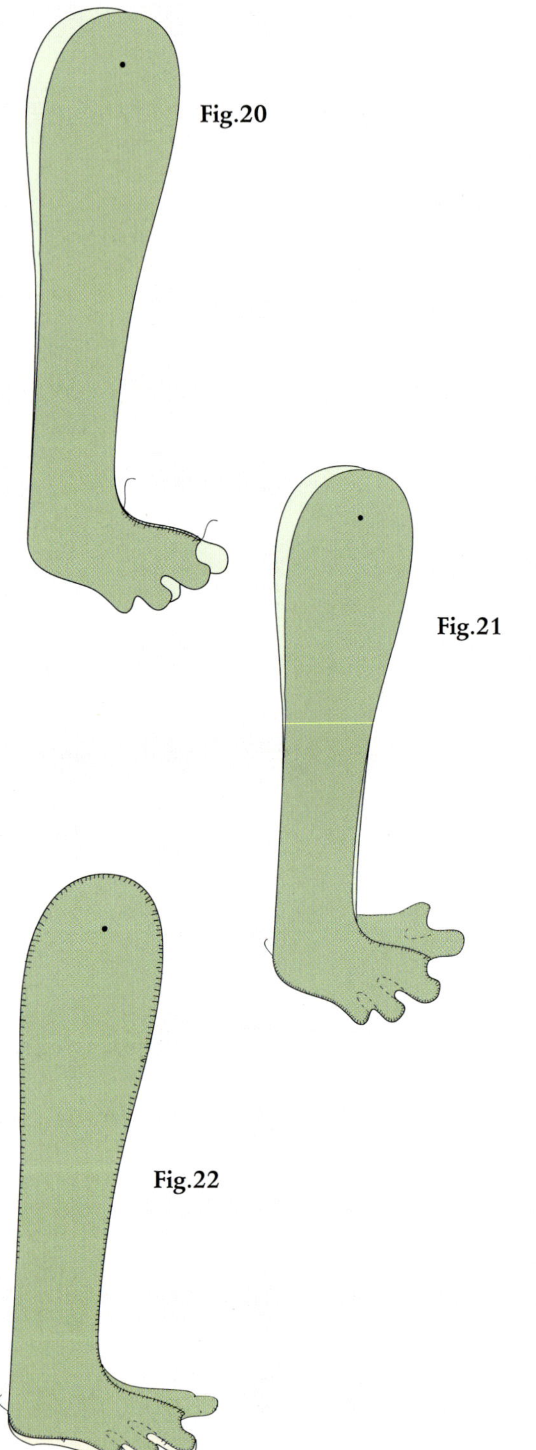

Making the Legs

1 Each leg has an inner and an outer leg piece to accommodate the shaped foot. With wrong sides together, match an inner leg to an outer leg and join together by oversewing along the upper foot, from the toe end to just before the ankle curve (**Fig.20**), leaving a long tail of thread to continue the sewing of the seam in step 4.

2 Take a couple of stitches to join the leg at the back heel and then position the footpad to match the shape of the now-joined leg and oversew around the edge until you get to the first toe, switching to backstitch to create a V shape between the toes, before continuing to oversew to the next toe. Continue in this way all the way round to your start point on the back leg seam (**Fig.21**).

3 Using a pair of tweezers or similar, take time to stuff the toes and then stuff the front of the foot.

4 Resume oversewing the leg pieces together, leaving a gap in the back for stuffing (**Fig.22**). Stuff the upper haunch less firmly for the first 4cm (1½in) or so, then continue to stuff firmly. Massage the legs as you stuff to ensure a smooth outer appearance, before sewing the opening closed by hand.

5 Repeat steps 1–4 to make a second leg, a mirror image of the first leg.

6 To attach the legs, thread a doll needle with a very long double thread. Attach the thread on one side of the body as marked on the pattern and pass the needle to the right side, through one leg (checking the feet are facing the correct way), then through a button, returning to bring the needle back through the button, through the leg, through the body fabric, to join the other leg in the same way on the other side. Repeat until secure, then gently pull the thread tight, to bring the legs into the body, compressing the body slightly, so the legs are snug. Cut the thread near the eye of the needle and use a smaller needle to fasten off invisibly between the leg and the body (**Fig.23**).

Attaching the Head to the Body

1 Turn the 1cm (⅜in) neck seam allowance up inside the head and add a little extra stuffing if you need to. Line up the front seams and, using double thread, slip stitch the head to the body, ensuring it is well attached by going around the neck at least twice. I tend to go around fairly loosely on round one and then tighten up in rounds two and three (**Fig.24**). The head should sit about 2.5cm (1in) down from the point of the body; make sure the angle of the face is sitting well.

Making the Arms

1 Match two arm pieces and oversew together starting at the back of the arm, over the top of the arm, and down the front to the hand. Sew the fingers using the same technique as you did for the toes on the feet. Stuff the fingers before continuing to sew around the arm, finishing about 4cm (1½in) away from where you started (**Fig.25**). Stuff the arm firmly, then close the opening. Repeat to make a second arm.

2 To attach the arms to the body, follow the instructions in How to Make Luna, Making the Arms, step 3.

Fig.23

Fig.24

Fig.25

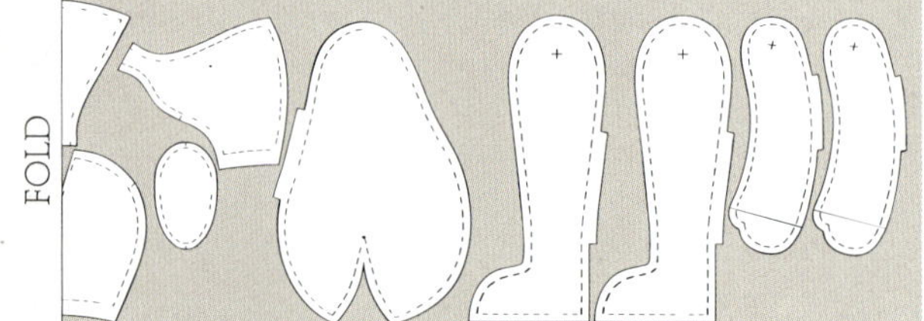

Fig.1

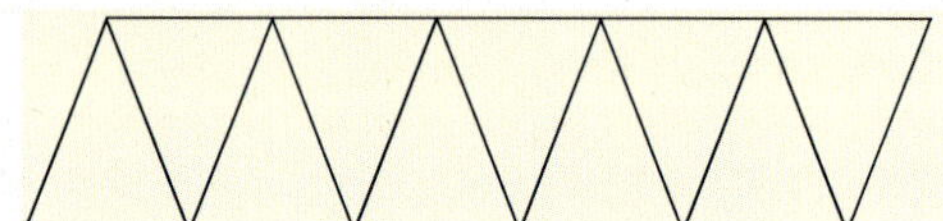

Fig.2

How to Make Maurice

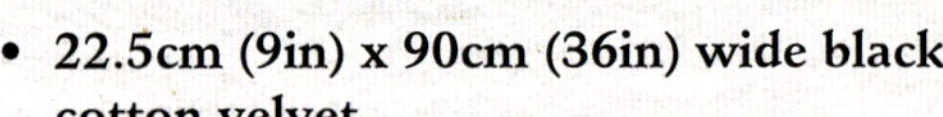

YOU WILL NEED

- **22.5cm (9in) x 90cm (36in) wide black cotton velvet**
- **5cm (2in) x 24cm (9½in) felt (boogie beige)***
- **Two 10mm (⅜in) safety eyes**
- **One 15mm (⅝in) x 10mm (⅜in) triangular safety nose**
- **Two 15mm (⅝in) buttons for arm joints and two 23mm (⅞in) buttons for legs**
- **1.5m (59in) of 0.8mm diameter beading elastic**
- **Toy stuffing about 120gm (4½oz)**
- **Basic sewing kit (see Materials)**

Use a 0.5cm (¼in) seam allowance, unless a different amount is stated.

*Required if making arms with talons rather than arms with hands (see Making the Arms).

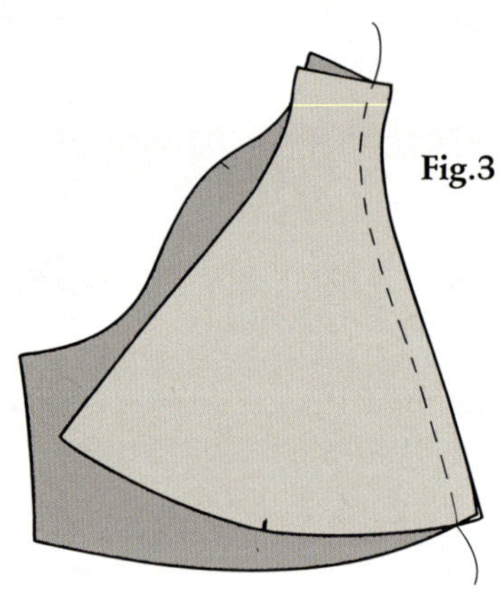

Fig.3

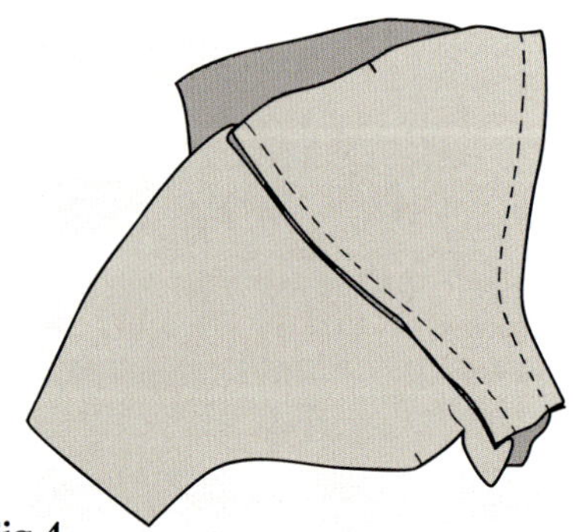

Fig.4

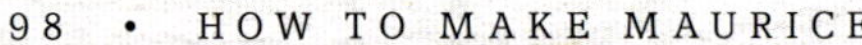

CUTTING OUT

1 When using velvet, all pattern pieces should be laid up and cut in the same direction. Run your hand down the fabric to establish the direction (it will feel smoother one way). Fold the fabric in half with right sides together to lay out your pattern pieces onto the wrong side. Pin your cut-out pattern pieces (see The Patterns) onto the fabric using **Fig.1** as a guide. Cut all pieces as stated on the pattern. Mark any notches with a tiny snip, including an 'on the fold' snip at the top of the upper head piece and at the bottom of the back head piece to mark the centre. Transfer any other markings to the fabric using a chalk pen. Velvet will fray and leave residue; a fabric glue product (e.g. Fraystop) on the cut edges prevents this.

2 If making the arms with talons option for Maurice, cut the talons from the felt using **Fig.2** as a guide.

MAKING UP

Note: Maurice is mainly machine sewn with some hand sewing finishing for assembly.

Making the Head

1 With right sides together, match and sew one edge of the upper head piece to one side head piece, easing in the side head slightly to fit (**Fig.3**). Repeat to join the other side head piece to the other edge of the upper head (**Fig.4**). Finger press seams open.

2 With right sides together, match the lower jaw seams on the side head pieces at the snout end; sew to the first notch, following the curves accurately. Snip into the seam allowance at the curves to allow the seams to sit flat when turned through (**Fig.5**).

3 Before completing the line of stitching along the bottom edge of the side head pieces, insert the safety nose. Bring the nose through the inside-out head to push the stalk out of the snout hole. Push the plastic washer on to be tight to the back of the nose (**Fig.6**) (it can be adjusted once turned through). Resume stitching to the neck edge although you may need to backstitch this by hand; cut into curves as before.

4 To fit the safety eyes, make a small snip at the marked eye position and push the eye stalk through from the inside. Press the plastic washer onto the stalk to be tight to the felt. Repeat to fit the second eye (**Fig 7**). Now turn the completed front head through to the right side; force the nose back through and adjust it to be the right angle, making sure no raw edges of fabric are showing.

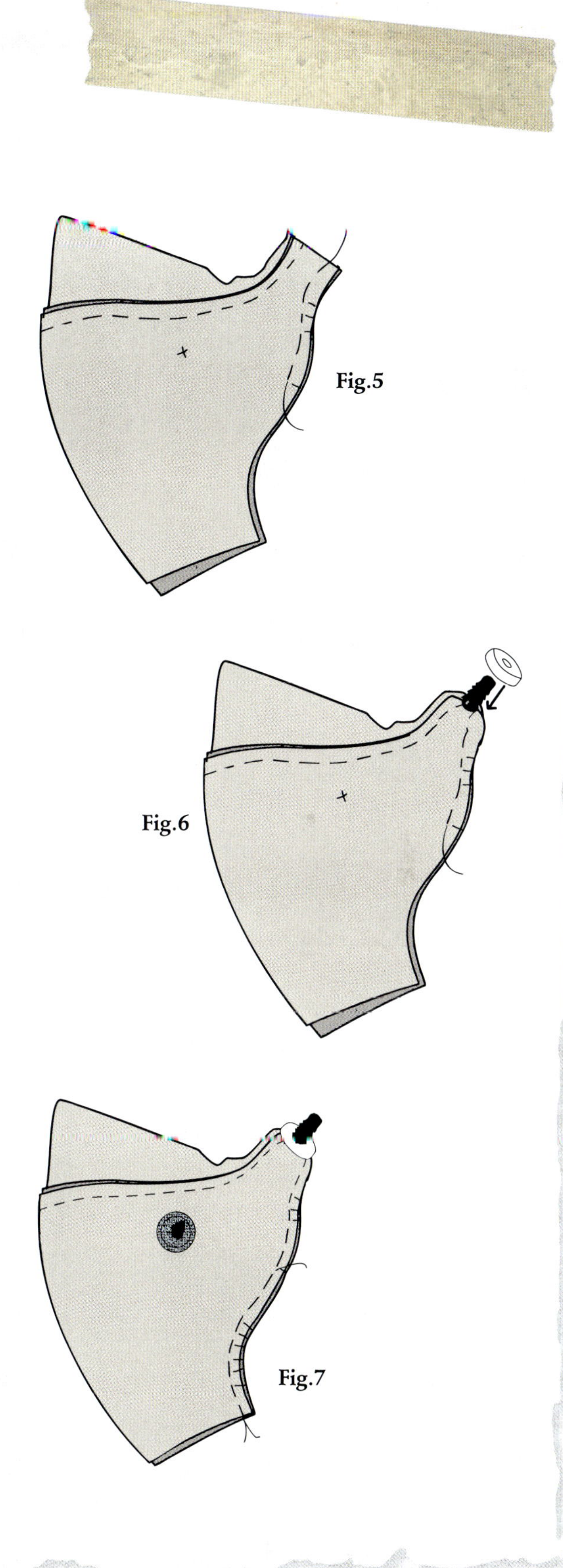
Fig.5

Fig.6

Fig.7

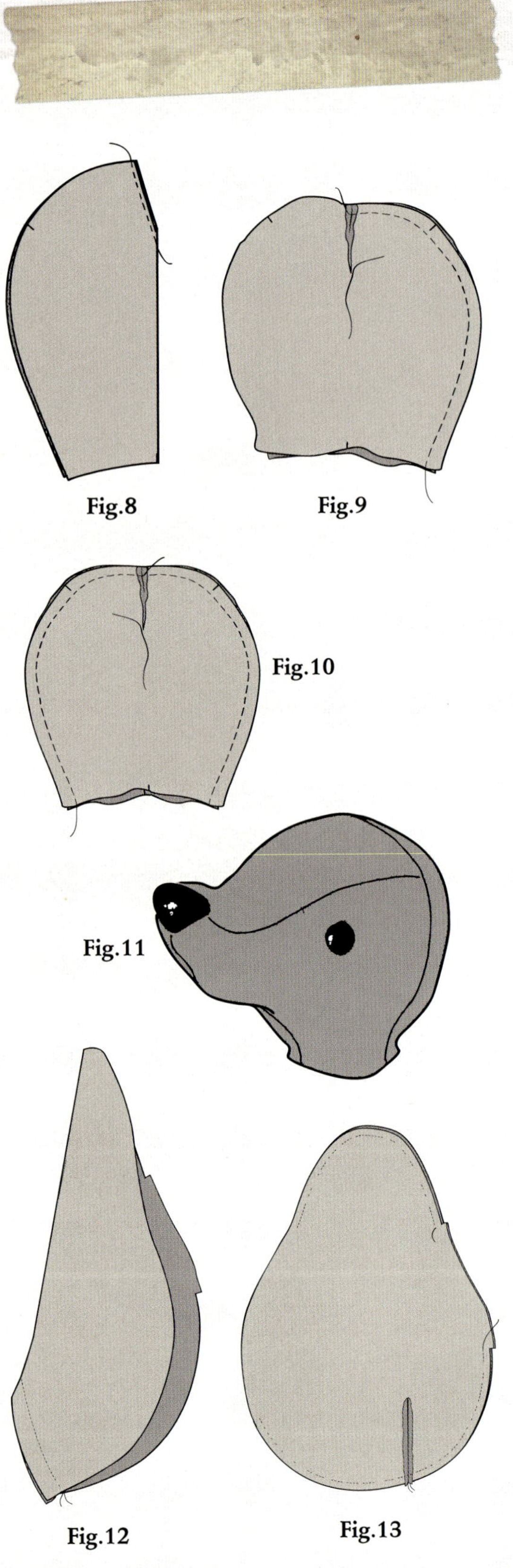

Fig.8 Fig.9 Fig.10 Fig.11 Fig.12 Fig.13

5 Take the back head piece and, with right sides together, fold it in half and sew along the dart edges with a 0.2cm (1⁄16in) seam allowance (**Fig.8**).

6 With right sides together, match and pin the front head to the back head, ensuring the front notch matches the back dart, and sew together to join (**Figs.9** and **10**). (I do this one side at a time, starting at the centre and sewing down to the neck edge, then flipping the project over and repeating on the other side.)

7 Stuff the head, using a knitting needle or similar tool to push the stuffing down into the snout first, then building up the main shape to be full and round. Check for a nice symmetrical shape and that the stuffing around the eye stalks hasn't altered the angle of the eyes. Turn the 1cm (3⁄8in) neck seam allowance up inside the head (**Fig.11**).

Making the Body

1 Start by sewing the body darts. Take one body piece and fold with right sides together so the curved dart edges match. Sew from the edge, following the curve to the dot, which marks the dart end (**Fig.12**). Repeat with the remaining body piece to make a mirror image.

2 With right sides together, match and then sew around the body shape, starting at the bottom of the seam extension and sewing all the way around to stop at the top of the seam extension (**Fig.13**). Turn through to the right side.

3 Stuff the body well, then turn in the 1cm (3⁄8in) seam allowance and slip stitch the opening closed.

Making the Legs

1 With right sides together, match and pin two leg pieces, then sew together starting at the front of the foot, stitching around the front of the leg to finish at the top of the seam extension on the back of the leg. Restart sewing at the bottom of the seam extension to finish at the back of the foot (**Fig.14**). Repeat to make a second leg.

2 Snip into the seam allowance at the curve of the ankles. Pin the footpad in place using the notches on the footpad to match up with the seams on the leg. Ease the footpad in and sew all the way around (note that this could be done by hand, using a double thread and backstitch) (**Fig.15**).

3 Turn each leg right side out through the opening in the back leg, and start stuffing, pushing pieces of stuffing down into the foot with a knitting needle or similar tool. The upper haunch can be less firmly stuffed than the lower leg; massage the leg as you stuff to ensure a smooth outer appearance. Turn the seam allowance in at the opening and slip stitch to sew closed (**Fig.16**).

4 To attach the legs, thread a doll needle with a very long double thread. Attach the thread on one side of the body at the end of the dart seam and pass the needle to the other side of the body, then through one leg (checking the feet are facing the correct way), then through a button. Returning, bring the needle back through the button, through the leg, through the body fabric, to join the other leg in the same way, and repeat until secure. Pull the legs in as you sew – the ideal distance button to button is 9cm (3½in). Gently pull the thread tight, to bring the legs into the body, compressing the body slightly so the legs are snug (**Fig.17**). Cut the thread near the eye of the needle and use a smaller needle to fasten off invisibly between the leg and the body.

Attaching the Head to the Body

1 Taking the head and making sure the 1cm (⅜in) neck seam allowance is turned up inside it, push the point of the body cone into the head, lining up the front seams. Using double thread in your needle, sew the head to the body using a slip stitch, ensuring it is well attached by going around the neck at least twice. I tend to go around fairly loosely on round one and then tighten up in rounds two and three. The head should sit about 2.5cm (1in) down from the top point of the body; check that the angle of the head is sitting well (**Fig.18**).

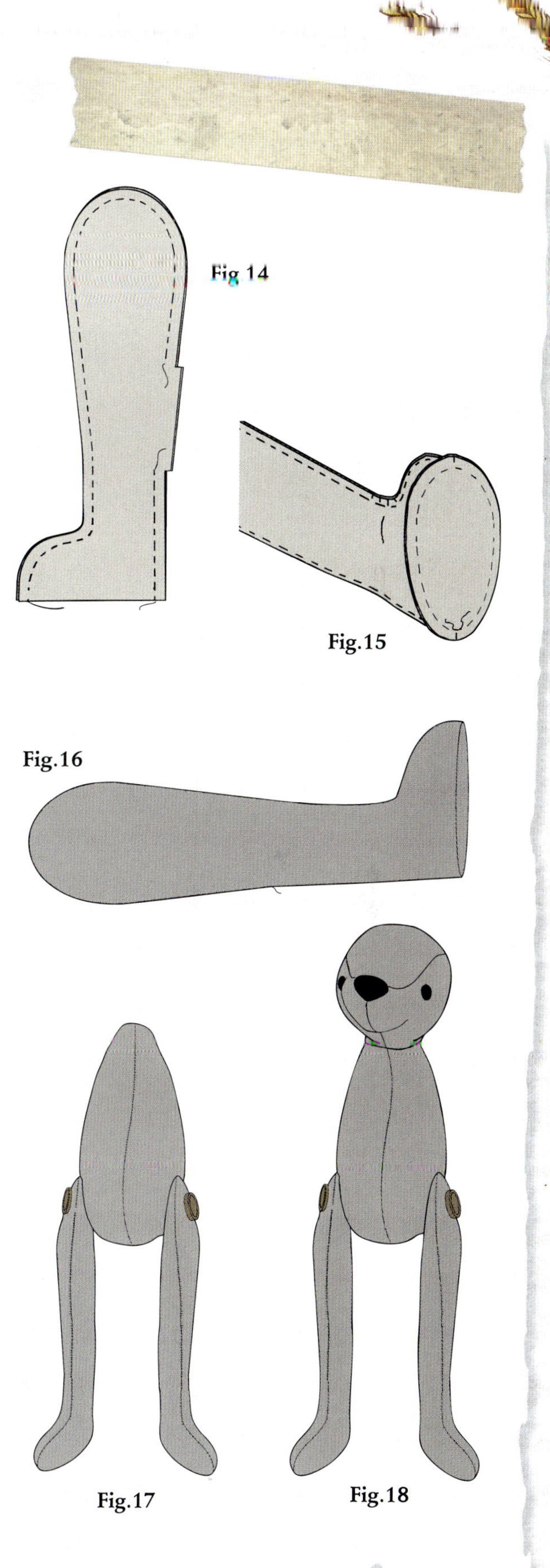

Fig.14

Fig.15

Fig.16

Fig.17

Fig.18

Making the Arms

Note: Decide on your preferred arm-making method and follow Method 1 to make a classic arm with a hand or Method 2 for an arm with talons.

Method 1: classic arm with hands

1 With right sides together, match two arm pieces and sew together around the outside, starting and finishing at the seam extensions. Take care at the thumb point: to turn the corner, leave your needle down in the fabric and lift the presser foot slightly to realign your seam (**Fig.19**). Snip into the seam allowance at the thumb pivot, then turn through to the right side.

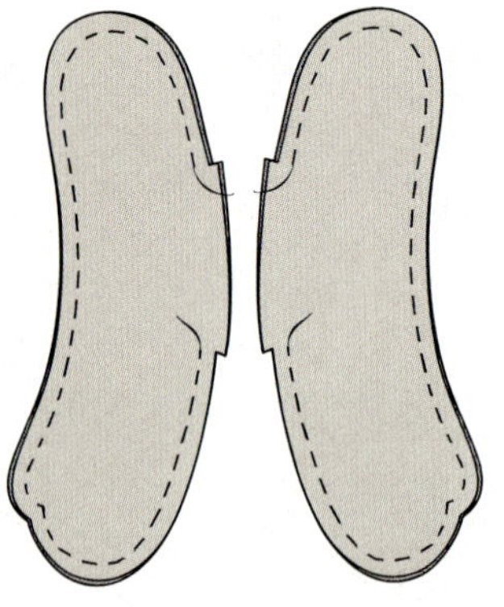

Fig.19

2 Stuff the arm firmly at the top and bottom, then fill the space next to the opening. Turn the 1cm (⅜in) seam allowance in on the opening gap and slip stitch closed (**Fig.20**). Repeat steps to make a second arm.

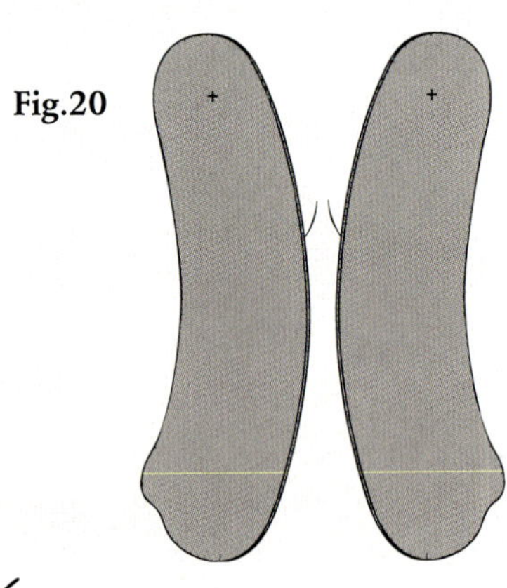

Fig.20

Method 2: arm with talons

1 Fold each of the felt triangles in half and sew along the long edges with a scant 1mm (less than 1/16in) seam allowance, at least two times. Trim excess seam allowance close to the stitching as necessary (**Fig.21**). To make the shorter thumb talons, cut off 0.5cm (¼in) from the wider end of two of the triangles (one for each arm). Flatten each triangle so the seam runs along the centre (**Fig.22**).

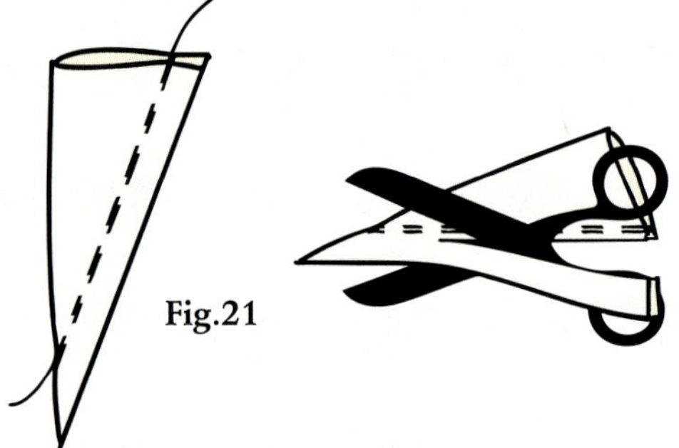

Fig.21

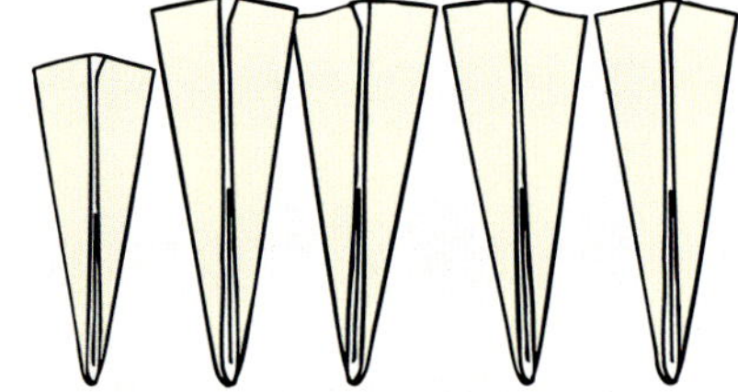

Fig.22

2 If you haven't already done so, cut the hands off the ends of the arm pieces using the line marked on the pattern as a guide. Take two mirrored arm pieces and lay them right side facing up. Working within the seam allowance, lay five talons (flattened seams facing up) across the straight edge of each arm, starting with a shorter thumb talon at the inside edge and so each talon overlaps the one positioned before it. Tack (baste) or staystitch in place 0.5cm (¼in) from the edge (**Fig.23**).

3 Take the remaining two arm pieces and match to the arm pieces with talons in place with right sides facing, making sure the talons are safely inside the seam allowance. Sew together around the outside, starting at the top of the seam extensions and finishing at the bottom (leaving a gap for turning through), pivoting at the corners (**Fig.24**).

4 Turn the arms through to the right side pushing the talons out. Stuff the arms firmly at the top and bottom, then fill the space next to the opening. Turn the seam allowance in at the opening and slip stitch closed (**Fig.25**). If you wish you can soften the talons by snipping off the spikey ends.

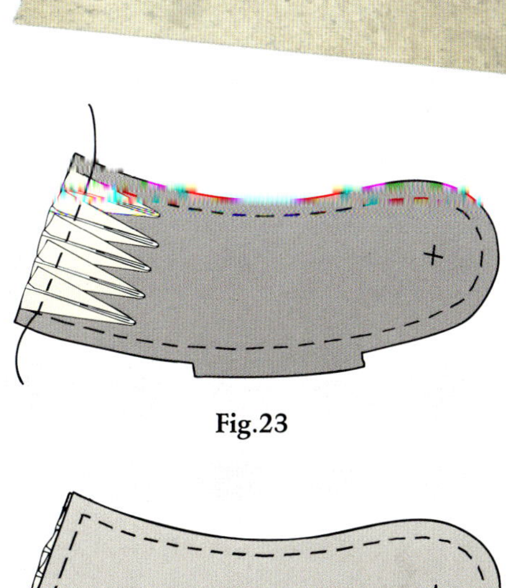

Fig.23

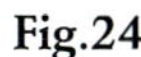

Fig.24

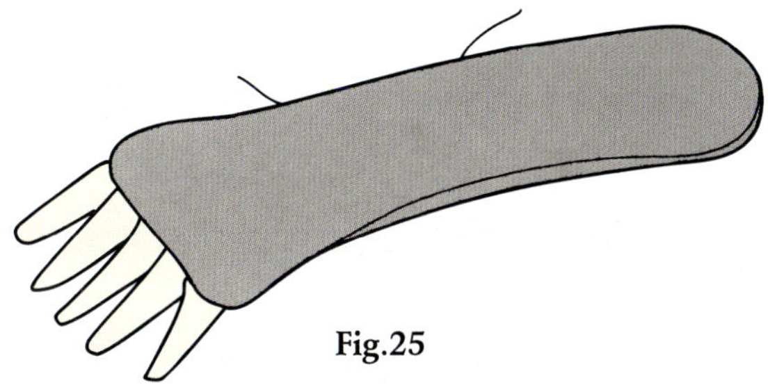

Fig.25

Attaching the Arms

1 To attach the arms to the body, follow the instructions in How to Make Luna, Making the Arms, step 3, being sure to check that the thumbs (i.e. the shorter talons) are facing forward.

Adding the Whiskers

1 Using the beading elastic, doubled through the eye of a needle, pass it through in various places around the snout, trimming it at varying lengths. The tight weave of the velvet should hold the whiskers in place without knotting.

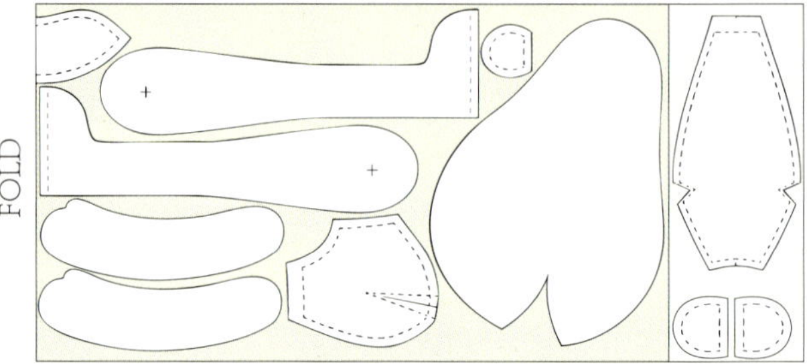

Fig.1

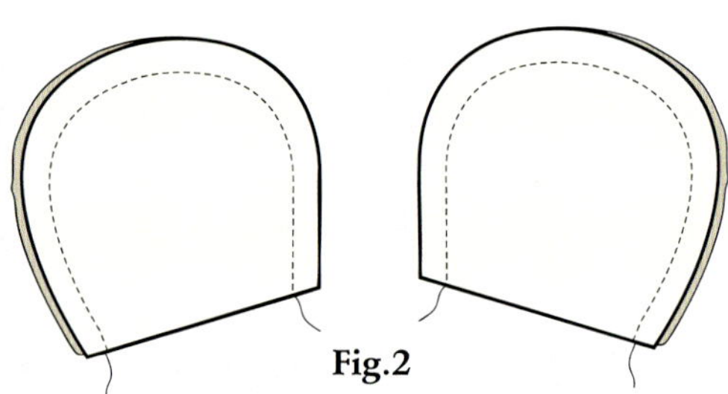

Fig.2

Fig.3

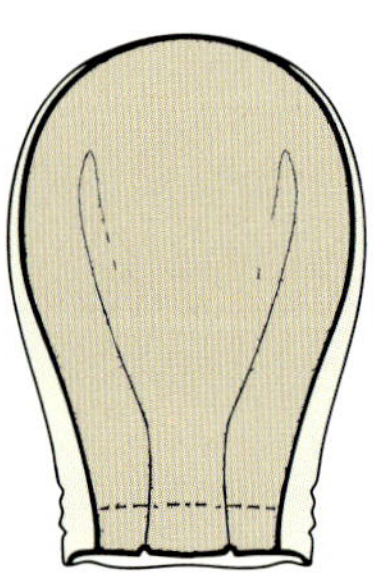

Fig.4

How to Make Erik

YOU WILL NEED

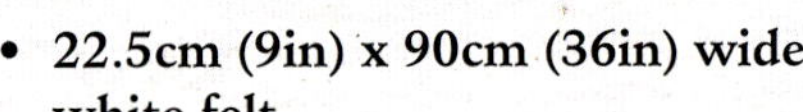

- 22.5cm (9in) x 90cm (36in) wide white felt
- 2.5cm (1in) square black felt for nose
- 15cm (6in) x 17cm (6¾in) cotton lawn fabric
- 60cm (24in) black embroidery thread
- Two 10mm (⅜in) safety eyes
- Two 15mm (⅝in) buttons for arm joints and two 23mm (⅞in) buttons for leg joints
- Toy stuffing about 120gm (4½oz)
- Basic sewing kit (see Materials)

Use a 0.5cm (¼in) seam allowance, unless a different amount is stated.

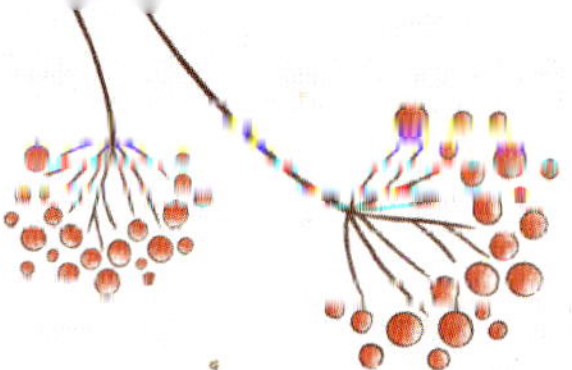

CUTTING OUT

1 Pin the cut-out pattern pieces (see The Patterns) onto the partially folded felt, using the layout in **Fig.1** as a guide. Cut the pieces out and mark any notches with a tiny snip in the felt, including an 'on the fold' snip to mark the centre fold of the muzzle. Transfer all other pattern markings using a water-soluble pen.

2 Cut out a pair of ears and a pair of footpads from the cotton lawn fabric. Mark the notches as before.

MAKING UP

Making the Ears

1 Place the right side of a cotton lawn ear onto a felt ear, matching edges. Sew around the outer edge, leaving the bottom edge open. You can machine sew or use a hand-sewn backstitch. Repeat to make the second ear, making sure it is a mirror image of the first (**Fig.2**).

2 Trim the sewn seam allowance down to 0.25cm (⅛in), then turn through. Roll the seams out to the edge between your fingers and press flat with a warm iron (**Fig.3**). Fold just a small amount of the felt over and tack (baste) or staystitch in place at the bottom edge (**Fig.4**).

Making the Head

1 Place the side head pieces so the straight (muzzle) edges are facing each other, having first cut along the head dart line as marked by the solid line on the pattern pieces. Place the ears on the side head pieces, cotton lawn side facing down, so that there is still about 0.75cm (5⁄16in) visible above the ear to allow for seam allowance. The short edge of the ears should match the cut edge of the felt on the head dart. Tack (baste) the ears into place (**Fig.5**).

2 Fold over the back of the side head pieces to enclose each ear, matching up the cut edges of the dart. Machine sew (or backstitch) through all layers starting at the depth of the notch, tapering to nothing at the dart end, as marked with a dot (**Fig.6**). Turn through to the right side; press ears towards the back so print side is visible (**Fig.7**).

3 Take the head gusset piece and sew the two mini darts, one at a time. To do this, match the edges of the small triangle notches, right sides together, and sew using a 0.2cm (1⁄16in) seam allowance (**Fig.8**) (if you are doing this by hand, oversewing to this depth will work just as well). Once both darts have been sewn in this way, trim the threads and turn to the right side (**Fig.9**).

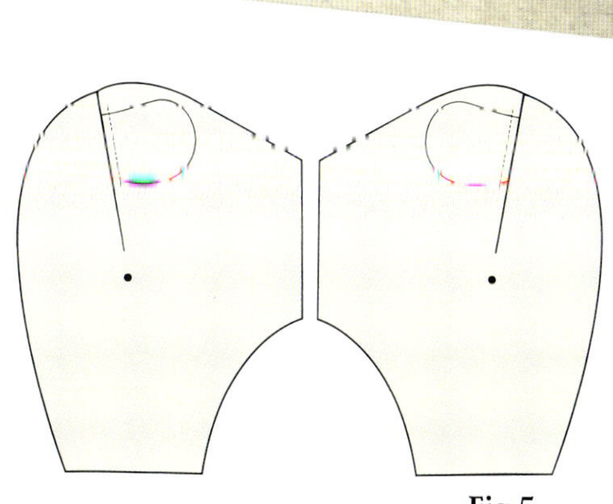

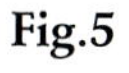

Fig.5

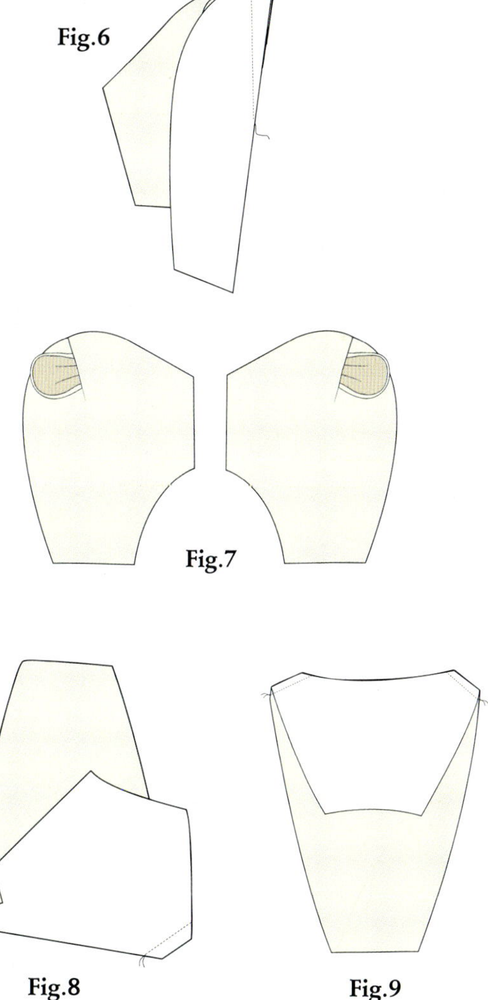

Fig.6

Fig.7

Fig.8

Fig.9

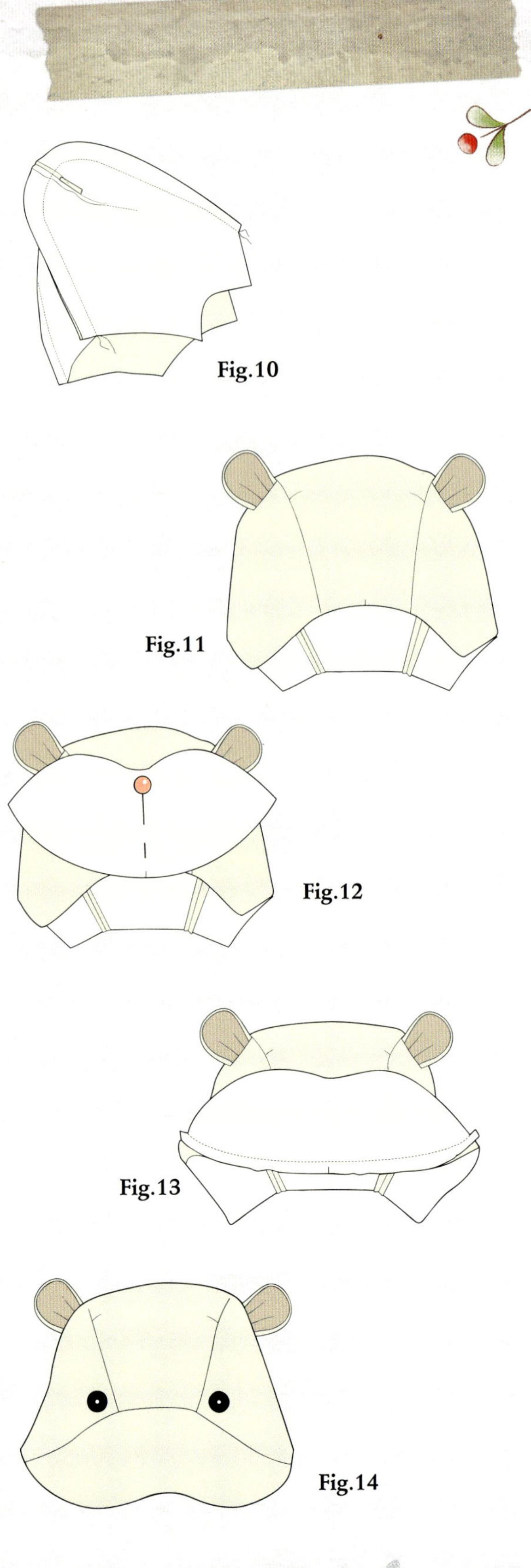
Fig.10
Fig.11
Fig.12
Fig.13
Fig.14

4 Making sure you have the narrower end of the head gusset at the back, and with right sides together, position and sew the gusset to one side head: sew up to the head dart point, then stop and realign everything before continuing with the second part. Repeat to sew the other side head piece to the other edge of the head gusset (**Fig.10**).

5 Turn the head piece through to the right side (**Fig.11**) and match the muzzle at the centre point (**Fig.12**). Matching up the rest of the seam, sew the muzzle to the front of the head (**Fig.13**).

6 Before continuing with the sewing of the muzzle, insert the safety eyes. With the head turned right side out, make a small snip in the felt at the eye positions as marked on the pattern. Now, working on one eye at a time, push the eye stalk through from the right side to the wrong side, then force the plastic washer onto the stalk and press until the washer is tight to the felt (**Fig.14**).

7 Fold the head in half with right sides together, matching at the lower edge and making sure the intersecting muzzle seam matches nicely. Sew from the end of the muzzle to the edge of the neck (**Fig.15**). Trim the corner off and push the head to be right side out – it's easiest to push the nose into the head, then pull it out through the neck. Push the nose point out but without stretching the felt too much.

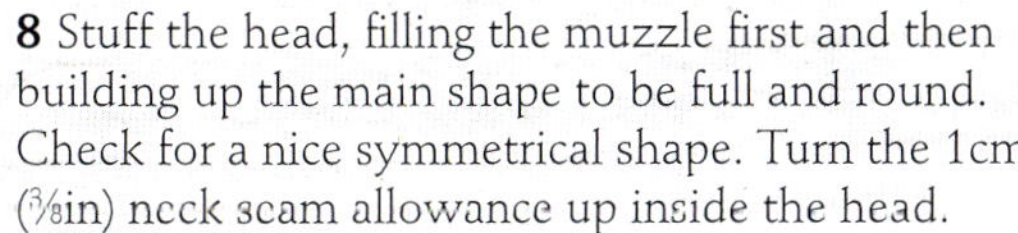

8 Stuff the head, filling the muzzle first and then building up the main shape to be full and round. Check for a nice symmetrical shape. Turn the 1cm (⅜in) neck seam allowance up inside the head.

9 Fold the black felt nose piece in half to find the centre, then position it centrally on the muzzle so that the top of the nose covers the end of the seam. Using two strands of black embroidery thread, oversew around the nose (**Fig.16**), then make one long stitch at the centre under the 'tip' of the nose (see detail photo).

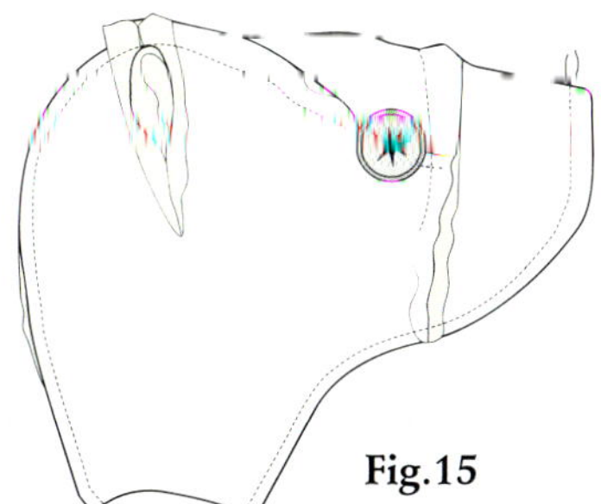

Fig.15

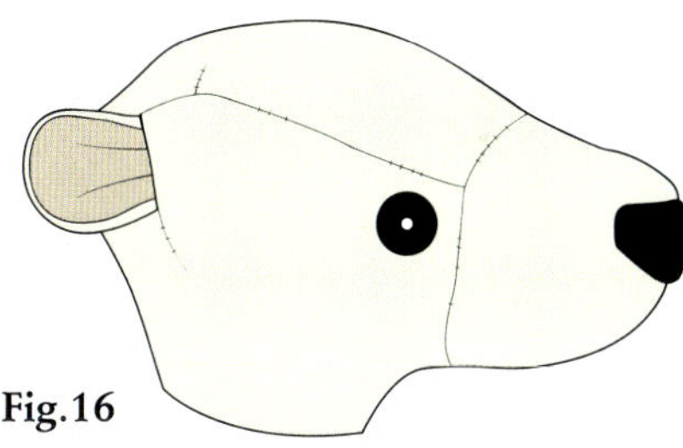

Fig.16

Making the Body

1 Start by sewing the body darts. Take one body piece and fold with right sides together so the curved dart edges match. Sew from the edge, following the curve to the dot, which marks the dart end (**Fig.17**). Repeat with the remaining body piece to make a mirror image.

2 With right sides together, match and then sew around the body shape, starting and stopping at back notches to leave a gap for turning (**Fig.18**). Turn through to the right side.

3 Stuff the body well, then fold in the seam allowance and slip stitch the opening closed.

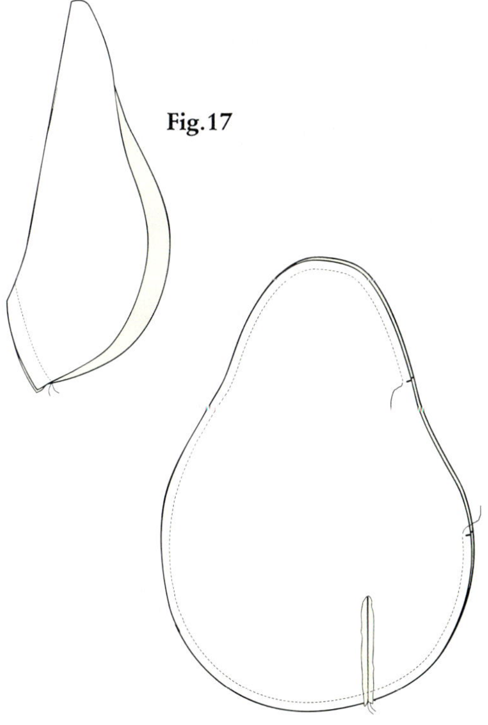

Fig.17

Fig.18

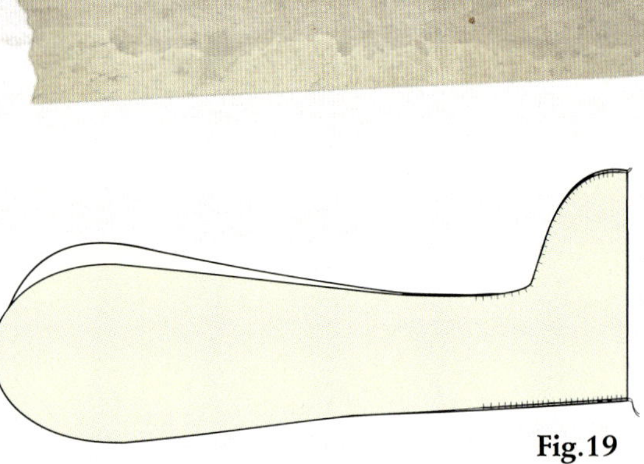

Fig.19

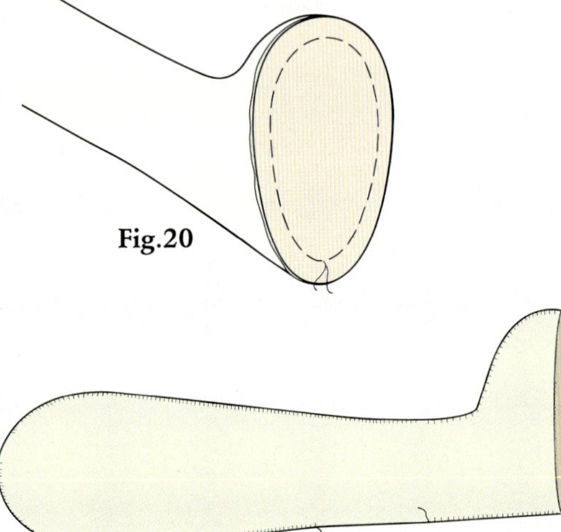

Fig.20

Fig.21

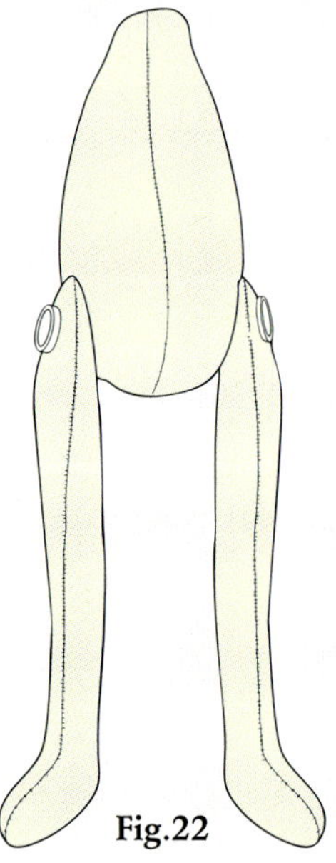

Fig.22

Making the Legs

1 Match two leg pieces and oversew the back seam to about 7cm (2¾in) above the heel. Then, starting from the toe, oversew the front seam to just above the ankle curve (**Fig.19**).

2 Now turn the leg so that these seams are to the inside, and pin the footpad in place using the notches on the footpad to match up with the seams you have just sewn. Note that the toe end of the footpad is slightly wider, so this should correspond with the toe end of the leg. Ease the footpad in and sew all the way around using a hand-sewn backstitch (**Fig.20**).

3 Turn the foot back out to the right side, so that the raw edges are enclosed, and stuff the foot firmly. Resume oversewing the leg pieces together, leaving a gap in the back seam for stuffing.

4 Stuff the upper haunch less firmly for the first 4cm (1½in) or so, then continue to stuff firmly. Massage the leg as you stuff to ensure a smooth outer appearance, then close the opening to finish (**Fig.21**). Repeat steps 1–4 to make a second leg.

5 Follow the instructions in How to Make Maurice for how to attach Erik's legs (**Fig.22**).

Attaching the Head to the Body

1 Follow the instructions in How to Make Maurice, Making the Legs, step 4, for how to attach Erik's head to his body (**Fig.23**).

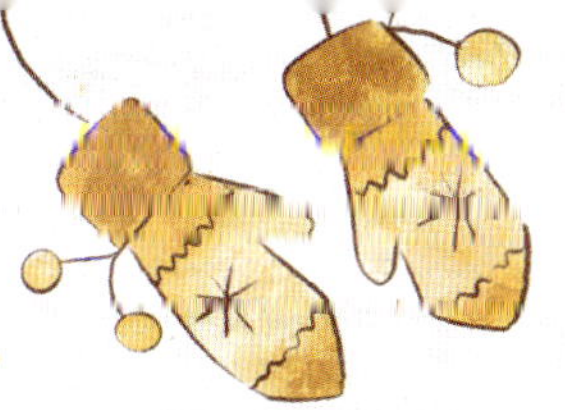

Making the Arms

1 Follow the instructions in How to Make Luna, Making the Arms, steps 1–3 for how to make and attach Erik's arms (**Figs.24** and **25**). (The method is exactly the same, although Erik's arm is gently curved.)

Making the Tail

1 Match the tail pieces and sew together using a backstitch (or machine sew) around the curved edges, leaving the straight edge open (**Fig.26**). Trim the seam down to 0.25cm (⅛in), then turn through to the right side. Roll the seams out to the edge between your fingers and press flat with a warm iron.

2 Oversew the straight edge of the tail onto the back of the body, level to the top of the leg button.

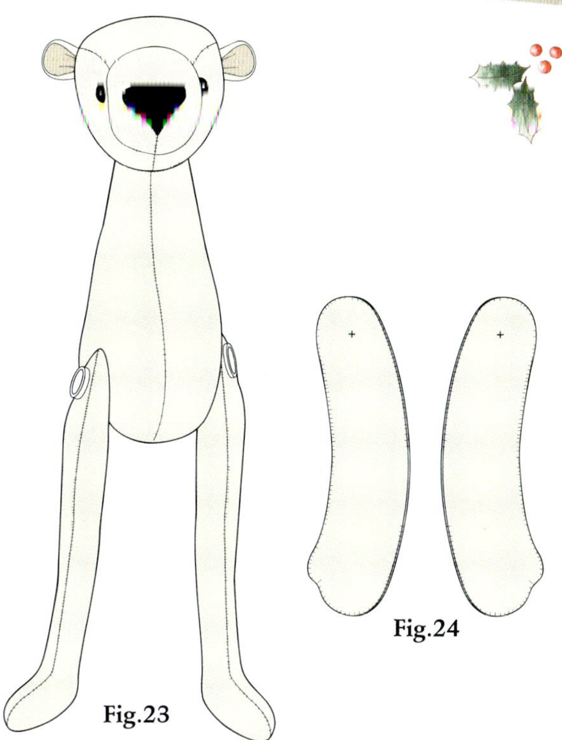

Fig.23

Fig.24

Fig.25

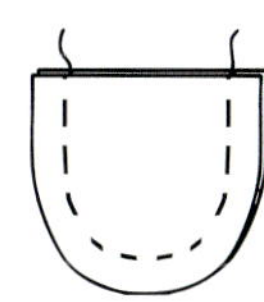

Fig.26

The Patterns

When using patterns follow these general guidelines:

- Refer to the pattern layout diagram(s) with each project to see which patterns are needed. The patterns have seam allowances included unless otherwise specified. The allowances are stated in the project instructions.
- All pattern pieces are shown actual size so there is no need to reduce or enlarge. However, some may need to be joined with adhesive tape to complete the pattern piece, so follow the advice given.
- Once copied, cut out your paper patterns. I like to cut on the black line, but to the outside not the inside.
- Iron the patterns before laying them out onto fabric that has also been ironed, to remove any creases.
- Some patterns only show half of the shape and these are clearly marked. In these cases, place the marked line along the fold of the fabric, so when the shape is cut out you will double the pattern. Where a pattern piece needs to be reversed when laying out onto the fabric, this is indicated on the pattern with an 'R', e.g. 'Cut 2 (1 and 1R)'.
- Cutting out is crucial to success so the use of pins when positioning a pattern on fabric will really improve your results. When pinning, keep the entire pin inside the pattern to avoid hitting the pin as you cut.
- Grainlines – placing pattern pieces on the fabric grainline helps cut-out pieces keep their shape. The grainline is parallel to the finished edges (selvedges) of a fabric. Try to follow our layouts as we have placed the shapes along the grainline, but at this scale it's not going to make or break your garment if you can't.

You will see symbols on the patterns – some of the common ones are shown and explained here.

⟷ Straight grain of fabric

– – – Sewing line

▼ I ● Triangle/notch and dot position markers

—✕— Buttonhole, button and press stud positions

Place on fold of fabric

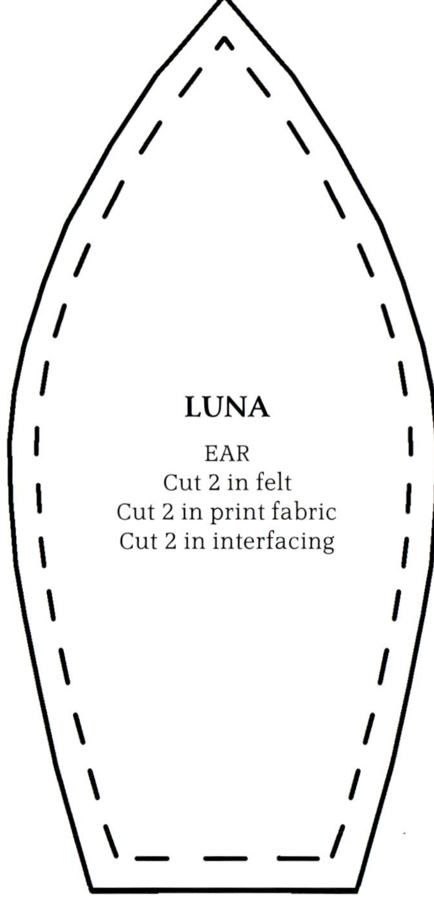

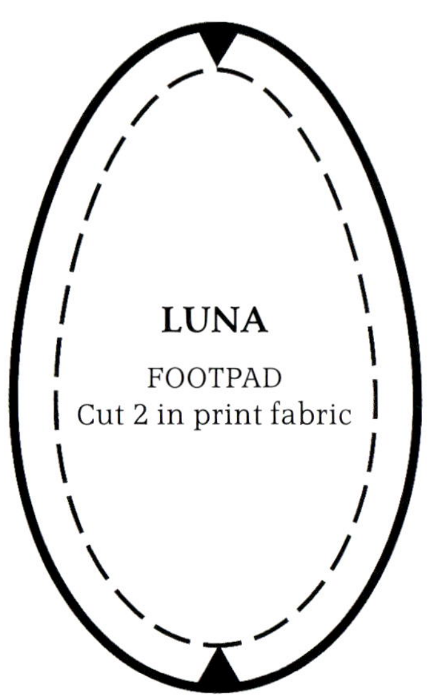

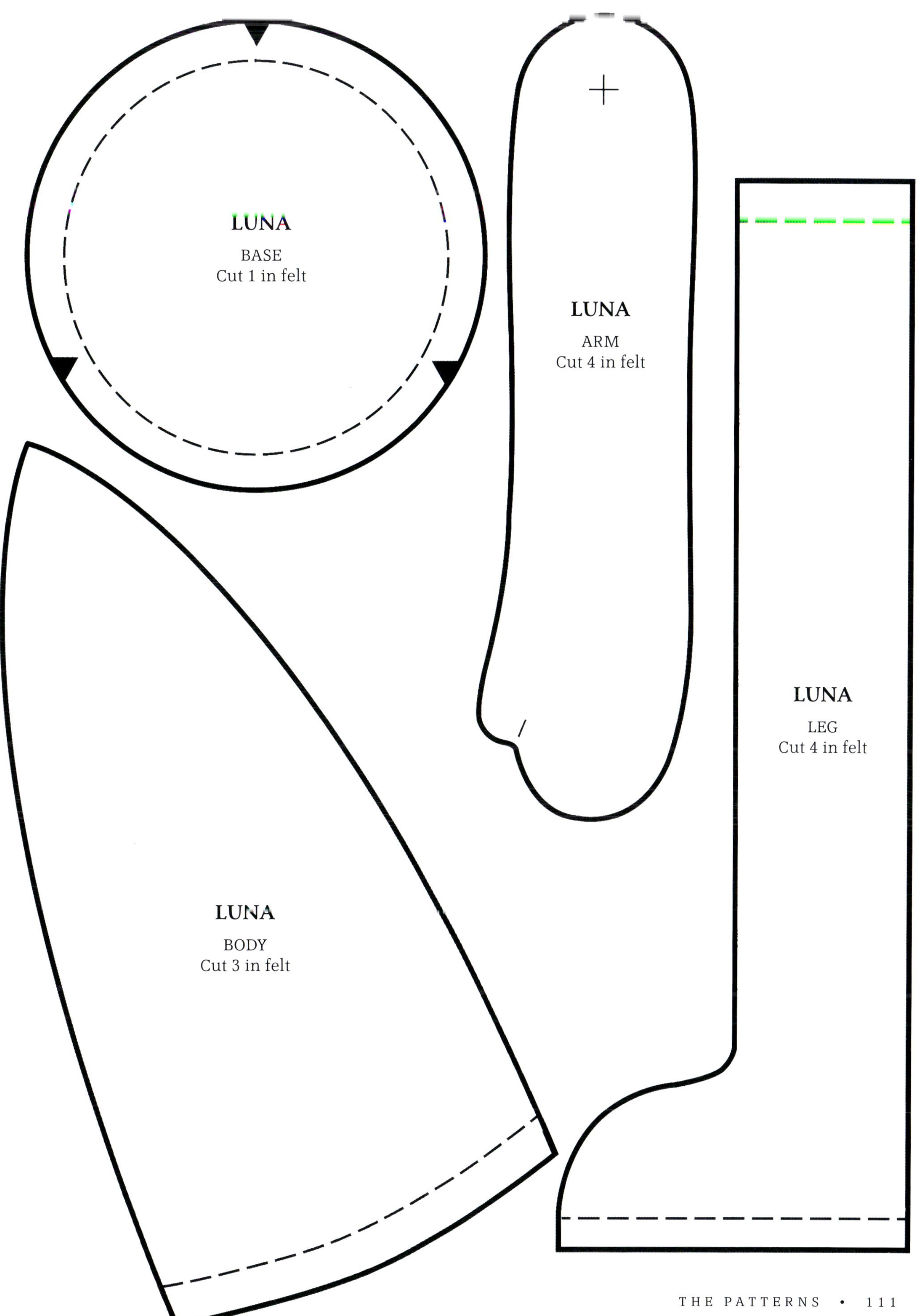
LUNA
BASE
Cut 1 in felt
LUNA
ARM
Cut 4 in felt
LUNA
LEG
Cut 4 in felt
LUNA
BODY
Cut 3 in felt

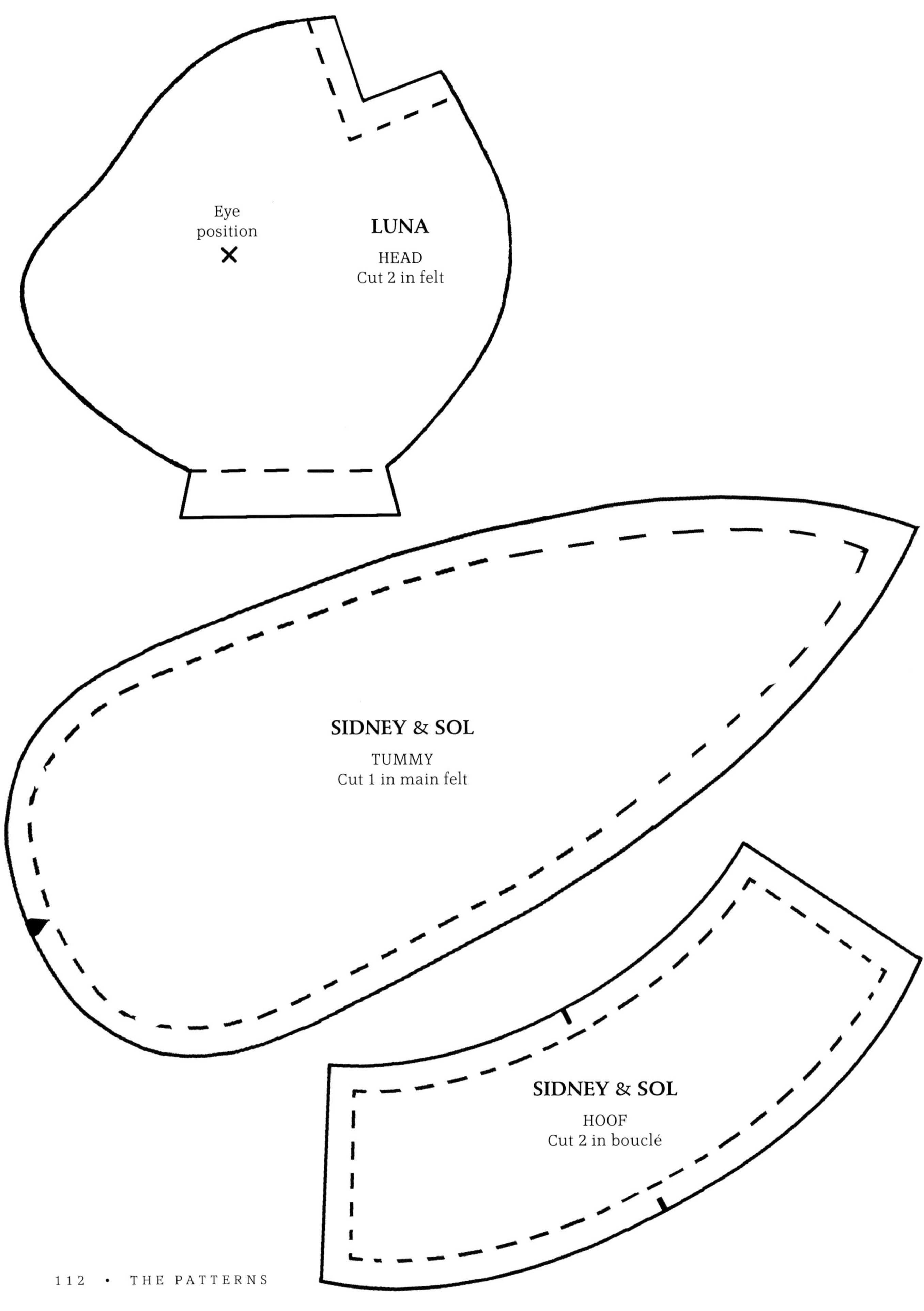
Eye
position
LUNA
HEAD
Cut 2 in felt
SIDNEY & SOL
TUMMY
Cut 1 in main felt
SIDNEY & SOL
HOOF
Cut 2 in bouclé

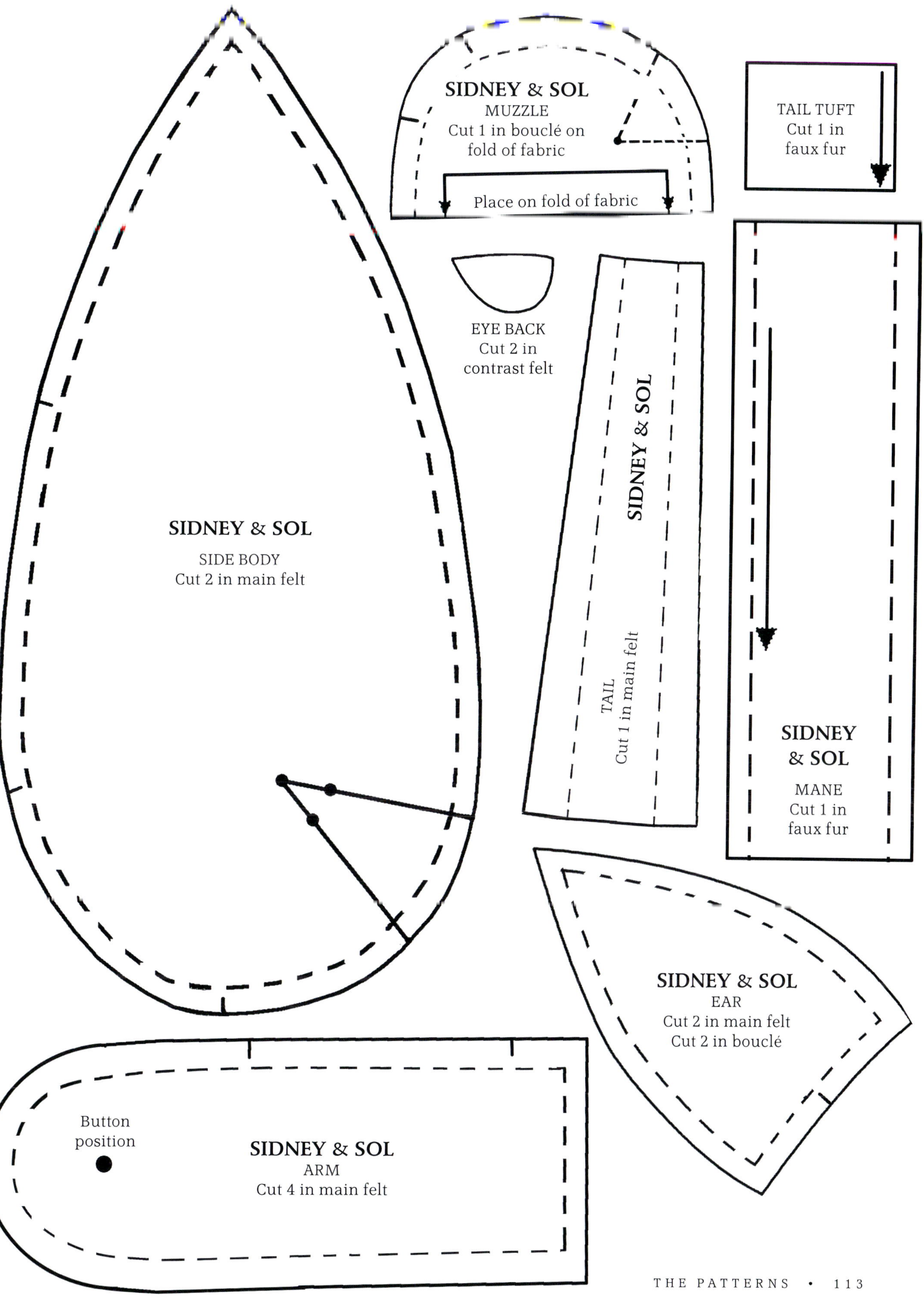
SIDNEY & SOL
MUZZLE
Cut 1 in bouclé on
fold of fabric
Place on fold of fabric
TAIL TUFT
Cut 1 in
faux fur
EYE BACK
Cut 2 in
contrast felt
SIDNEY & SOL
TAIL
Cut 1 in main felt
SIDNEY & SOL
SIDE BODY
Cut 2 in main felt
SIDNEY
& SOL
MANE
Cut 1 in
faux fur
SIDNEY & SOL
EAR
Cut 2 in main felt
Cut 2 in bouclé
Button
position
SIDNEY & SOL
ARM
Cut 4 in main felt

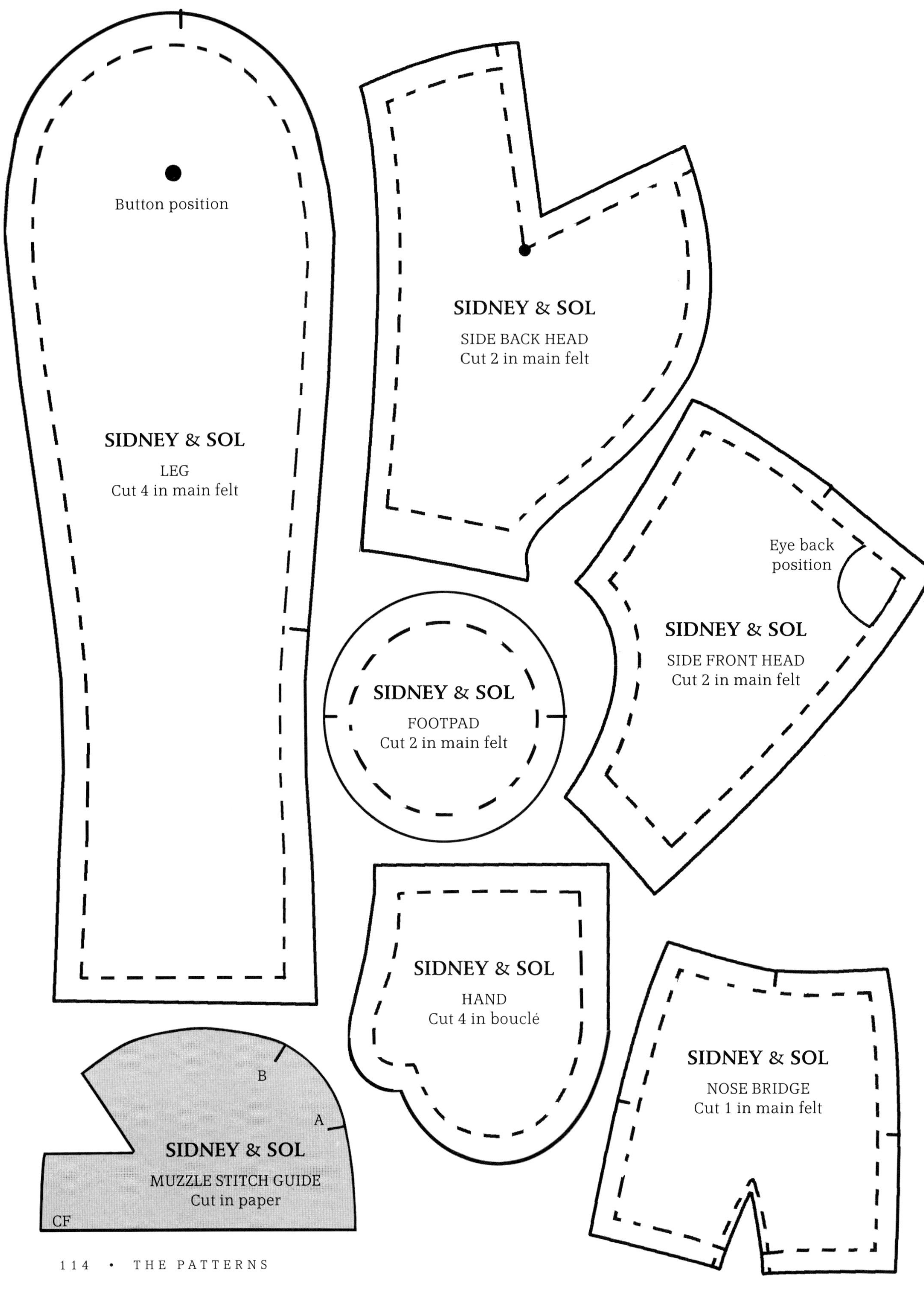
Button position
SIDNEY & SOL
LEG
Cut 4 in main felt
SIDNEY & SOL
SIDE BACK HEAD
Cut 2 in main felt
Eye back
position
SIDNEY & SOL
SIDE FRONT HEAD
Cut 2 in main felt
SIDNEY & SOL
FOOTPAD
Cut 2 in main felt
SIDNEY & SOL
HAND
Cut 4 in bouclé
B
A
SIDNEY & SOL
MUZZLE STITCH GUIDE
Cut in paper
CF
SIDNEY & SOL
NOSE BRIDGE
Cut 1 in main felt

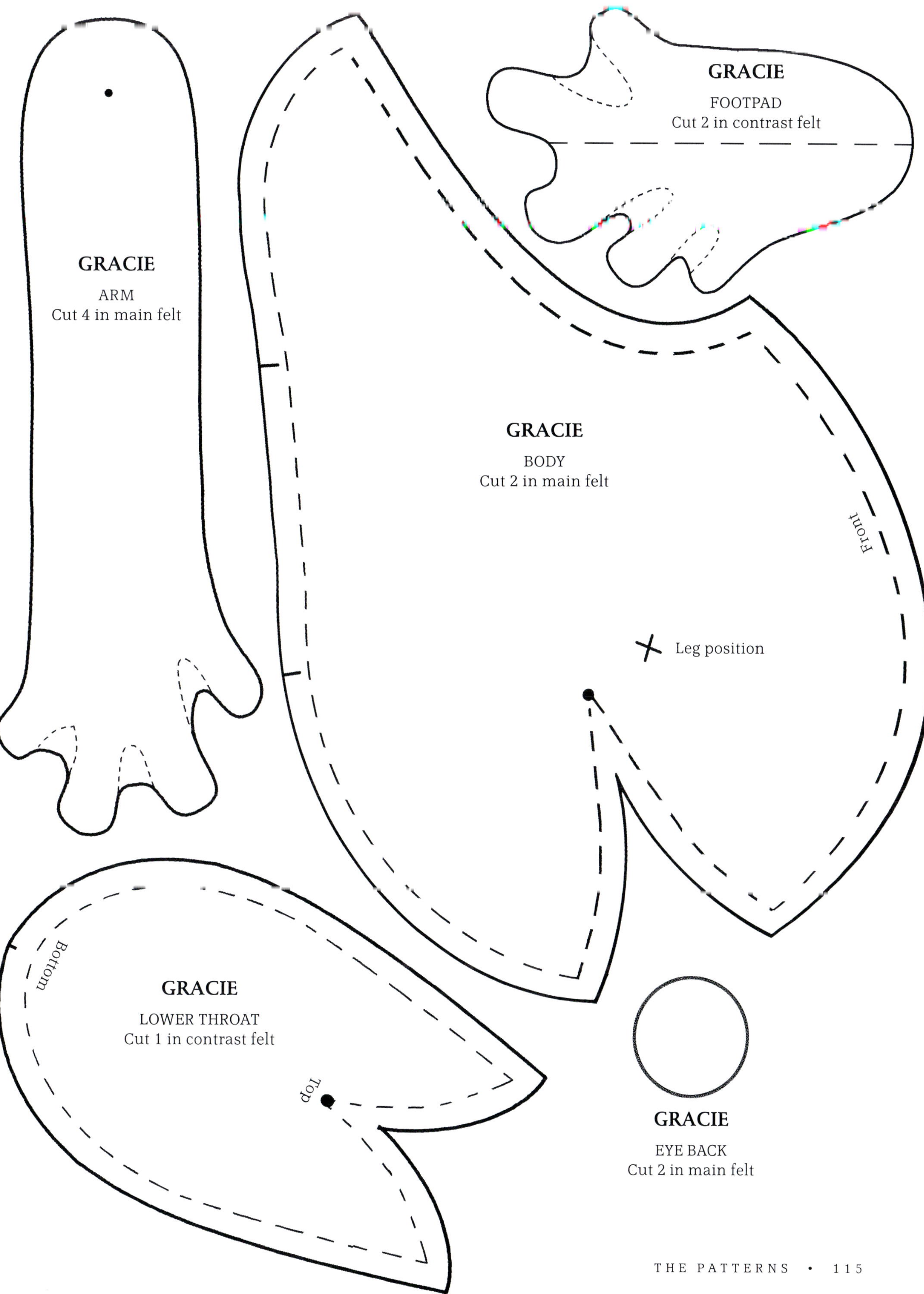
GRACIE
ARM
Cut 4 in main felt
GRACIE
BODY
Cut 2 in main felt
Front
Leg position
GRACIE
FOOTPAD
Cut 2 in contrast felt
GRACIE
LOWER THROAT
Cut 1 in contrast felt
Bottom
Top
GRACIE
EYE BACK
Cut 2 in main felt

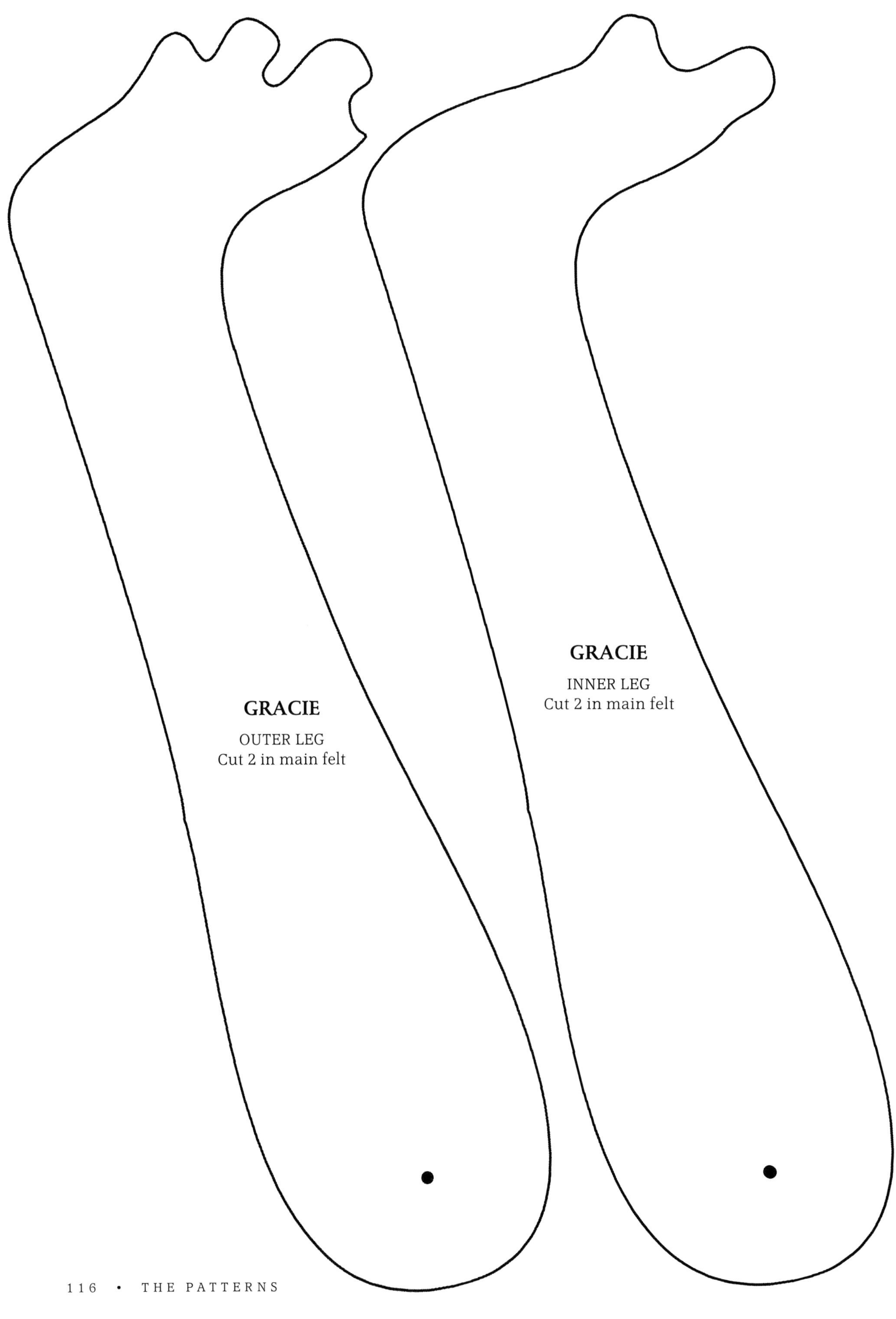
GRACIE
OUTER LEG
Cut 2 in main felt
GRACIE
INNER LEG
Cut 2 in main felt

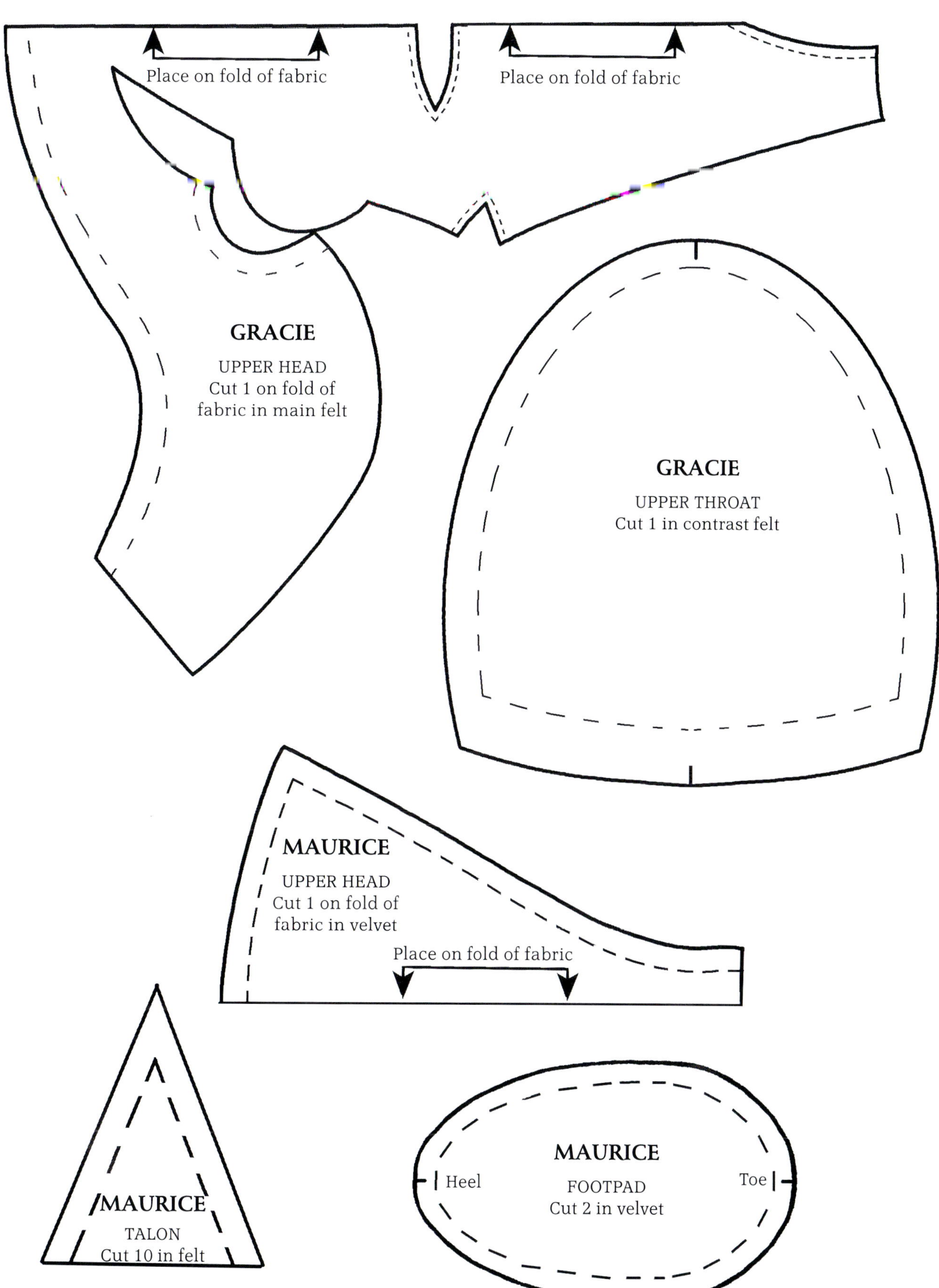
Place on fold of fabric
Place on fold of fabric
GRACIE
UPPER HEAD
Cut 1 on fold of
fabric in main felt
GRACIE
UPPER THROAT
Cut 1 in contrast felt
MAURICE
UPPER HEAD
Cut 1 on fold of
fabric in velvet
Place on fold of fabric
MAURICE
TALON
Cut 10 in felt
Heel
MAURICE
FOOTPAD
Cut 2 in velvet
Toe

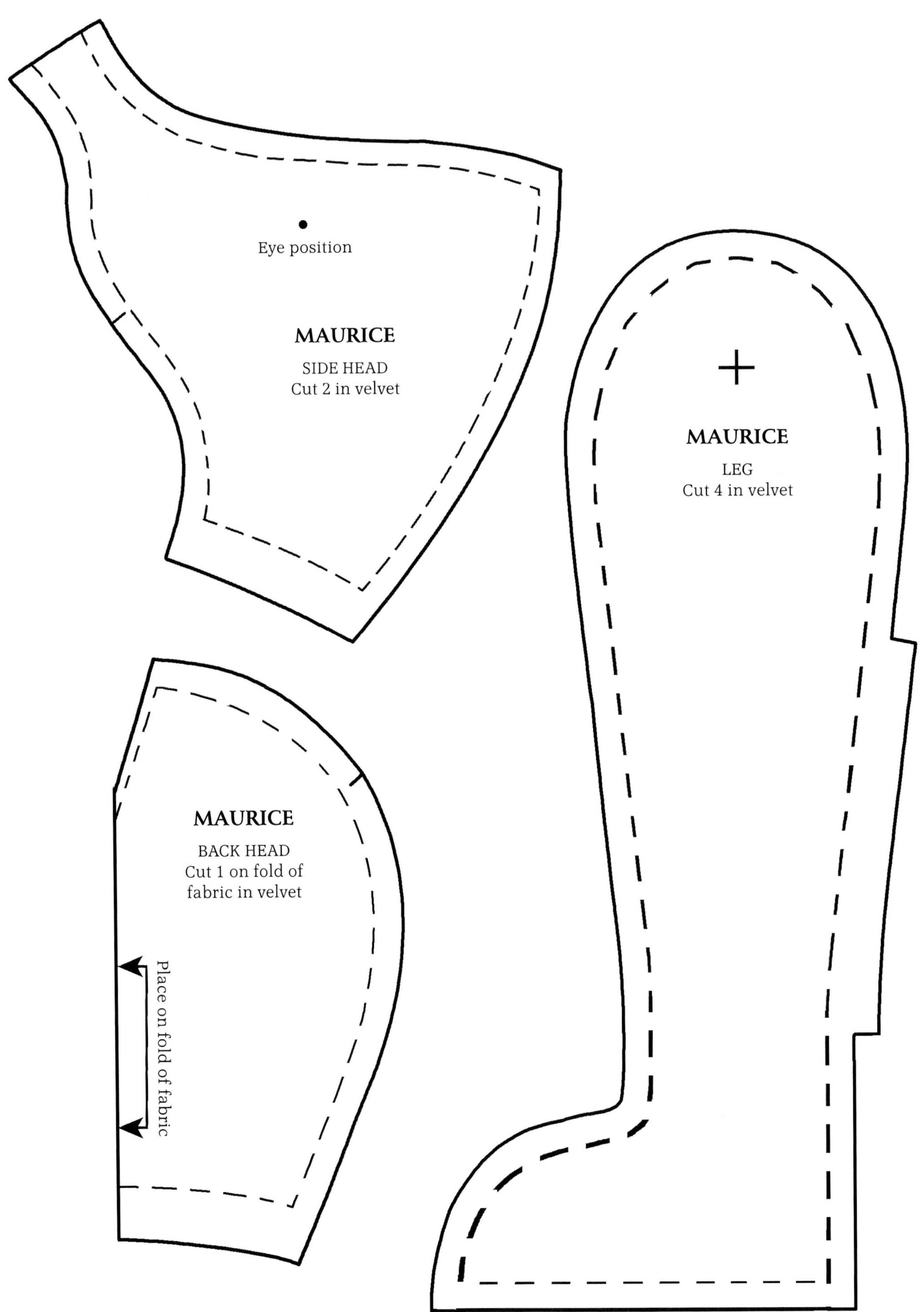
Eye position
MAURICE
SIDE HEAD
Cut 2 in velvet
MAURICE
LEG
Cut 4 in velvet
MAURICE
BACK HEAD
Cut 1 on fold of
fabric in velvet
Place on fold of fabric

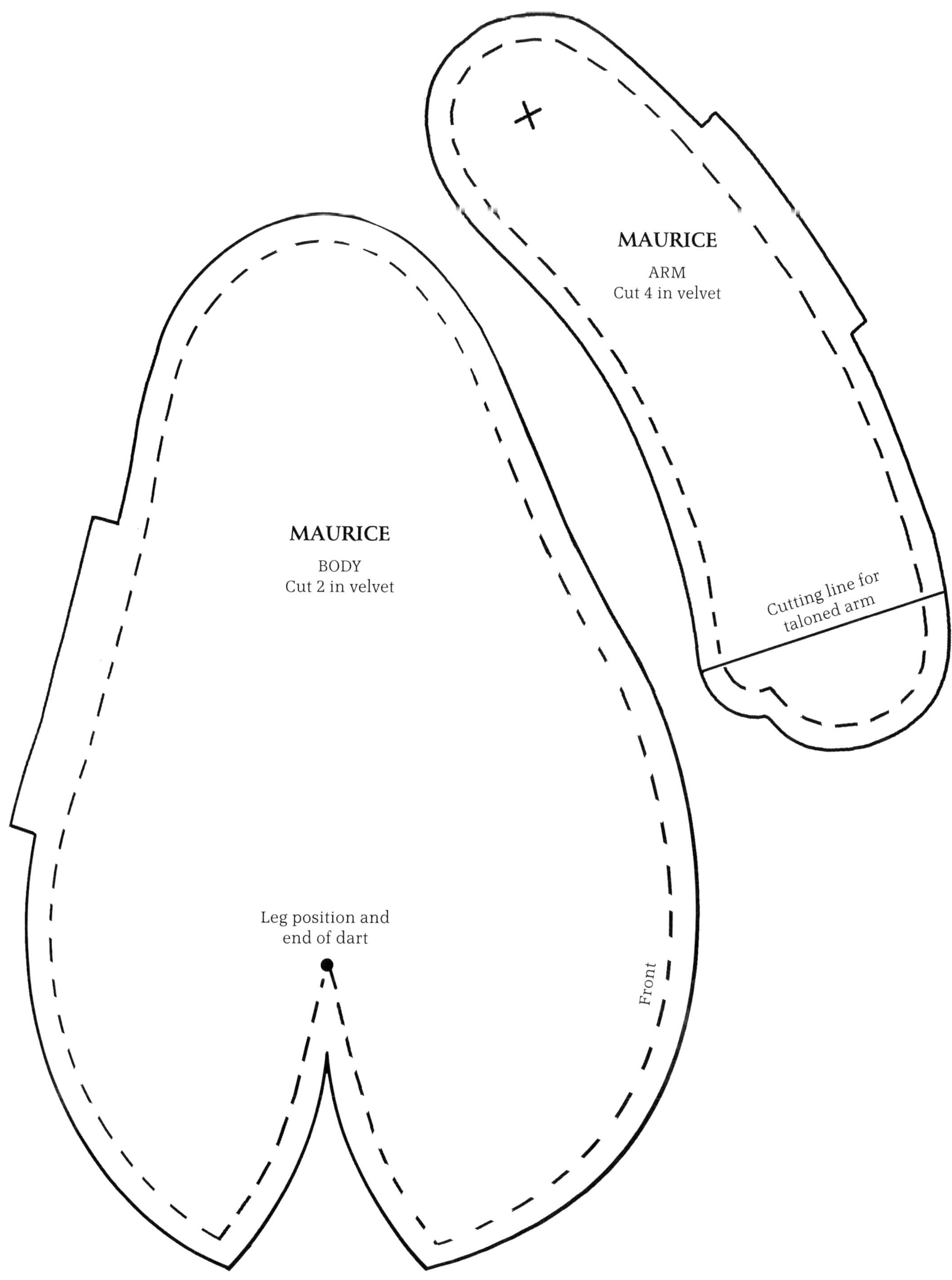
MAURICE
ARM
Cut 4 in velvet
Cutting line for taloned arm
MAURICE
BODY
Cut 2 in velvet
Leg position and end of dart
Front

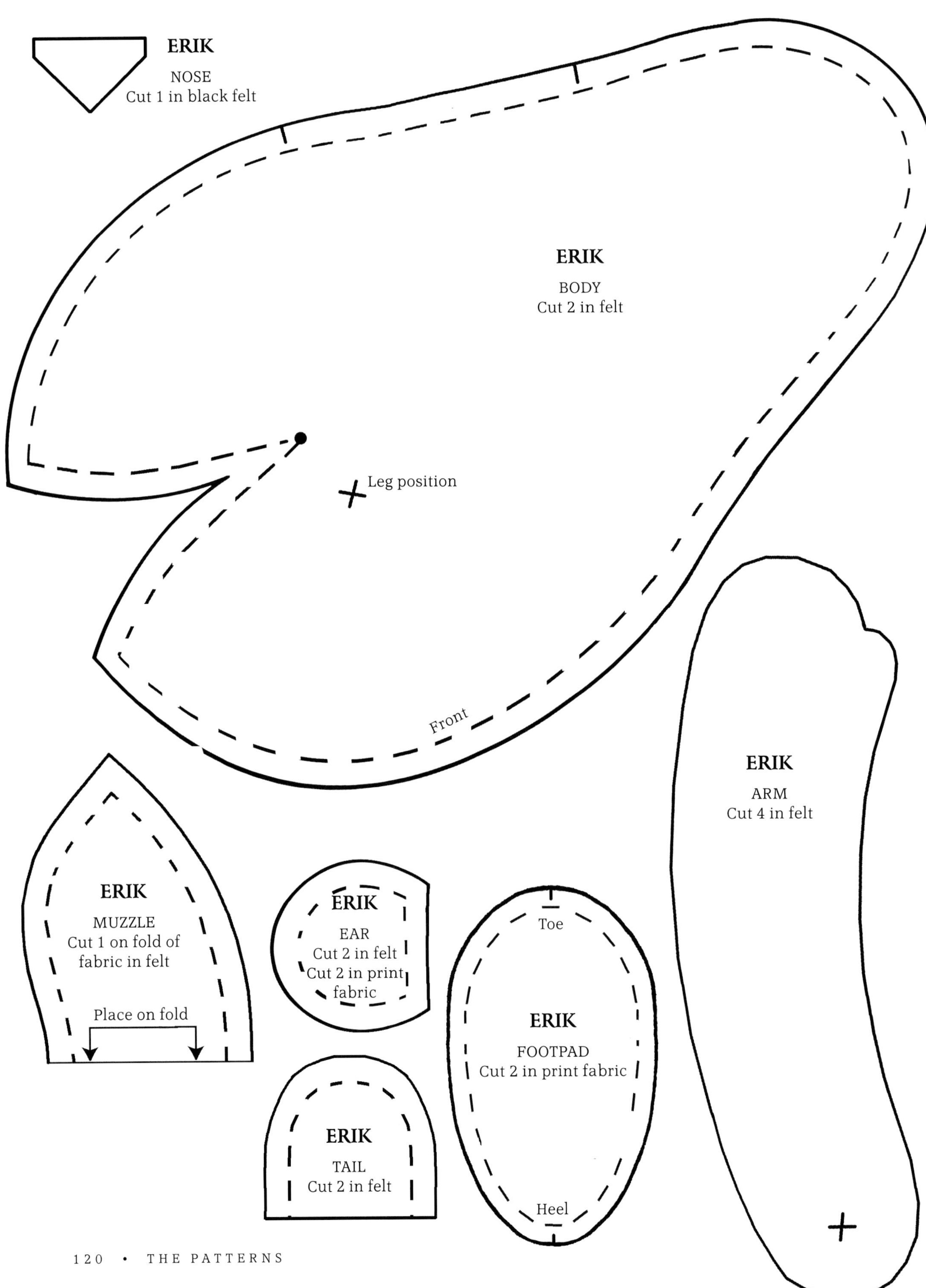
ERIK
NOSE
Cut 1 in black felt
ERIK
BODY
Cut 2 in felt
Leg position
Front
ERIK
ARM
Cut 4 in felt
ERIK
MUZZLE
Cut 1 on fold of
fabric in felt
Place on fold
ERIK
EAR
Cut 2 in felt
Cut 2 in print
fabric
ERIK
FOOTPAD
Toe
Cut 2 in print fabric
Heel
ERIK
TAIL
Cut 2 in felt

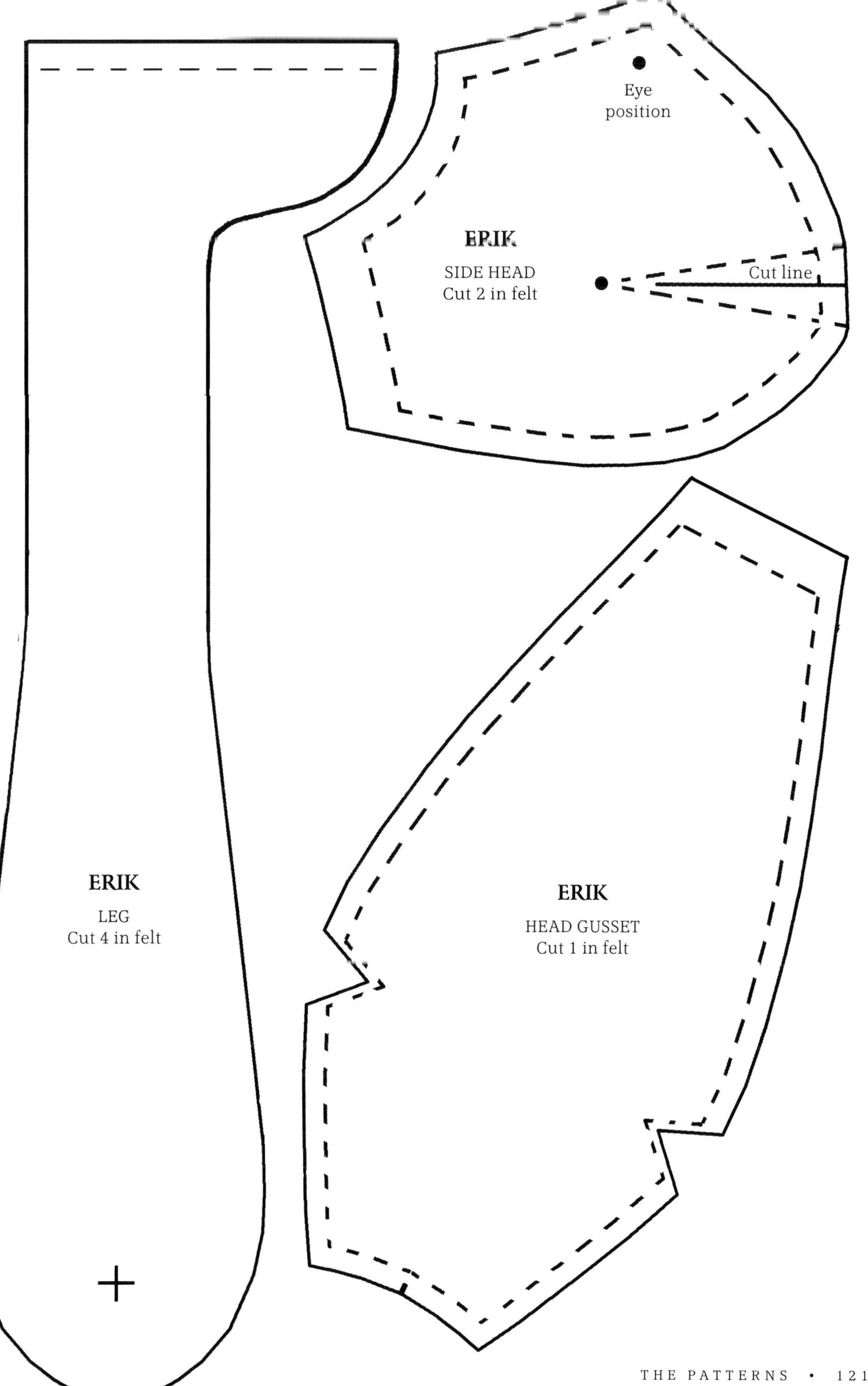
Eye
position
ERIK
SIDE HEAD
Cut 2 in felt
Cut line
ERIK
LEG
Cut 4 in felt
ERIK
HEAD GUSSET
Cut 1 in felt

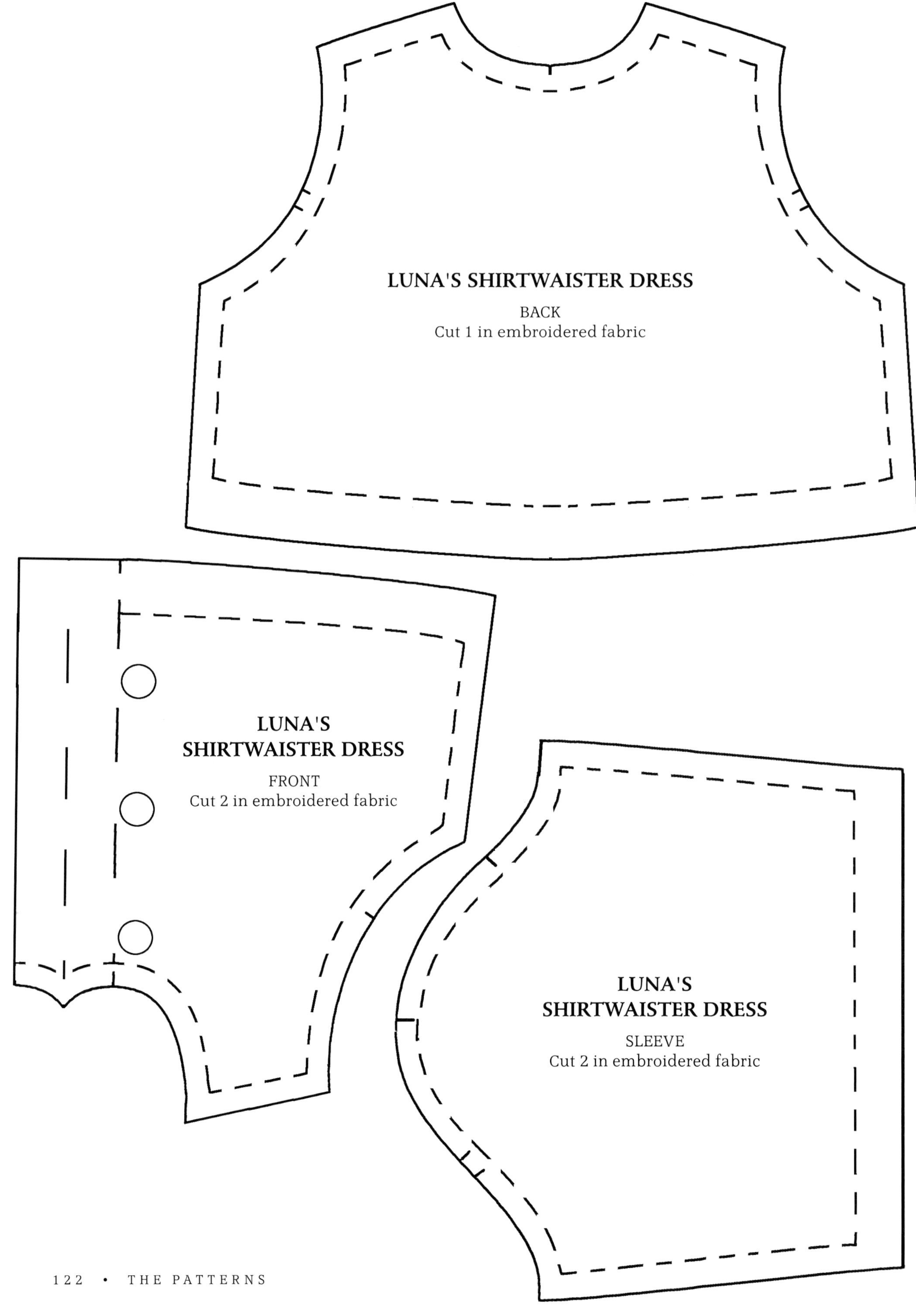
LUNA'S SHIRTWAISTER DRESS
BACK
Cut 1 in embroidered fabric
LUNA'S
SHIRTWAISTER DRESS
FRONT
Cut 2 in embroidered fabric
LUNA'S
SHIRTWAISTER DRESS
SLEEVE
Cut 2 in embroidered fabric

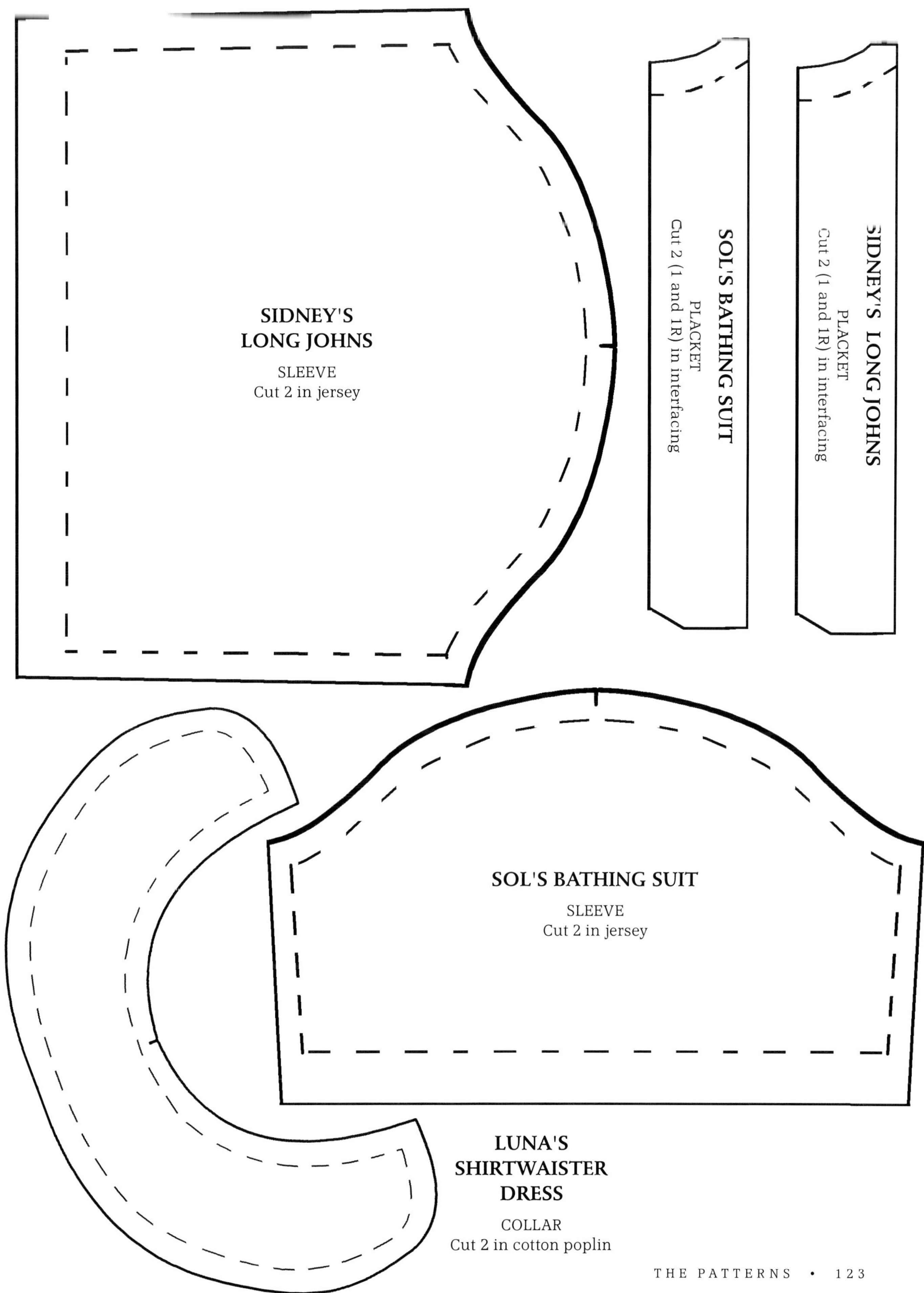

SIDNEY'S
LONG JOHNS
SLEEVE
Cut 2 in jersey
SOL'S BATHING SUIT
PLACKET
Cut 2 (1 and 1R) in interfacing
SIDNEY'S LONG JOHNS
PLACKET
Cut 2 (1 and 1R) in interfacing
SOL'S BATHING SUIT
SLEEVE
Cut 2 in jersey
LUNA'S
SHIRTWAISTER
DRESS
COLLAR
Cut 2 in cotton poplin

A

SIDNEY'S LONG JOHNS

BACK
Join at Points A and B to complete pattern piece
Cut 2 in jersey

B

SIDNEY'S LONG JOHNS

FRONT
Join at Points A and B to complete pattern piece
Cut 2 in jersey

A

B

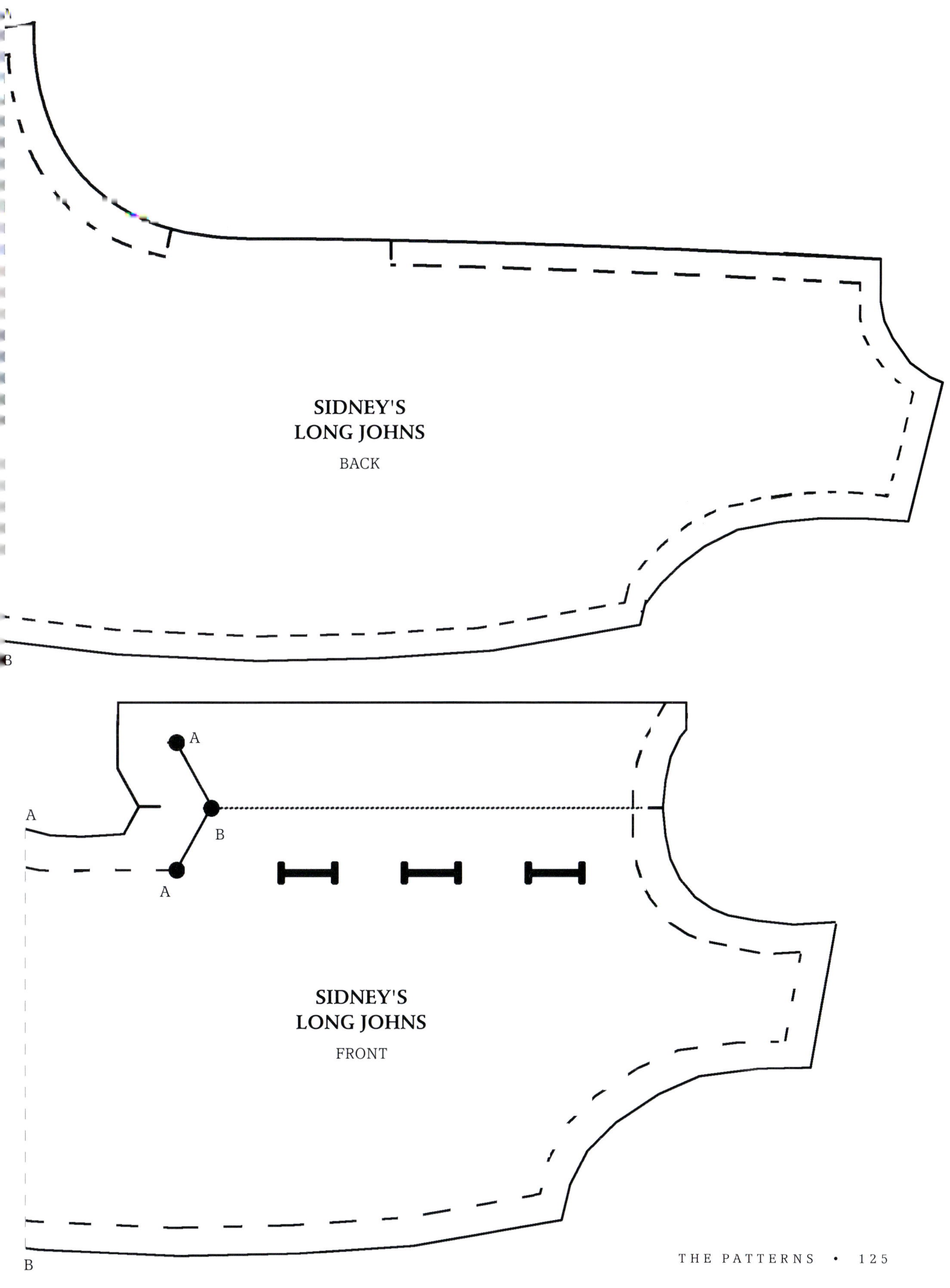
SIDNEY'S
LONG JOHNS
BACK
B
A
A
B
A
SIDNEY'S
LONG JOHNS
FRONT
B

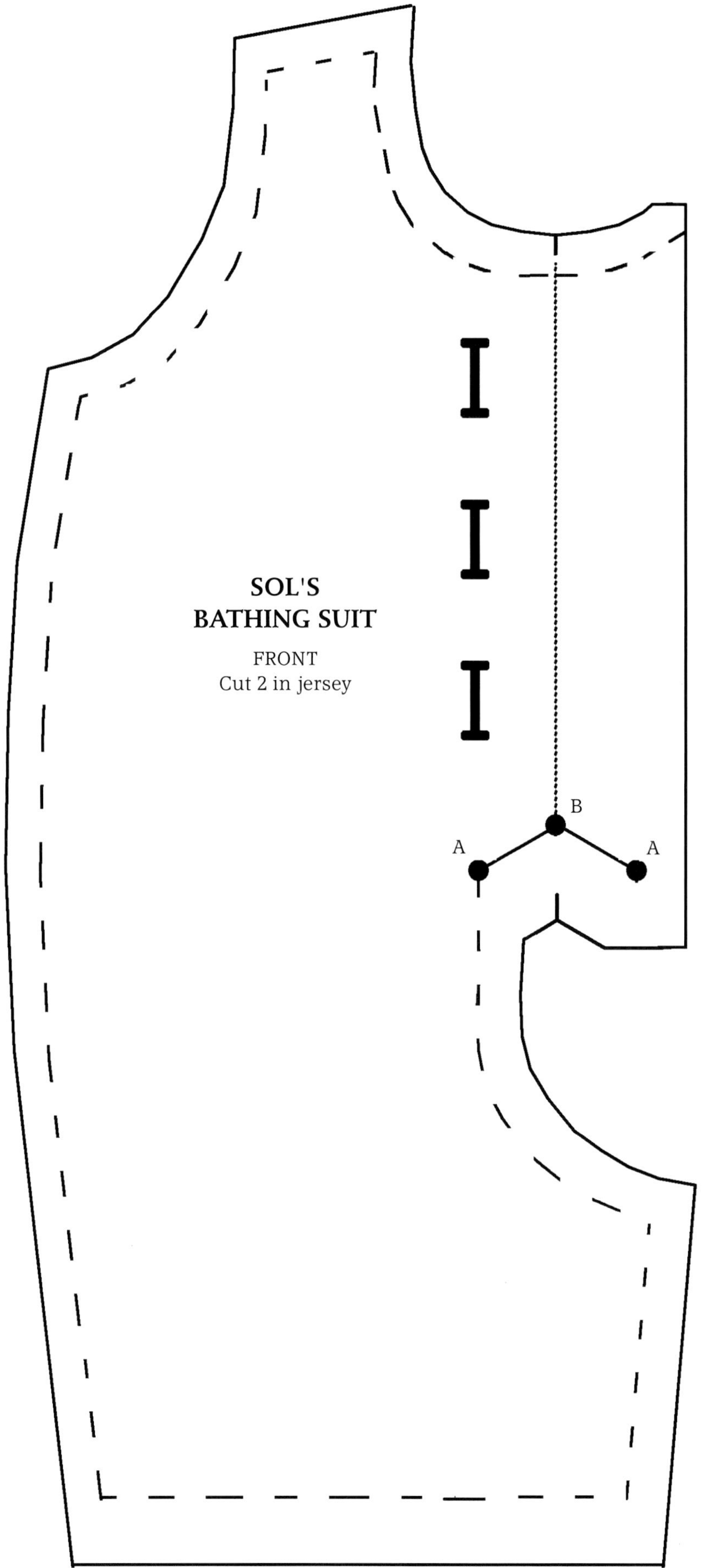
SOL'S
BATHING SUIT
FRONT
Cut 2 in jersey
B
A
A

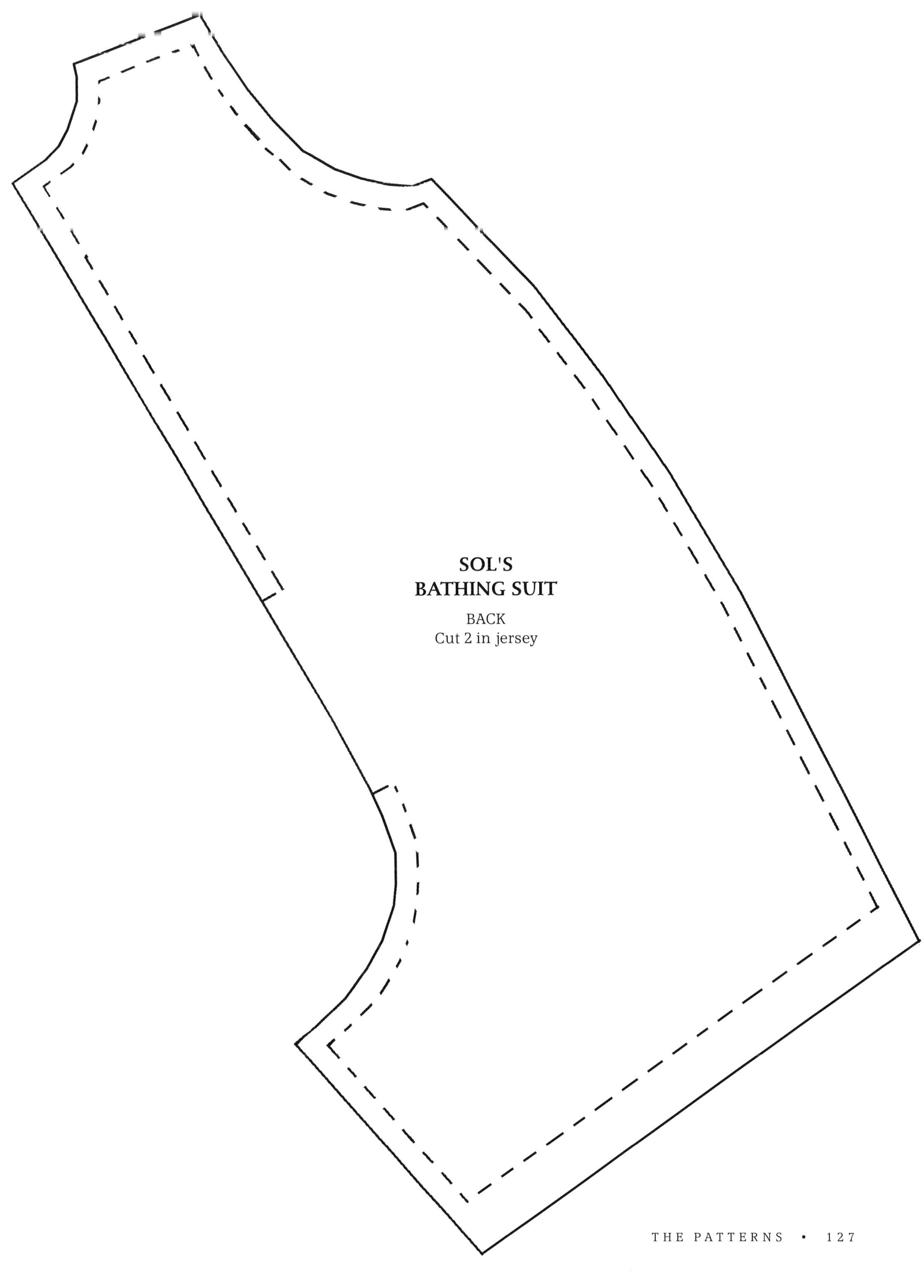
SOL'S
BATHING SUIT
BACK
Cut 2 in jersey

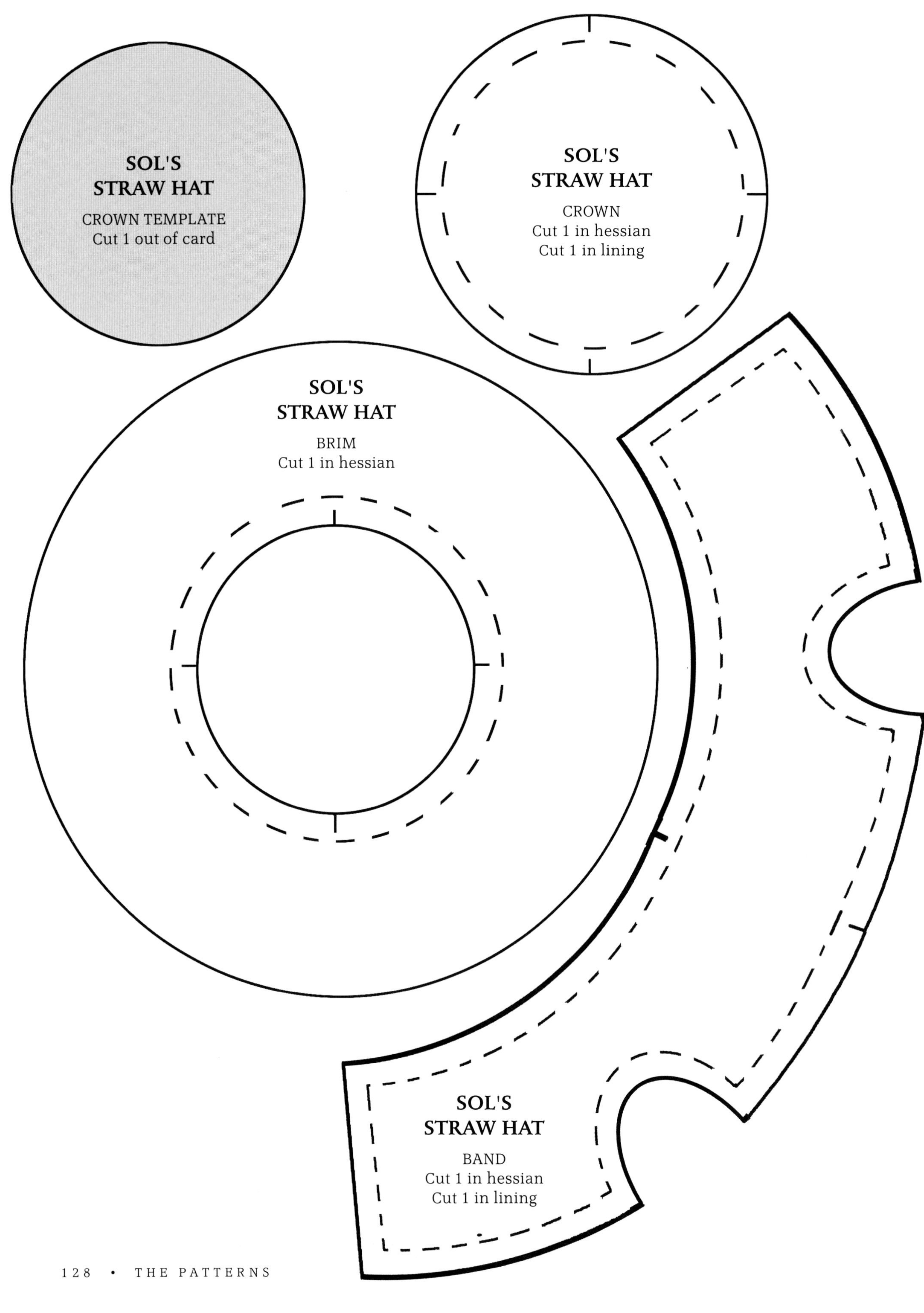
SOL'S
STRAW HAT
CROWN TEMPLATE
Cut 1 out of card
SOL'S
STRAW HAT
CROWN
Cut 1 in hessian
Cut 1 in lining
SOL'S
STRAW HAT
BRIM
Cut 1 in hessian
SOL'S
STRAW HAT
BAND
Cut 1 in hessian
Cut 1 in lining

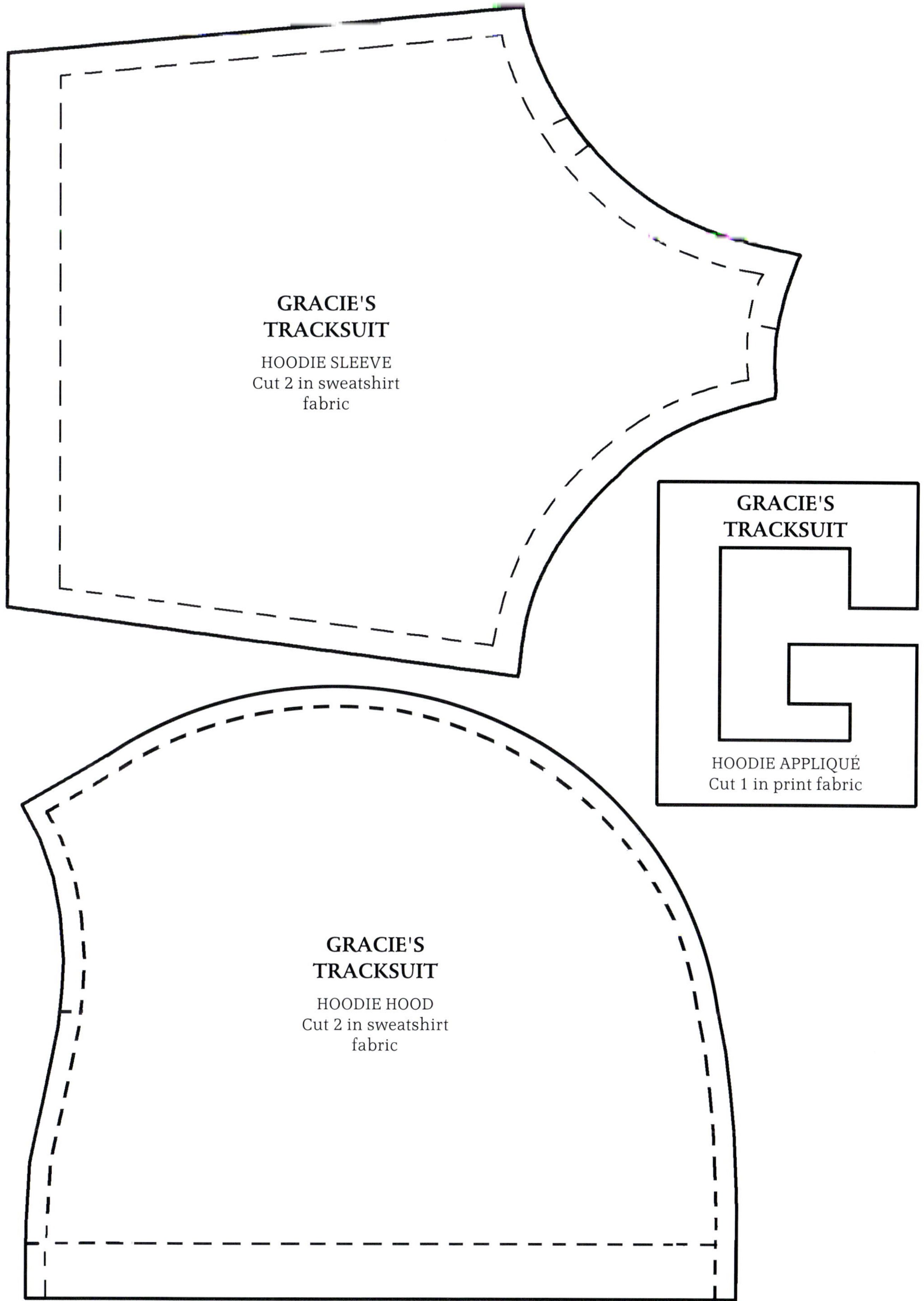
GRACIE'S
TRACKSUIT
HOODIE SLEEVE
Cut 2 in sweatshirt fabric
GRACIE'S
TRACKSUIT
HOODIE APPLIQUÉ
Cut 1 in print fabric
GRACIE'S
TRACKSUIT
HOODIE HOOD
Cut 2 in sweatshirt fabric

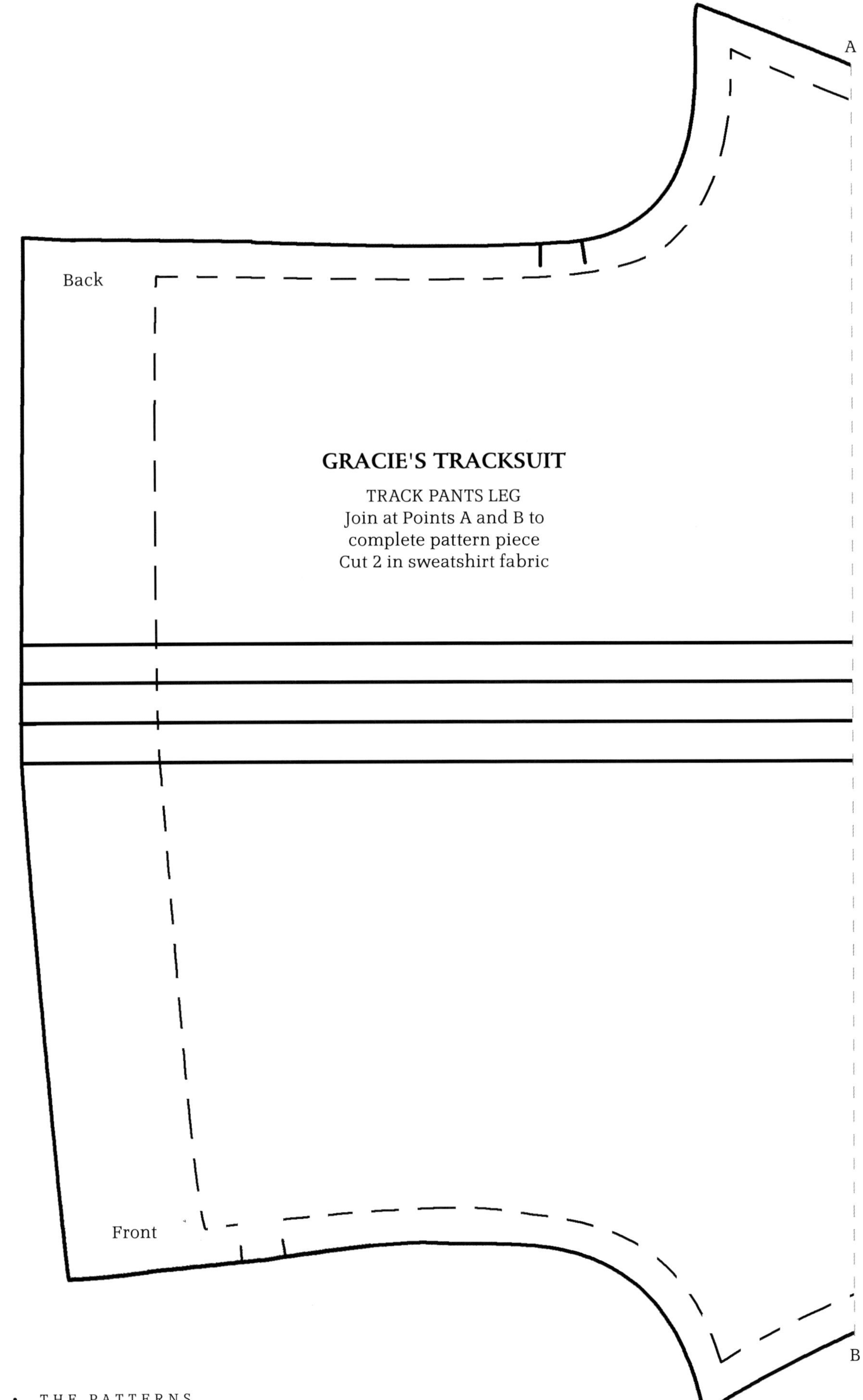
A
Back
GRACIE'S TRACKSUIT
TRACK PANTS LEG
Join at Points A and B to
complete pattern piece
Cut 2 in sweatshirt fabric
Front
B

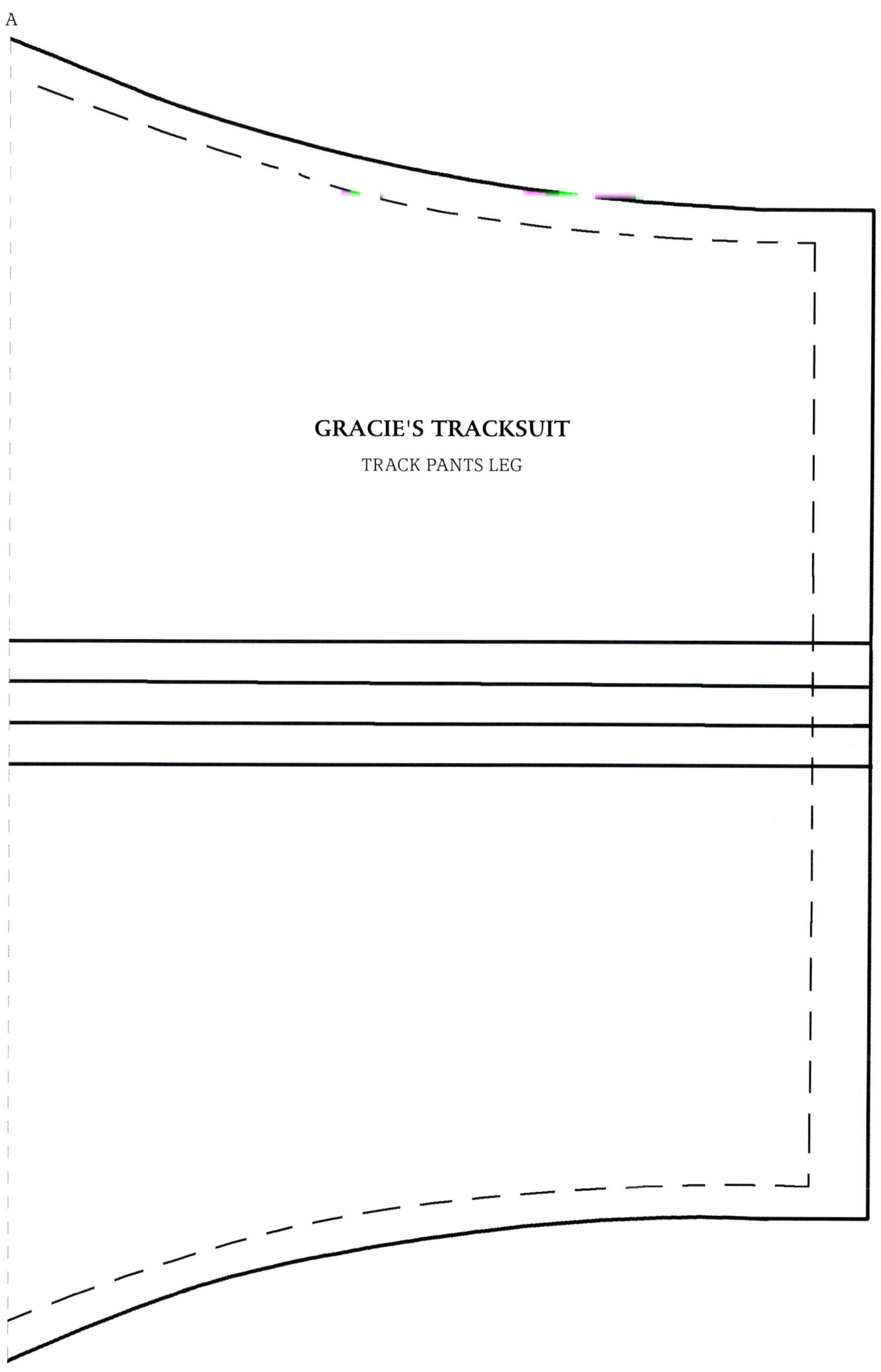
A
GRACIE'S TRACKSUIT
TRACK PANTS LEG
B

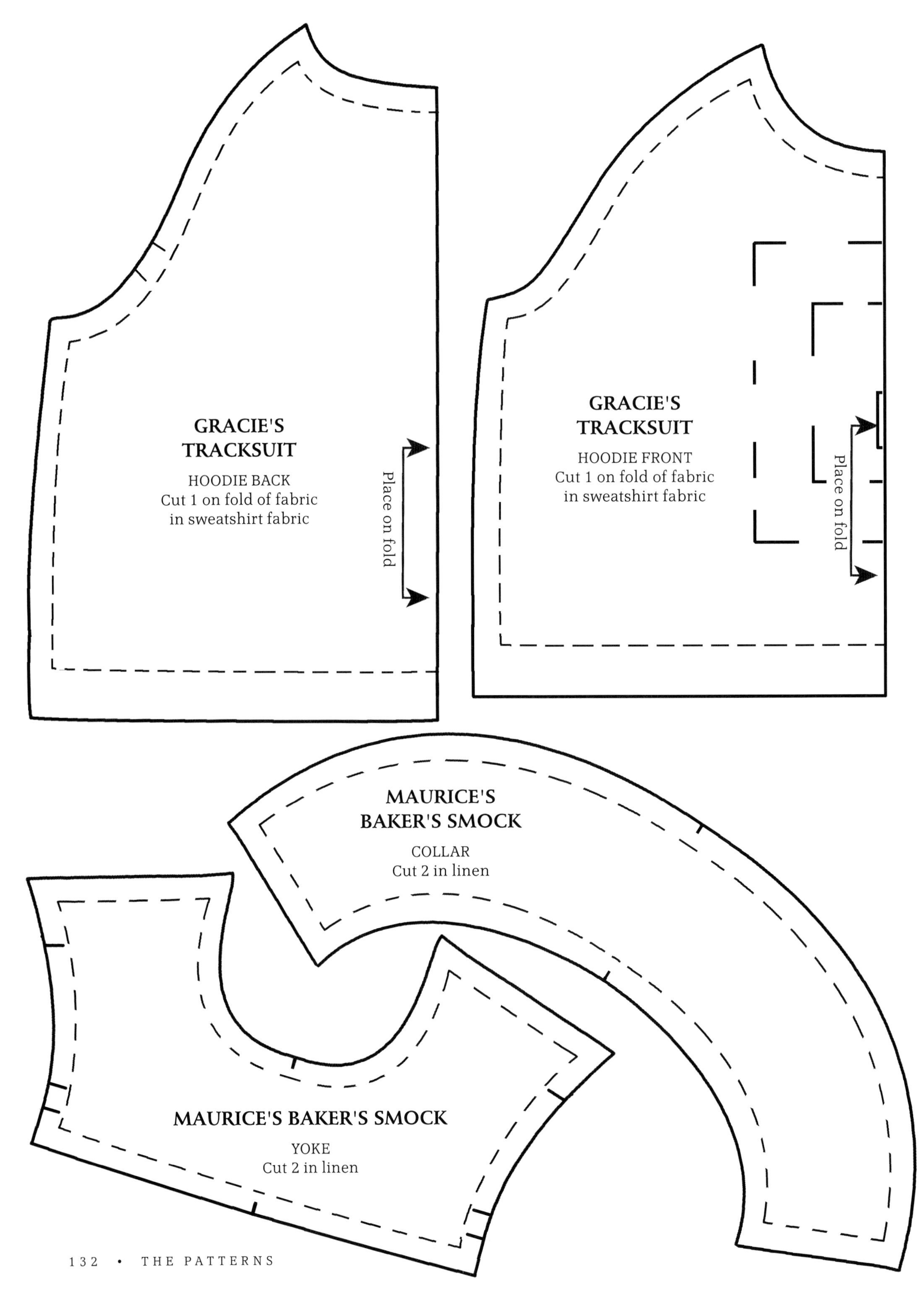
GRACIE'S
TRACKSUIT
HOODIE BACK
Cut 1 on fold of fabric
in sweatshirt fabric
Place on fold
GRACIE'S
TRACKSUIT
HOODIE FRONT
Cut 1 on fold of fabric
in sweatshirt fabric
Place on fold
MAURICE'S
BAKER'S SMOCK
COLLAR
Cut 2 in linen
MAURICE'S BAKER'S SMOCK
YOKE
Cut 2 in linen

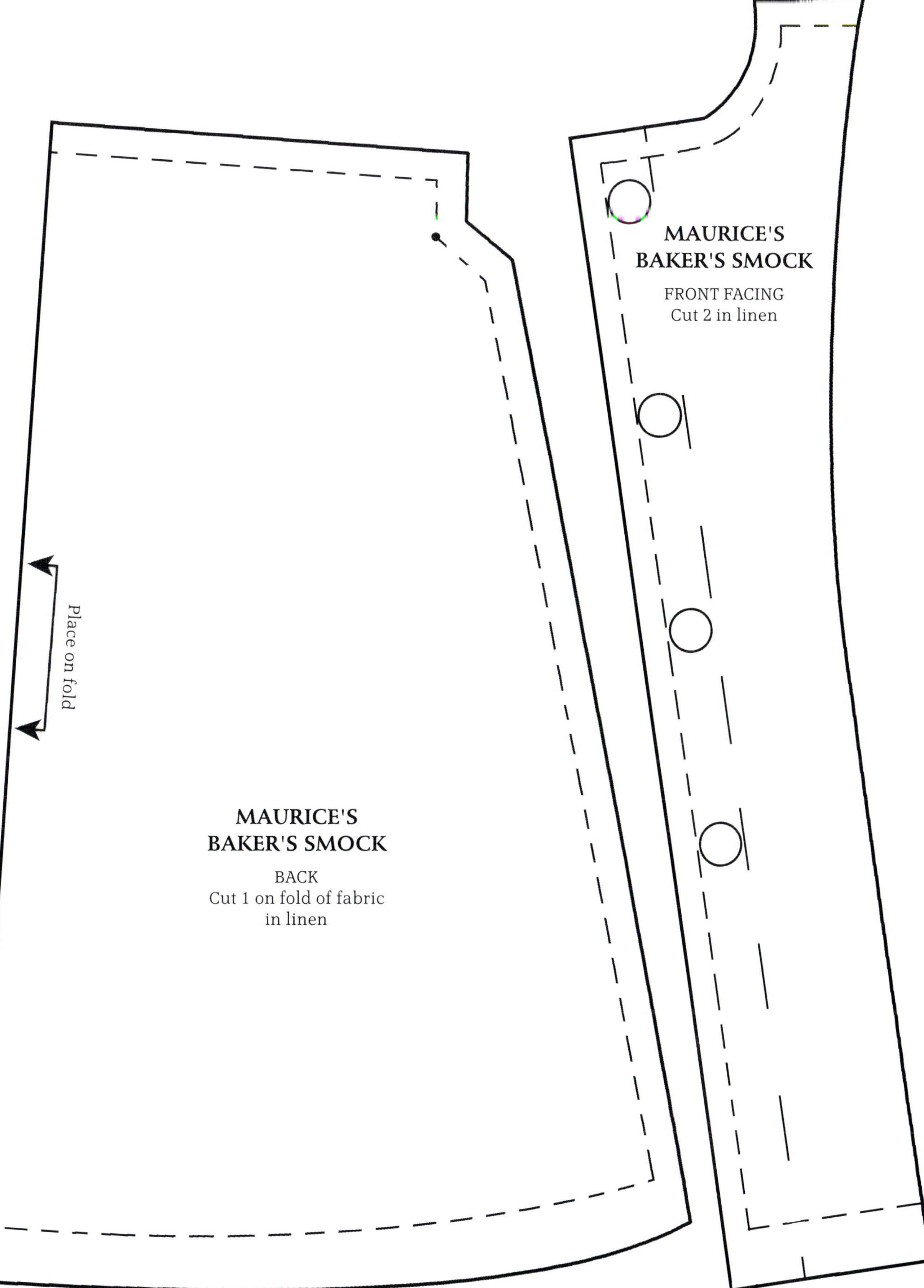
MAURICE'S
BAKER'S SMOCK
FRONT FACING
Cut 2 in linen
Place on fold
MAURICE'S
BAKER'S SMOCK
BACK
Cut 1 on fold of fabric
in linen

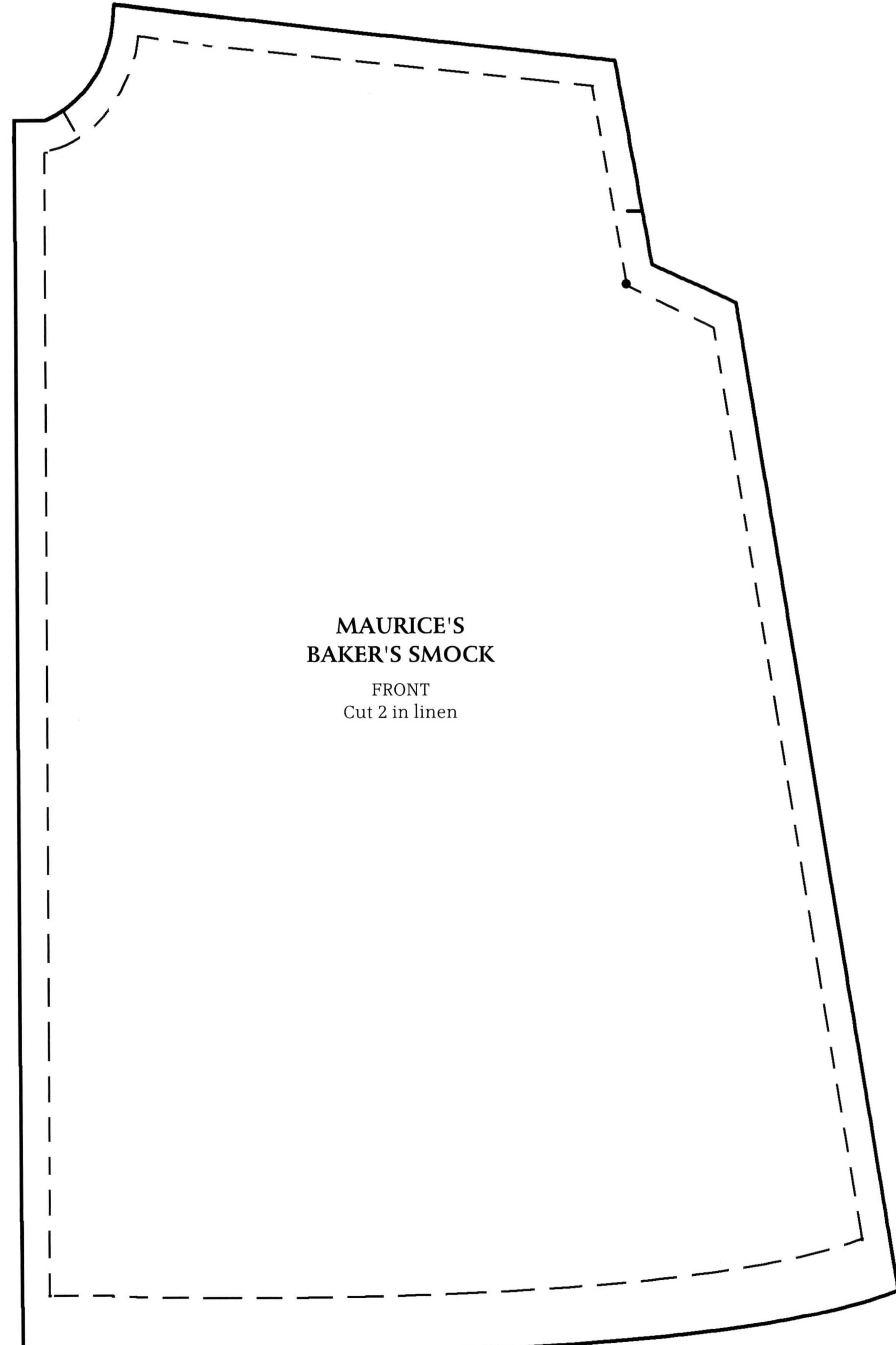
MAURICE'S
BAKER'S SMOCK
FRONT
Cut 2 in linen

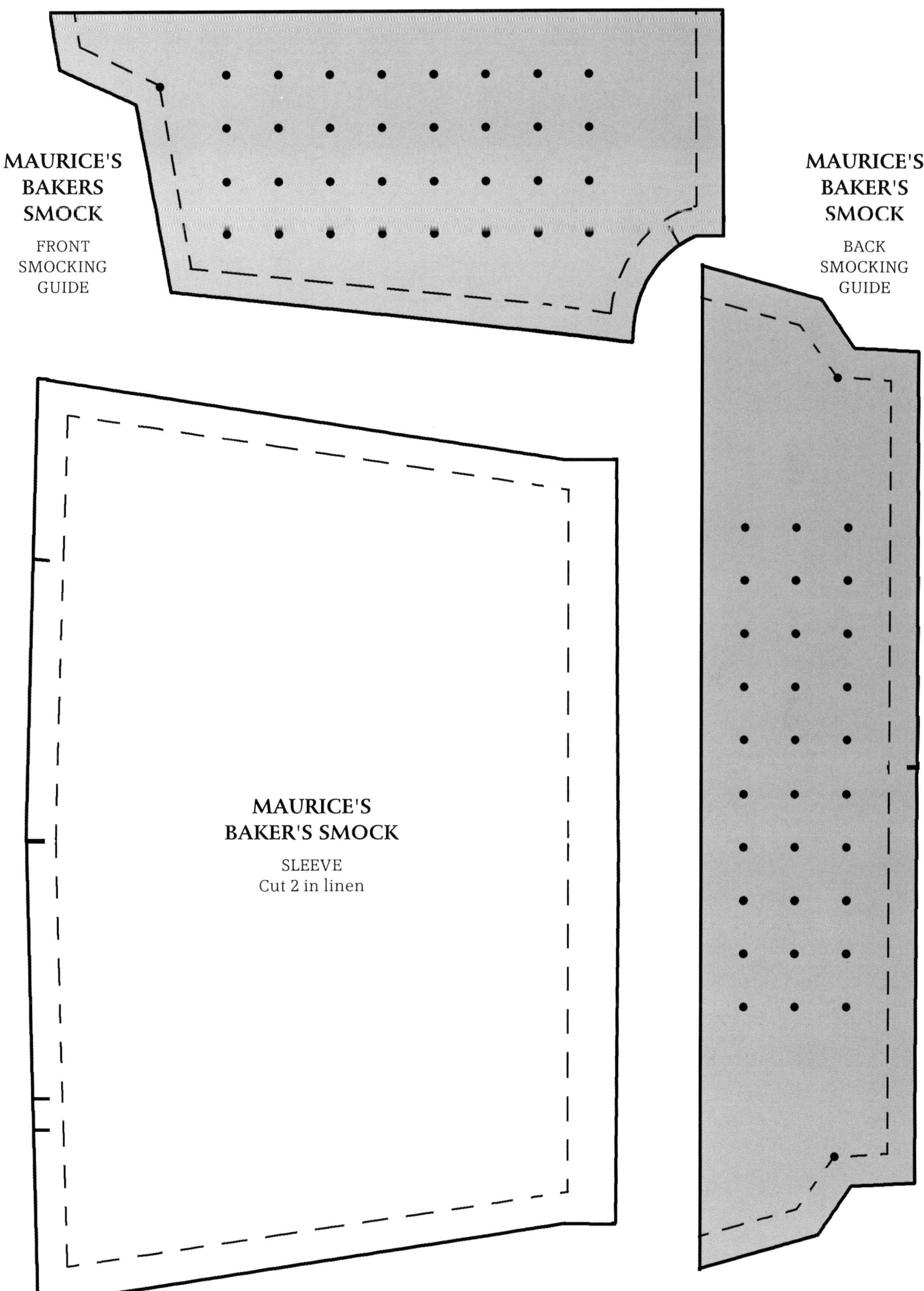
MAURICE'S
BAKERS
SMOCK
FRONT
SMOCKING
GUIDE
MAURICE'S
BAKER'S
SMOCK
BACK
SMOCKING
GUIDE
MAURICE'S
BAKER'S SMOCK
SLEEVE
Cut 2 in linen

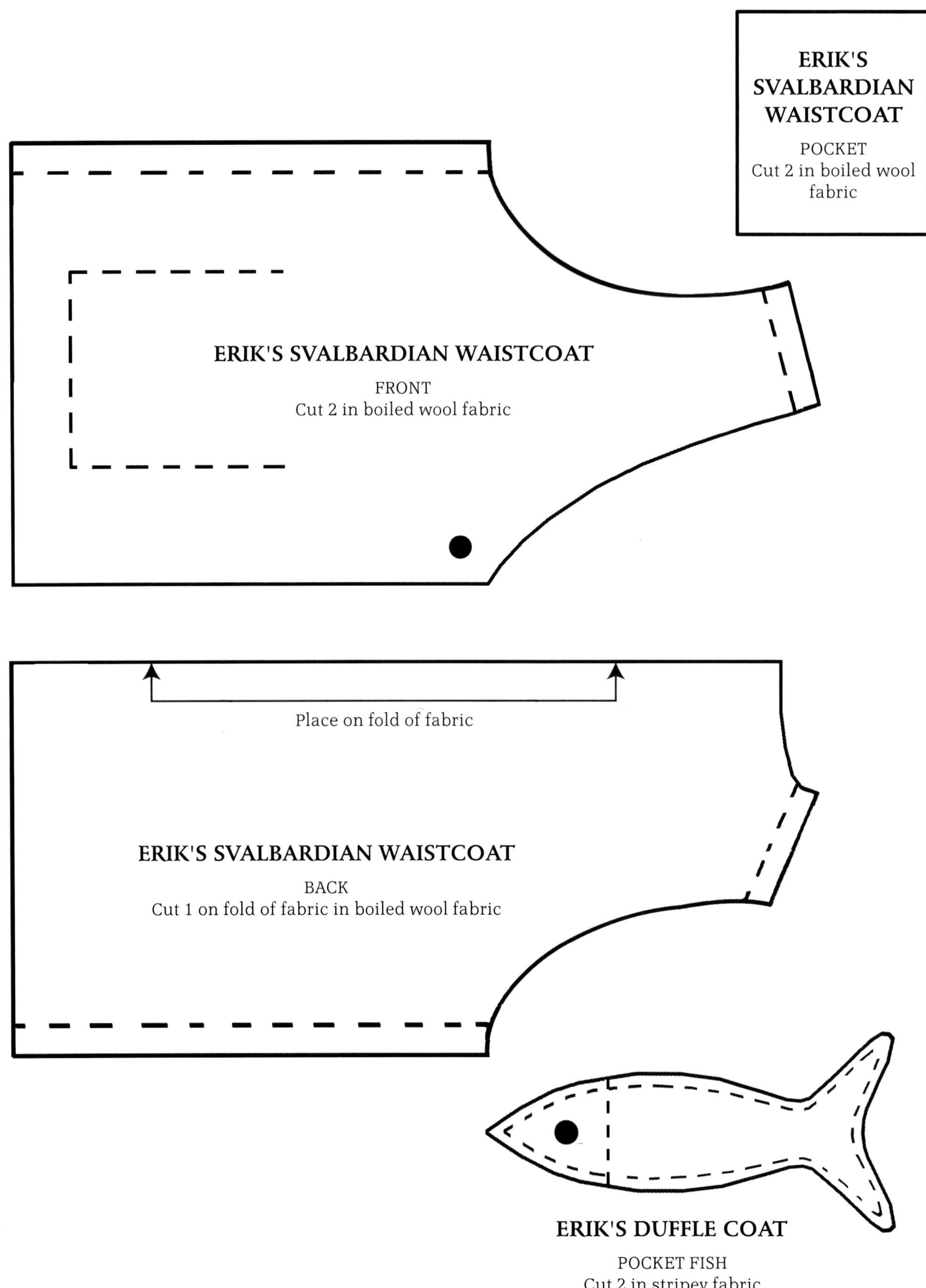
ERIK'S SVALBARDIAN WAISTCOAT
POCKET
Cut 2 in boiled wool fabric
ERIK'S SVALBARDIAN WAISTCOAT
FRONT
Cut 2 in boiled wool fabric
Place on fold of fabric
ERIK'S SVALBARDIAN WAISTCOAT
BACK
Cut 1 on fold of fabric in boiled wool fabric
ERIK'S DUFFLE COAT
POCKET FISH
Cut 2 in stripey fabric

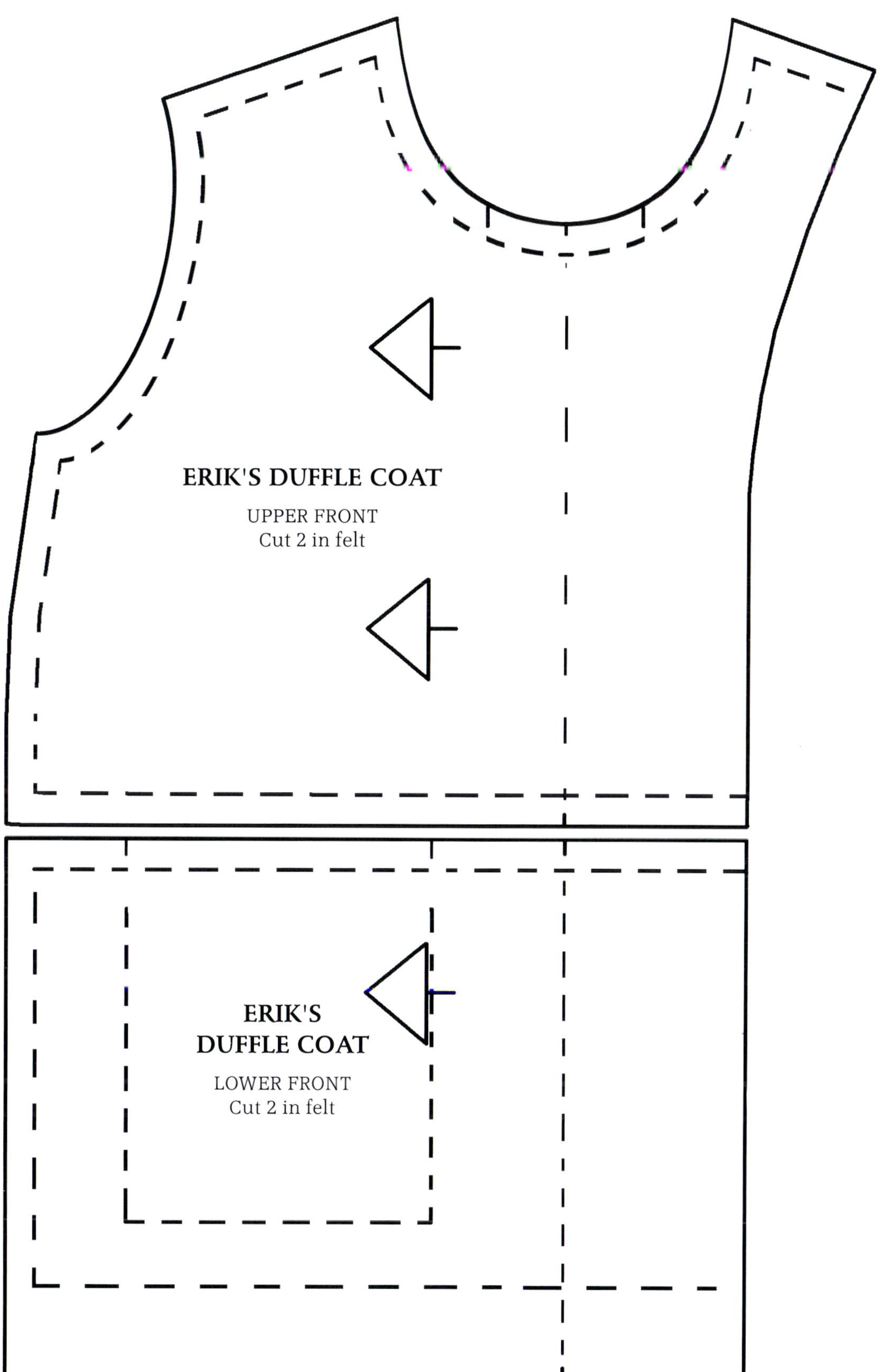
ERIK'S DUFFLE COAT
UPPER FRONT
Cut 2 in felt
ERIK'S
DUFFLE COAT
LOWER FRONT
Cut 2 in felt

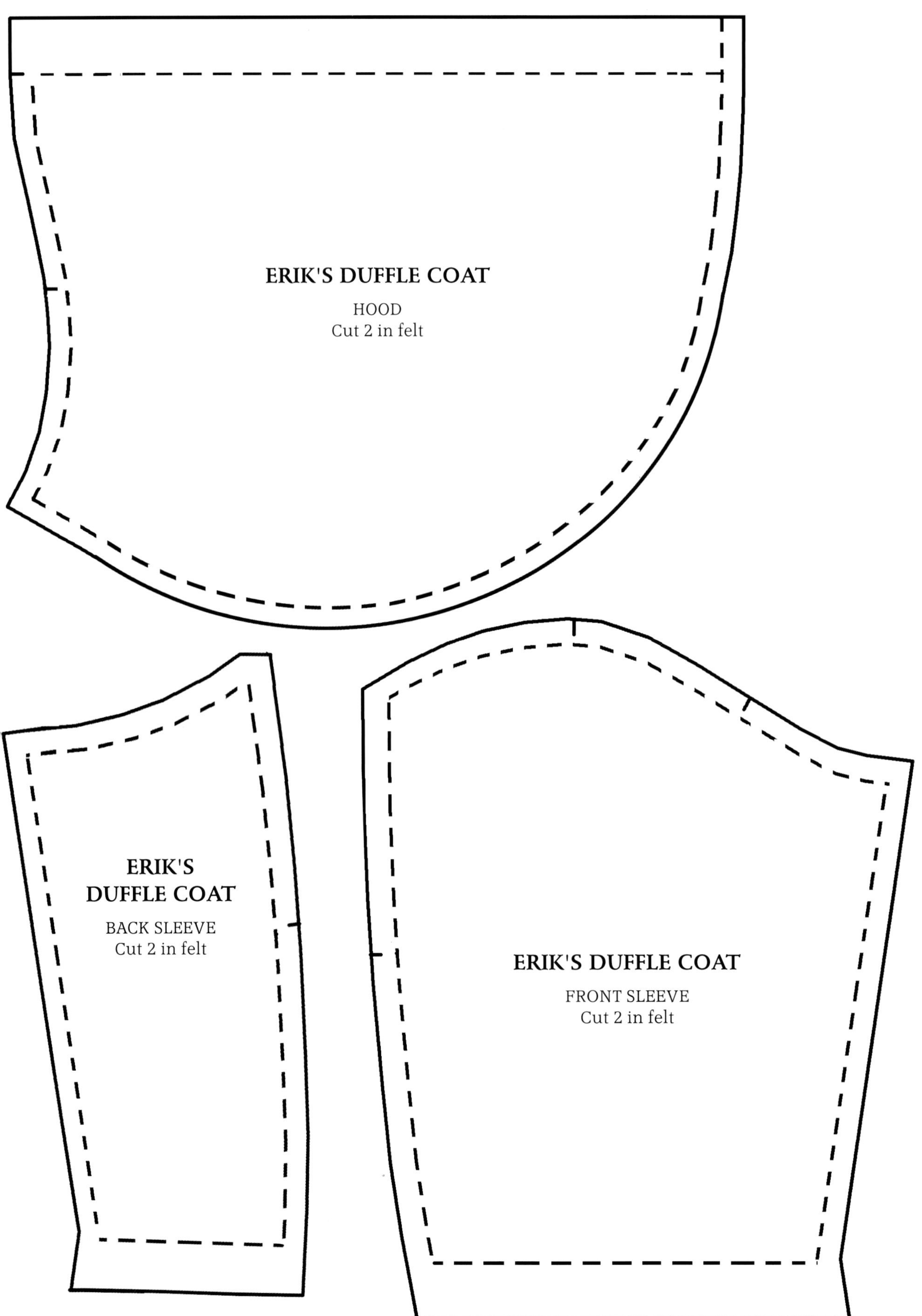
ERIK'S DUFFLE COAT
HOOD
Cut 2 in felt
ERIK'S
DUFFLE COAT
BACK SLEEVE
Cut 2 in felt
ERIK'S DUFFLE COAT
FRONT SLEEVE
Cut 2 in felt

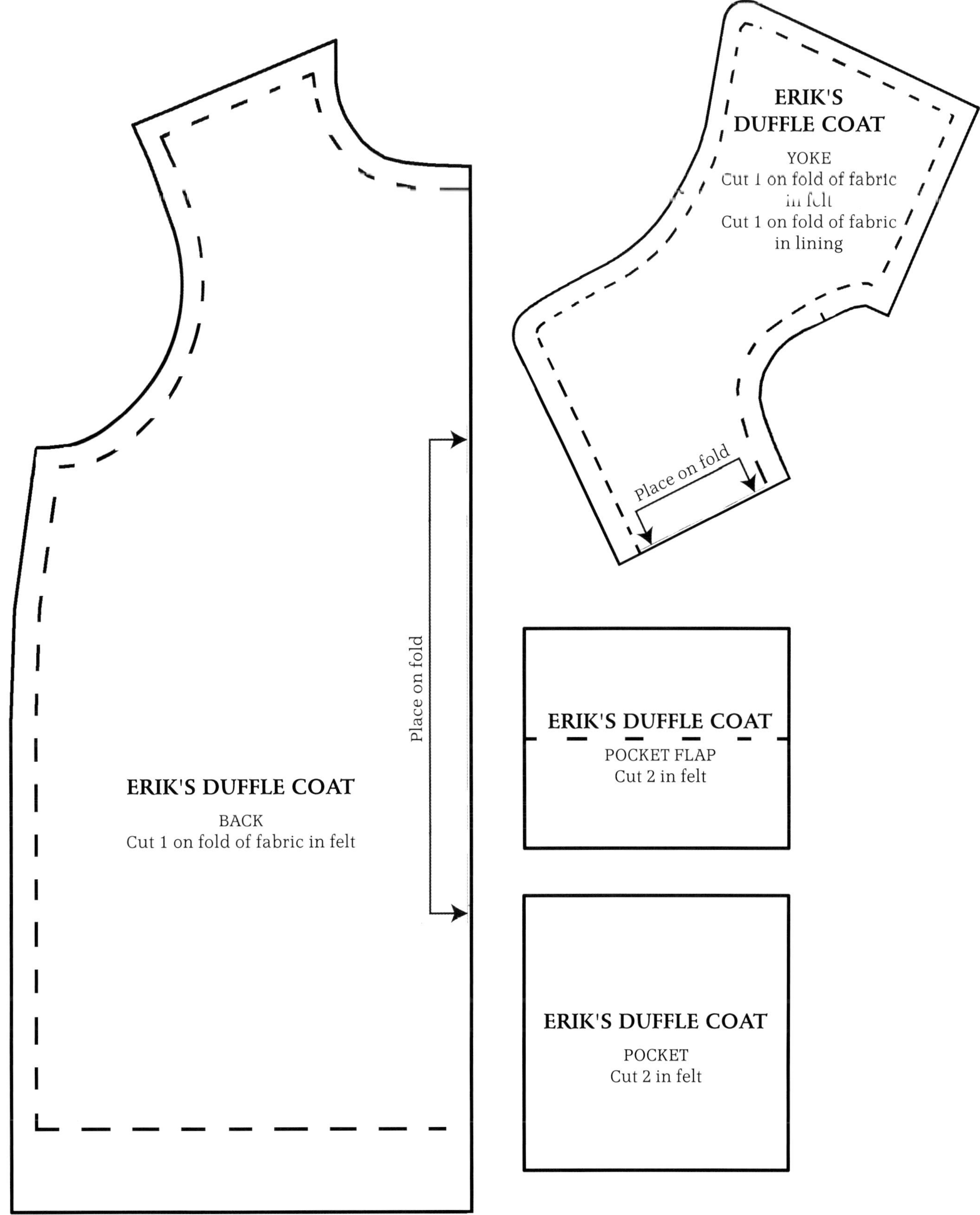
ERIK'S DUFFLE COAT
BACK
Cut 1 on fold of fabric in felt
Place on fold
ERIK'S DUFFLE COAT
YOKE
Cut 1 on fold of fabric
in felt
Cut 1 on fold of fabric
in lining
Place on fold
ERIK'S DUFFLE COAT
POCKET FLAP
Cut 2 in felt
ERIK'S DUFFLE COAT
POCKET
Cut 2 in felt

A

ERIK'S BARREL LEG TROUSERS

BACK LEG
Join at Points A and B to complete pattern piece
Cut 2 in cotton check fabric

B

A

ERIK'S BARREL LEG TROUSERS

FRONT LEG
Join at Points A and B to complete pattern piece
Cut 2 in cotton check fabric

B

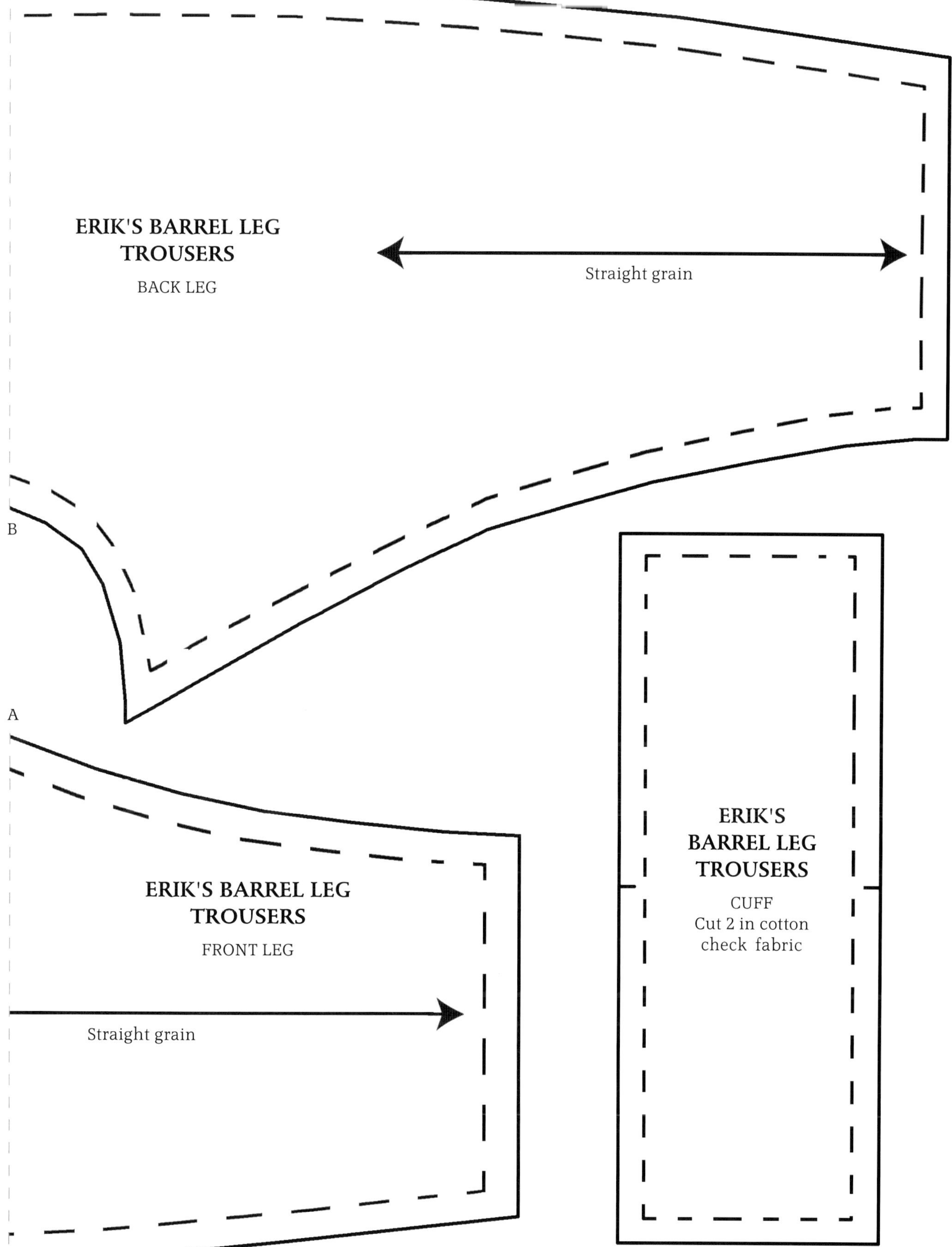
A
ERIK'S BARREL LEG
TROUSERS
BACK LEG
Straight grain
B
A
ERIK'S BARREL LEG
TROUSERS
FRONT LEG
Straight grain
B
ERIK'S
BARREL LEG
TROUSERS
CUFF
Cut 2 in cotton
check fabric

Suppliers

Think first, what do you already have? It might not be exactly as we have prescribed, but will it do the job, will it improve the job, will it bring an undefinable element of 'your story' to the end project? If you are wanting these pieces to mean more, try to incorporate little bits of your life into them. It could be a 'past its best' shirt or an old pair of leather gloves – but tiny amounts can equal tiny clothes and accessories. While I would encourage you to let your imagination go to work on the clothes, I would advise that you to use the best felt you can for the animal characters themselves.

If you fancy something specific, do support your local fabric experts – the little haberdasheries on the high street who need you to shop with them – even if it's just for the odd bobbin of thread or a fat quarter.

Big supermarket chains don't care about fabric, they haven't chosen the prints with excitement or love.

Shop local, shop small.

Speaking of which...

About the Author

Sarah Peel is the founder of CoolCrafting, established in 2011 to deliver crafting and sewing inspiration. Today, the business is primarily driven by Luna Lapin and her friends. With a team of 14 staff, CoolCrafting is based at the very top of Kendal's famously picturesque Branthwaite Brow. With two floors of sewing and knitting gorgeousness and plenty of space for creating new projects, we can't wait for Luna lovers from all over the world to make the pilgrimage to the home of Luna Lapin.

With a background in fashion pattern cutting, womenswear design, and buying, Sarah's ultimate aim is to move you on from making beautiful clothes for Luna to making your own clothes! As well as supplying kits for the miniature characters, the business provides contemporary dressmaking supplies and yarns for the modern handmade wardrobe.

Sarah lives on the edge of the English Lake District in Hincaster, Cumbria, with her partner Anthony and rescue dog Harvey. Occasionally, her grown-up sons live in the rather untidy house too, and Grace comes for a regular sleepover. Having found a smidgen more time, Sarah has a passion for playing tennis and her greenhouse is doing rather well. Heir to Luna's empire, Grace continues to breathe magic into Sarah's clever creations, through beautiful storytelling that contains tiny nuggets of real family and business life. Grace lives on the Furness Peninsula with her wonderful husband Paul and their poodle Lenny and two cats, in a house much too small for them all.

To find out more about the CoolCrafting business go to www.coolcrafting.co.uk or join us on Facebook at Luna Lapin's Little World.

COOLCRAFTING – HOME OF LUNA LAPIN

The shop for everything featured in this book – kits, remake kits, felt, Liberty prints, tiny buckles and buttons, and all the latest Luna frippery. Worldwide shipping.

40 Market Place
Kendal
Cumbria
LA94TN
Tel: 01539 724099
Email: info@coolcrafting.co.uk
Website: www.coolcrafting.co.uk

ACKNOWLEDGEMENTS

To all the hands who threaded a needle to stitch our quiet, kind rabbity hare. Luna People are the best people. To all the people who made this fifth Luna book possible – my thanks.

And to my mum, Joan Peel. We talk about you every day.

Index

A DAVID AND CHARLES BOOK

David and Charles is an imprint of David and Charles, Ltd
Suite A, Tourism House, Pynes Hill, Exeter, EX2 5WS

First published in the UK and USA in 2025

A catalogue record for this book is available from the British Library.

ISBN-13: 9781446316078 paperback
ISBN-13: 9781446316085 EPUB

This book has been printed on paper from approved suppliers and made from pulp from sustainable sources.

Printed in China through Asia Pacific Offset for:
David and Charles, Ltd
Suite A, Tourism House, Pynes Hill, Exeter, EX2 5WS

10 9 8 7 6 5 4 3 2 1

Publishing Director: Ame Verso
Senior Commissioning Editor: Sarah Callard
Publishing Manager: Jeni Chown
Editor: Jessica Cropper
Project Editor: Cheryl Brown
Lead Designer: Sam Staddon
Designer: Lucy Ridley
Pre-press Designer: Susan Reansbury
Diagrams and Patterns: Sarah Peel
Decorative Illustrations: Prudence Rogers
Art Direction, Layout and Design: Prudence Rogers
Photography: Jason Jenkins
Production Manager: Beverley Richardson

Full-size printable versions of the templates are available to download free from www.bookmarkedhub.com. Search for this book by the title or ISBN: the files can be found under 'Book Extras'. Membership of the Bookmarked online community is free.

David and Charles publishes high-quality books on a wide range of subjects. For more information visit www.davidandcharles.com.

Share your makes with us on social media using #dandcbooks and follow us on Facebook and Instagram by searching for @dandcbooks.

Layout of the digital edition of this book may vary depending on reader hardware and display settings.